May 2002

Congratulations on a very successful practicum Jennifer! You have worked hard and learned so much. All the best of luck in your future teaching career. I hope this book will be helpful and provide some useful ideas.

Sincerely
Lindsey

Editors
Sharon Coan, M.S. Ed.—Part 1
Dona Heweck Rice—Part 2

Editor-in-Chief
Sharon Coan, M.S. Ed.

Managing Editor
Ina Massler Levin, M.A.

Cover Artist
Denise Bauer

Illustrator
Howard Chaney

Art Coordinator
Denice Adorno

Imaging
James Grace
Alfred Lau
Ralph Olmedo Jr.

Product Manager
Phil Garcia

Publishers
Rachelle Cracchiolo, M.S. Ed.
Mary Dupuy Smith, M.S. Ed.

Brain Games

Part 1 Contributing Authors

*Dona Herweck Rice, Ina Massler Levin,
Michael H. Levin, Patti Sima, and Neil Jacob*

Part 2 Author

Kathleen Christopher Null

Teacher Created Materials

Teacher Created Materials, Inc.
6421 Industry Way
Westminster, CA 92683
www.teachercreated.com
ISBN-0-7439-3670-1
©2000 Teacher Created Materials, Inc.
Reprinted, 2001
Made in China

Table of Contents

Part 1

Part 2

Introduction

Brain Games provides many different ways to exercise and develop brain power. Puzzles are designed for solving individually or by a group. Many can be used to teach research skills as answers can be found through searching enclyclopedia, the Internet, or other resource materials.

The activities in this book are designed to help children develop the following skills:

- critical thinking
- research
- creative thinking
- math
- vocabulary
- memory
- spelling
- general knowledge

For ease of use, this book has been divided into Part 1 and Part 2 with a separate answer key for each part. In Part 1 the puzzles and games are progressively more challenging.

Brain Games
Part 1

Backwards ABC

Follow the letters of the alphabet backwards to find the picture. Color the picture.

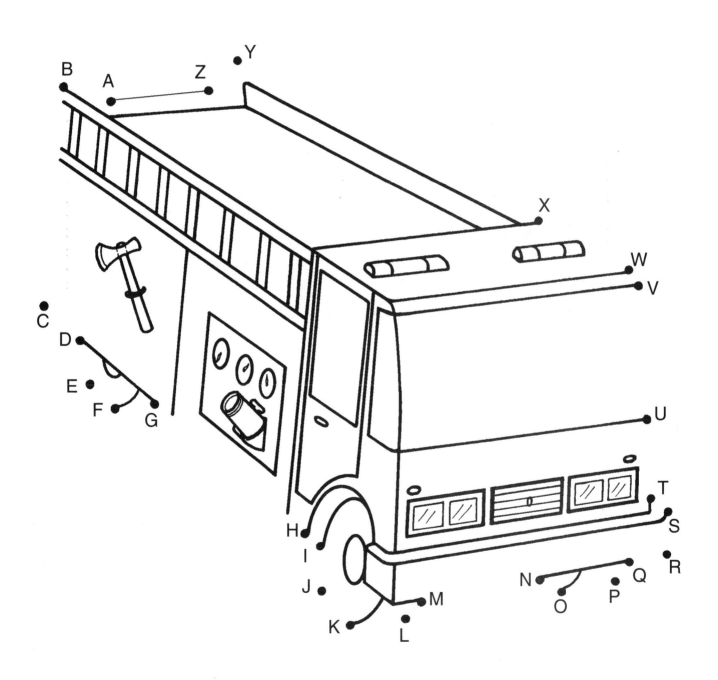

It's Amazing!

Follow the maze to help the dog find the bone.

What Comes Next?

Draw the next thing in each series.

1. ○ □ ○ □ ○	
2. ♡ ☆ ♡ ☆ ♡	
3. □ ○ △ □ ○	
4. ☆ □ ☆ □ ☆	
5. ○ ○ ▭ ○ ○	

Number Series

Write the next number in each series.

a. 1 2 3 1 2 3 1 2 _____

b. 1 3 3 1 3 3 1 3 _____

c. 1 5 1 5 1 5 1 5 _____

d. 2 2 2 3 3 3 4 4 _____

e. 1 2 3 4 1 2 3 4 _____

f. 1 2 2 3 3 3 4 4 4 _____

g. 115 116 117 _____

h. 2 4 6 8 10 12 _____

i. 105 110 115 _____

j. 5 10 15 20 25 _____

Letter Series

Write the next letter in each series.

1. J K L M N O P _____

2. R S T U V W X Y _____

3. B A B B B C B D B E _____

4. A B B C C C D D D _____

5. X Y Z A B C X Y Z A _____

6. X X X Y Y Y Z Z _____

7. A E I O U A E I O U _____

8. M N O M N P M N Q _____

9. Z A A Z B B Z C _____

10. Z Y X W V U T S R Q _____

8

Alphabet Snake

Fill in the missing uppercase letters on the snake.

A B ___ D ___

___ G H ___ J

___ ___ ___ M ___ O

P Q ___ ___ ___

U ___ W ___ ___ Z

Alphabetical Order

Put the words in alphabetical order.

run

book

map

apple

elephant

zebra

jump

cat

skate

kite

dog

tree

1. _____

2. _____

3. _____

4. _____

5. _____

6. _____

7. _____

8. _____

9. _____

10. _____

11. _____

12. _____

Pairs

Color the item in each row that makes a pair with the first item.

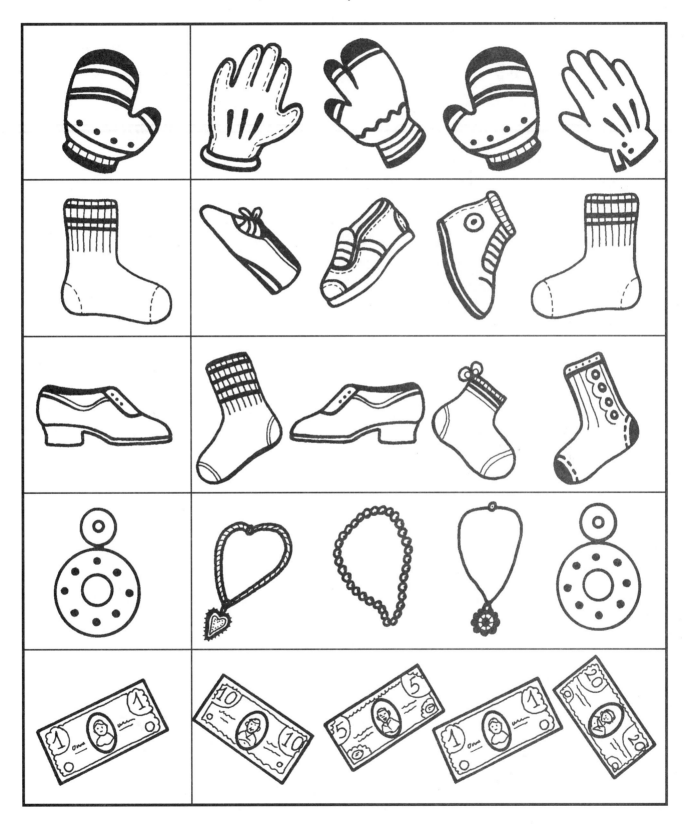

What Goes Together?

Draw a line to match the things that go together. Color the pictures.

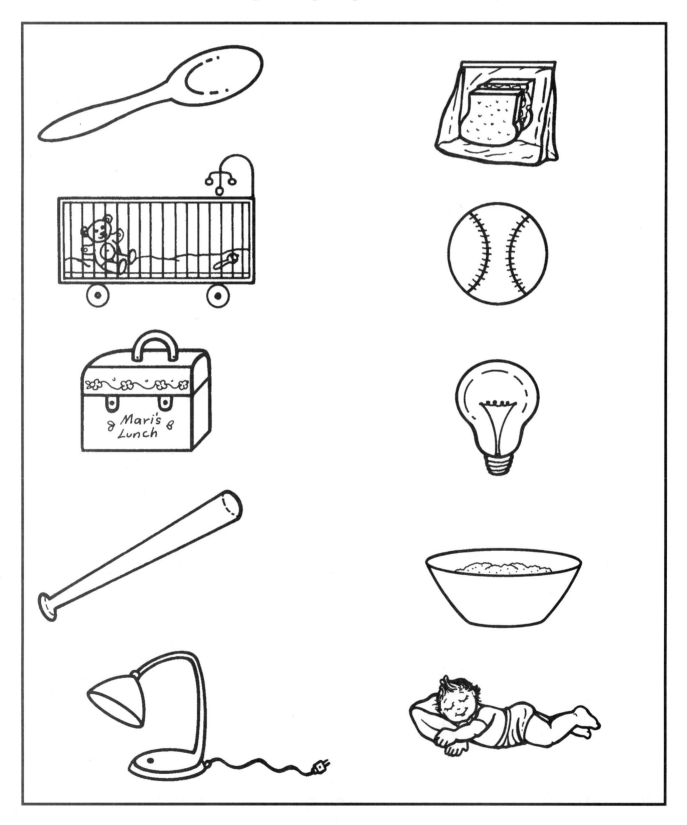

Hooves and Paws

Draw lines to match the animal faces and feet. Color the pictures.

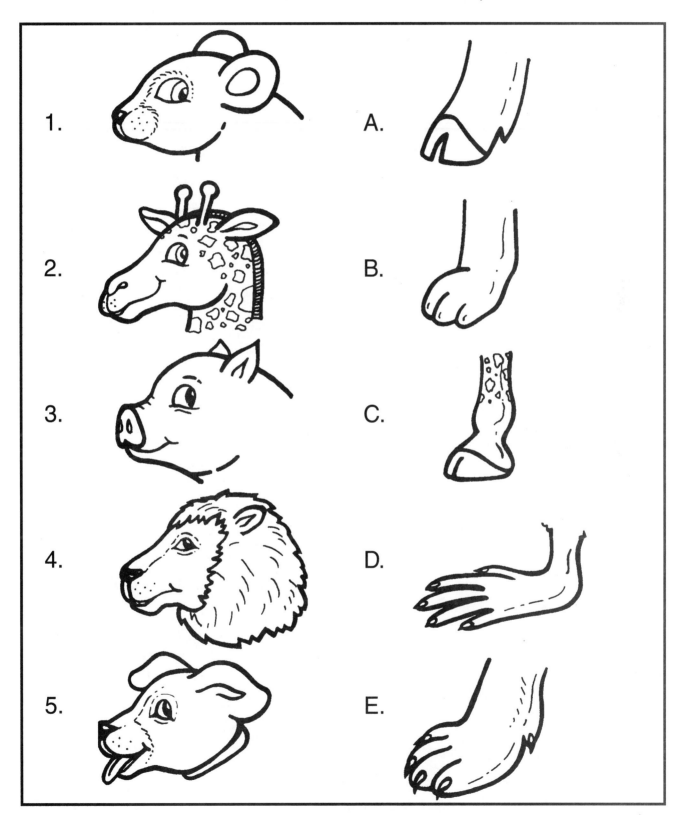

1.

2.

3.

4.

5.

A.

B.

C.

D.

E.

It Doesn't Belong

Circle everything in the picture that does not belong. Color the picture.

A Present for Everyone

Can you match each present to each child? Write the present on the line under each child. **Hint:** The ones that go together have something in common.

Picnic Math

Complete the problem on each picnic basket. The answer will be a clue to what is inside. Write the answer on the line under each picnic basket.

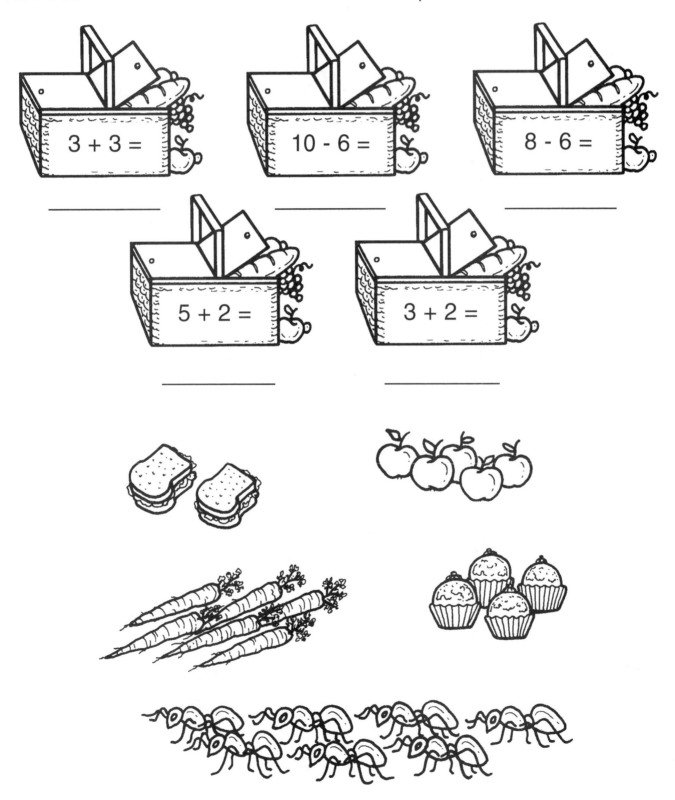

Favorite Sports

Three friends, Jose, Mike, and Latanya, each enjoy a different sport. When they play together, they take turns choosing the game they will play. Use the clues below to figure out each child's favorite sport. Draw a line to connect each child to his or her favorite sport.

1. Jose's favorite sport uses a helmet.

2. Mike's favorite sport uses a racquet.

3. Latanya's favorite sport does not use a helmet or a racket.

Jose

Latanya

Mike

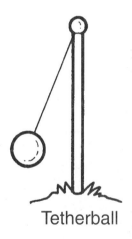

Tetherball

Football

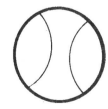

Tennis

Whose Toy?

Follow the strings to see who is connected to each. Write the number of the toy above each child. Color the pictures.

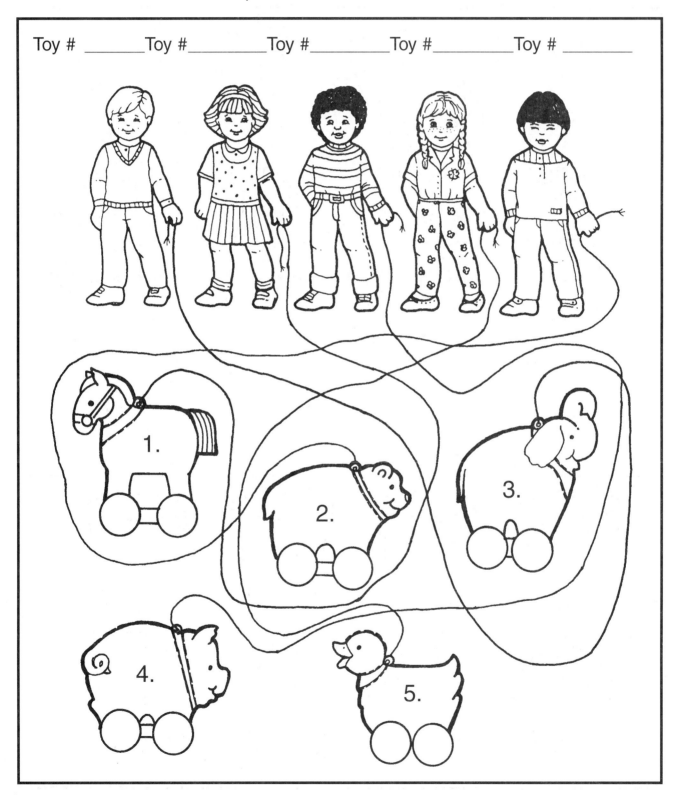

Toy # _____ Toy #_____ Toy #_____ Toy #_____ Toy # _____

1.

2.

3.

4.

5.

Which Is Different?

One picture in each row is different. Color the picture that is different.

How Many?

Fill in the number that completes the title of the rhyme or fairy tale.

1. Snow White and the _____ Dwarfs

2. _____, _____ Buckle My Shoe

3. Goldilocks and the _____ Bears

4. The _____ Little Kittens

5. The _____ Dancing Princesses

6. Ali Baba and the _____ Thieves

7. The _____ Little Pigs

8. The _____ Swans

9. _____ Dalmatians

10. _____ Blind Mice

What's Missing?

Draw in the missing part of each picture from these things that go.

Car

Wagon

Wheel barrow

Bike

Ice skates

Airplane

Opposites

List the opposites.

1. full _____

2. down _____

3. sad _____

4. near _____

5. dry _____

6. straight _____

7. out _____

8. hard _____

9. low _____

10. under _____

11. short _____

12. on _____

13. light _____

14. dirty _____

15. cold _____

Name Something

1. Name something orange. _____

2. Name something square. _____

3. Name something slow. _____

4. Name something wet. _____

5. Name something light. _____

6. Name something noisy. _____

7. Name something yellow. _____

8. Name something cute. _____

9. Name something flat. _____

10. Name something sweet. _____

11. Name something pretty. _____

12. Name something scratchy. _____

13. Name something bumpy. _____

14. Name something smooth. _____

15. Name something gooey. _____

Rhymes

Write four words that rhyme with each word below.

cat

top

feet

pie

bow

tree

Dot to Dot

Follow the numbers to find the picture. Color the picture.

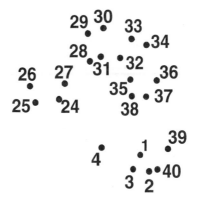

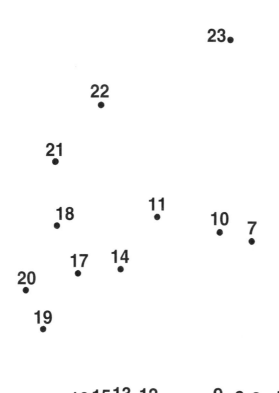

Follow the Dots

Follow the even numbers to find the picture. Color the picture.

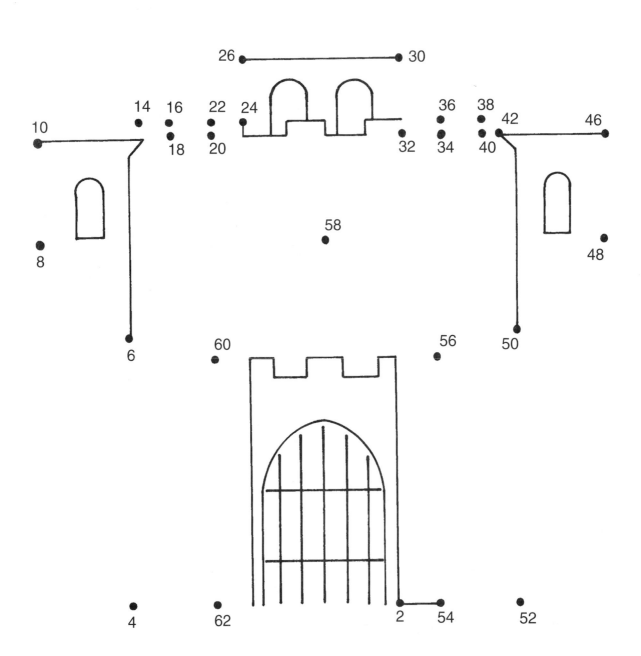

26

Follow the Letters

Follow the letters of the alphabet to find the picture. Color the picture.

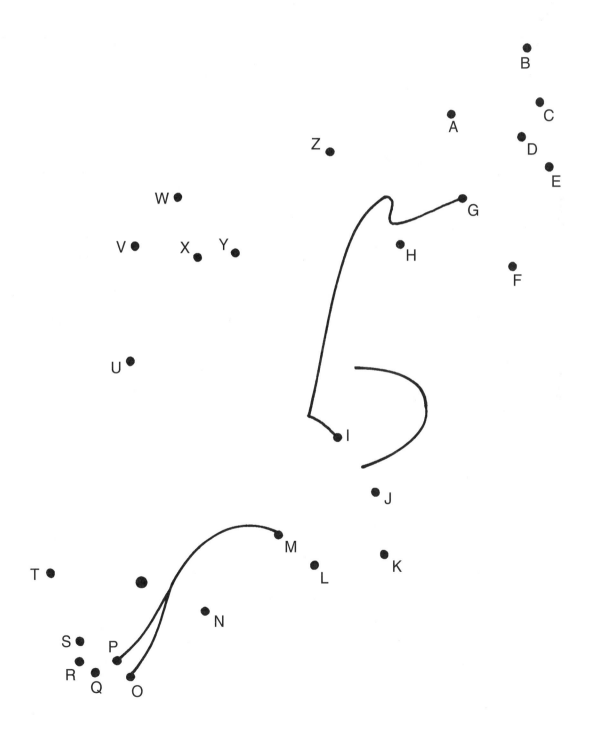

Backwards ABC

Follow the letters of the alphabet backwards to find the picture. Color the picture.

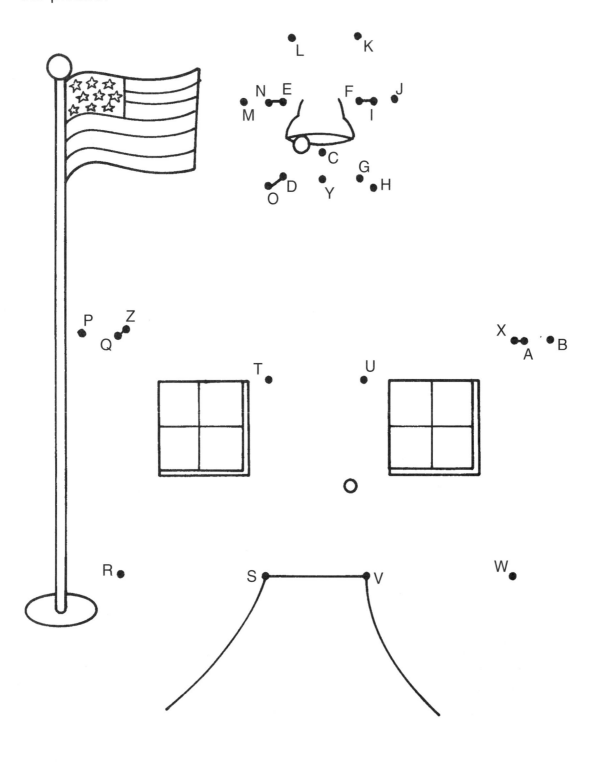

It's Amazing

Follow the maze to get the goldfish to the bowl.

A Maze of Letters

Follow the alphabet through the maze to get the children to school.

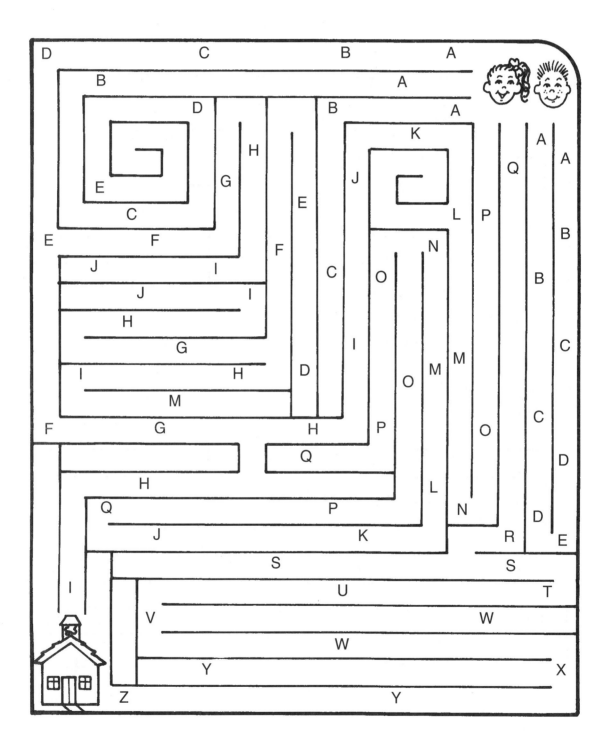

30

Amazing Numbers

Follow the numbers 1 through 20 to get the bear cub to its mother.

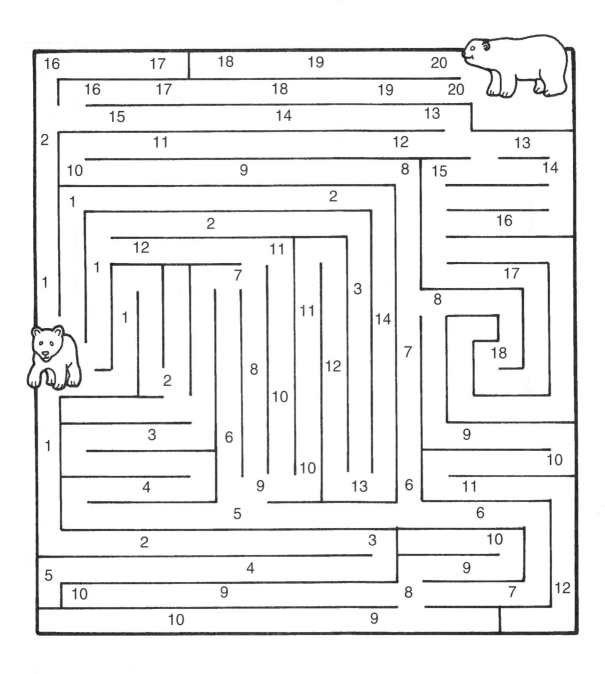

Body Works

Find all the words from the Word Box in the word search puzzle. The words can be found down or across.

```
L R J T X L V F D G N B L R N J Y B J S D H Y C
M F Q W Q B Y Q X F H T X T H T N K B D S X P F
C M H W T B B S Q S M G D G Q X V R B X F T Q G
L D P R S V C G S Y X Y L S N V P P W M N Z W R
G X V V Q R L T H S D V X X J Y B H G P G D K K
K F C X L Q S V O F P X L B W H D T N L Z X V B
N T C L R Y Z S U N V T C N V L S Q J A R M M C
D S H B K H B X L N P F H R G D F R G N X T R C
Q D M T J A L B D D L G E A M K O M S K T C Y B
X X B G G I L Y E R Z R E H Z T O X L L L R N D
F I N G E R F F R N E C K W W M T O E E L B O W
F H T M R M Y Z M M B T K R Z N Y F Y A G H S G
H B D H K W V R H O X M N W N C V C E R X E E L
Z N L B V N L B N U M K E P D S L B J M F A L C
H E E L H A N D Q T Y G E S T O M A C H Y D X G
B R G K Z C X P X H Z B C L J H J Y L R P Z S S
M S P B C V V F V C P T M C J Z B D J P G D X G
```

Word Box

head	knee	nose	heel
arm	toe	ear	ankle
leg	finger	eye	stomach
foot	shoulder	mouth	cheek
elbow	neck	hand	hair

Things That Go

Find all the words from the Word Box in the word search puzzle. The words can be found down or across.

```
S Y B M T R N L Q J P V R Q S T C C C S N B V
H K G F R G F X T T G X C V W C L W W D W D W T
I H G Q I L W L F K F B J W S P C B F P Y K F M
P M M L C L X G F Z Y F S C J S H B S X R L M S
R S F W Y P V G K W Q K D B J X R M B S L D K H
N S B Z C M H Y T M T S B G K J L D Z W Y V K Z
J V Y R L B Z T Q W H M H Y D Y L S C Y J T L B
D M B K E Y J Y G Z G O P D C P V K G V B C K H
T B P V T F C G Y S P T T S L E D S Z L G W B V
R T V X R R T V N S S O B R C Z G C Q S T N J B
P L D B A S K A T E S R C N L L V O W A G O N J
L L X Y I S M G B S K C C X G Z N O J E E P B P
A C A R L D H L O G L Y P K K Z T T Y A G B V V
N H S A E N N A A J S C V C A S L E N X E O A M
E B R T R A I N T R O L L E Y K T R U C K P N D
Z U F P V W G M N E S E P V A H Z N S J C B Y H
Y S U R F B O A R D S M F D K B I C Y C L E J M
```

Word Box

train	car	truck	bus
plane	bicycle	jeep	trolley
van	trailer	boat	kayak
ship	skates	surfboard	scooter
tricycle	wagon	sled	motorcycle

I Only Have I's for You

Find the "I" words hidden in the word search puzzle. The words can be found down or across.

```
D D R T L B H M R V H C Q D F H H B Y R M B D R
Y H M X Y S S F T X T W S P T H Z D B Q V V F H
Q L K Q N J J Z X K Y K J P T Q P P G B F Y P Q
D Q H M N N Z J S Y S K M N Y P J R M W D H R
  I H W F R C X V Z V F J G M V N B Y H Z
  G H T Y I H L T Q C W K M V S G W I S P
  U I L L C C X R V W W V Q Z V C W G X Y
  A K I Z I R J P T B I X M H F Y J L W L
  N W S J C M B I Z P C V C I F Q Y O F M
  A I D O L C P F I T E M G T Y N R O R C
  M F Y P E C T J B S F X K L B B C M M S
  B Y N R J T H F P G Z X C Q P S M M Y N
  J P Z I J B I W D M B V Q F S K J P T H
  B N O N C V T E W X F T U I J K L M B V
  P L N T Y B M L P A A S D E W Y U I O P
F J T L B O I R I S W Z Q M L G S C T T W V X W
Q J F G W S F V C G L K B Y S B C P Q Z G K W N
M K R L J Q F M X C R R V Z R G W P X M T J V V
S N H F D M P Y N W W B M H J T Y V C B D P W V
```

Word Box

it	ill	if
item	iguana	into
igloo	iris	is
ice	idol	icicle

Lights, Camera, Action!

Find the action words from the Word Box in the word search puzzle.
The words can be found down, across, or diagonally.

```
N R N B S W S P M R N J N L R L B S H K M J R Z
X R N L G V S C P L G W N P A G I U F Q R H J K
S R M X J H B V C N G F D L R U R S I S E Y U V
M L B T L D N Z V A L F H A E U G X T L A G M S
S L O O K F P A I N T C R Y A W N H J E D Q P X
K W Y R V Q S Q P T H C F O T M T R O E N X R M
I B I V L N L N X N R B H C W L Z L G P H C K J
P W R M H Q I D P V O R X O P N T D L S F W V H
C S G E X P D F F K W D H U X J H H D M Z N D F
L J K K A N E R N F B Y N G W F K O H I T Y T Q
I B Q T C K X Y Y D M C Y H X M H W P L Z W S B
M P N M M D Y R X G S L M Q T B X G L E D Y G C
B H W G V D C R V S V C Y G Z Z B Y H T X G S H
T V D W V W C P V W R F N P Y K Y M F T H Y V F
Q J V D R L F M Z M L Y G K S T T R N W K Q S D
N S V B F P H L K S J L B M D L G Y S Y Q X G R
D K Q V L T S K Z C M Y M T L B T V S B R X F J
```

Word Box

swim	climb	jog	build	laugh
run	read	throw	break	smile
jump	sleep	catch	eat	frown
skip	play	look	paint	cry
hop	slide	listen	yawn	cough

Words

Find the word "word" twenty times in the word search puzzle. It can be found across, down, or diagonally.

```
W O R D Z Y T Z W O R D Q Z B W S V Q W V M H P
M T X R S R F X C Q G P L R T W O R D N Z V X T
G T S X S V C C W L T G M W H L B Q X T W O R D
K Y B G Q C V C M O K R H O T V M G J K N K C G
J V V P W W K Y T Y R J M R K D M R V E S N R W
D K V P D O V P F Q F D R D V T G R D H H P L O
Y T S J R R R V Z R Y P C Z G Y T R W W O R D R
D Z W Y H D N G W Y W O R D B G O F T R G D G D
J Z O W P N W B F O L F F Y L W M G R D H J T J
W O R D D M V T J T R L L Y F P Y X S V W X X H
T C D X F Y X J S R M D Q Z V C D Z Y C O P W G
H T R D N G N Y R W B P V P C Z V Y W F R M M D
T P W W Q F K K D O F J P N F M D C N H D J K S
X B L C W D D Q S R M S J T R R B V Y M T W V C
T D Y J S K K Z D G R B F O Z X V C F F O V N
B V R S W Y C D T Q Y N G W N V W G D Z G R X R
M B B P D W O R D V B D M N R C F Q W O R D S H
T F U P K V G B M F W R T F U P K V G B M F W R
V Z R P K T F D V J Y L V Z R P K T F D V J Y L
L K V T F R E S C V H U L K V T F R E S C V H U
J C L P S C Z X M N Y B J C L P S C Z X M N Y B
K G D S A V T H J A V I K G D S A V T H J A V I
```

    36   ©Teacher Created Materials, Inc.

Scrambled Words

Unscramble the letters to find the barnyard animals.

1. neh _____

2. gip _____

3. rhsoe _____

4. owc _____

5. osgeo _____

6. kdcu _____

7. srotore _____

8. lume _____

9. gato _____

10. tca _____

11. hpsee _____

12. gdo _____

More Scrambled Words

Unscramble the letters to find the musical instruments.

1. rmsdu   _____

2. lutef   _____

3. utrgia   _____

4. opani   _____

5. joanb   _____

6. olinvi   _____

7. buta   _____

8. angtrlie _____

9. arhp   _____

10. booe   _____

11. lceol   _____

12. goran   _____

Word Jumbles

Unscramble the letters to find the things used in a house.

1. dbe   _____

2. mlpa   _____

3. voen   _____

4. lvsnteeiio   _____

5. batle   _____

6. nkis   _____

7. salgs   _____

8. hraic   _____

9. lewto   _____

10. lptea   _____

11. ubt   _____

12. rkfo   _____

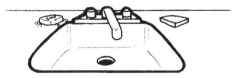

Decoding

Match each number to the letter in the code to find the color names.

<u>A</u>	<u>B</u>	<u>C</u>	<u>D</u>	<u>E</u>	<u>F</u>	<u>G</u>	<u>H</u>	<u>I</u>	<u>J</u>	<u>K</u>	<u>L</u>	<u>M</u>
1	2	3	4	5	6	7	8	9	10	11	12	13

<u>N</u>	<u>O</u>	<u>P</u>	<u>Q</u>	<u>R</u>	<u>S</u>	<u>T</u>	<u>U</u>	<u>V</u>	<u>W</u>	<u>X</u>	<u>Y</u>	<u>Z</u>
14	15	16	17	18	19	20	21	22	23	24	25	26

1. 2 12 21 5 _____

2. 18 5 4 _____

3. 16 21 18 16 12 5 _____

4. 7 18 5 5 14 _____

5. 2 12 1 3 11 _____

6. 25 5 12 12 15 23 _____

7. 23 8 9 20 5 _____

8. 19 9 12 22 5 18 _____

9. 15 18 1 14 7 5 _____

10. 16 9 14 11 _____

11. 7 15 12 4 _____

12. 2 18 15 23 14 _____

Word Codes

To decode the words below, write the letter of the alphabet that comes after each letter given. The words you spell will be things found at school. (**Note:** Use "Z" as the letter before "A.")

1. odmbhk   _____

2. bgzkj   _____

3. rstcdms   _____

4. fknad   _____

5. okzxfqntmc   _____

6. sdzbgdq   _____

7. cdrj   _____

8. dqzrdq   _____

9. bqzxnmr   _____

10. ozodq   _____

11. oqhmbhozk   _____

12. qtkdq   _____

What Comes Next?

Draw the next thing in each series.

1.

2.

3.

4.

5.

Number Series

Write the next number in each series.

1. 1 2 3 1 2 3 1 2   _____

2. 1 2 2 1 2 2 1 2   _____

3. 1 2 1 2 1 2 1 2   _____

4. 1 1 1 2 2 2 3 3   _____

5. 1 2 3 4 1 2 3 4   _____

6. 1 2 3 2 1 2 3 2   _____

7. 1 2 2 3 3 3 4 4 4   _____

8. 1 1 2 2 1 1 3 3 1   _____

9. 1 1 2 1 1 3 1 1 2   _____

10. 1 5 1 10 1 15 1 20 1   _____

11. 10 9 8 7 6 5 4 3 2   _____

12. 1 2 4 8 16 32   _____

Letter Series

Write the next letter in each series.

1. A B C D E F G H I J _____

2. L M N O P Q R S T U _____

3. Z Y X W V U T S R Q _____

4. A A B B C C D D E E _____

5. A B A C A D A E A F _____

6. A B B C C C D D D D _____

7. A B C X Y Z A B C X _____

8. A A A B C C C D E E _____

9. A E I O U A E I O U _____

10. A A A B B B C C C D _____

11. A Z Z Z A Z Z Z A Z Z A _____

12. A B C B A B C B A B _____

Alphabet Train

Fill in the missing uppercase letters of the alphabet.

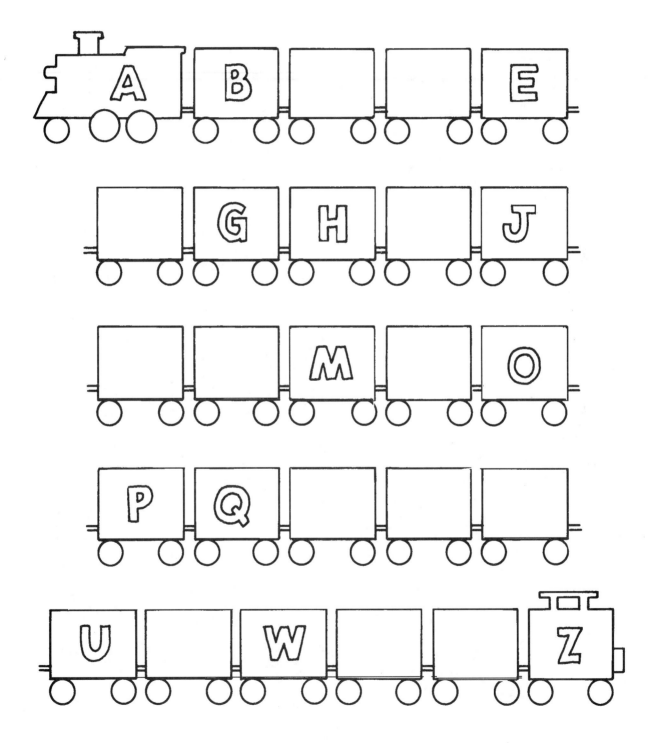

Alpha-Bug

Fill in the missing lowercase letters of the alphabet.

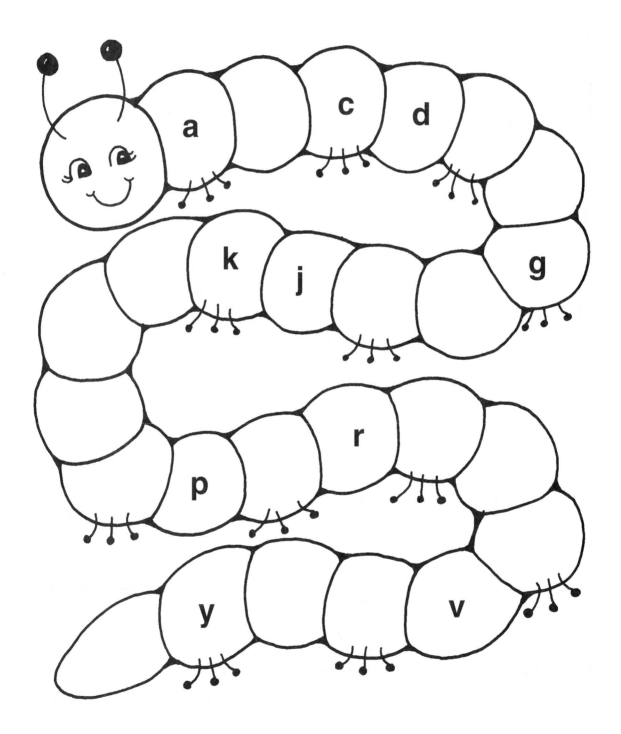

Alphabetical Order

Put the words in alphabetical order.

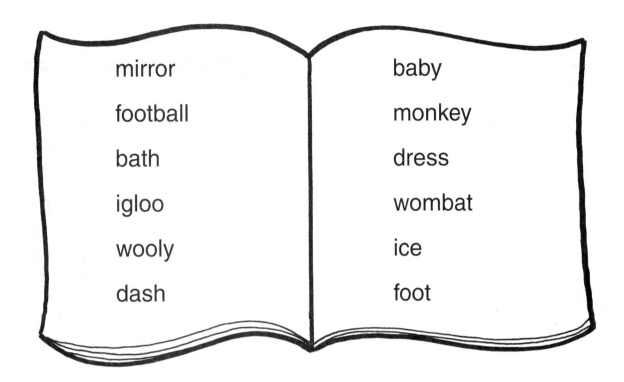

mirror

football

bath

igloo

wooly

dash

baby

monkey

dress

wombat

ice

foot

1._____

2._____

3._____

4._____

5._____

6._____

7._____

8._____

9._____

10._____

11._____

12._____

More Alphabetical Order

Put the words in alphabetical order.

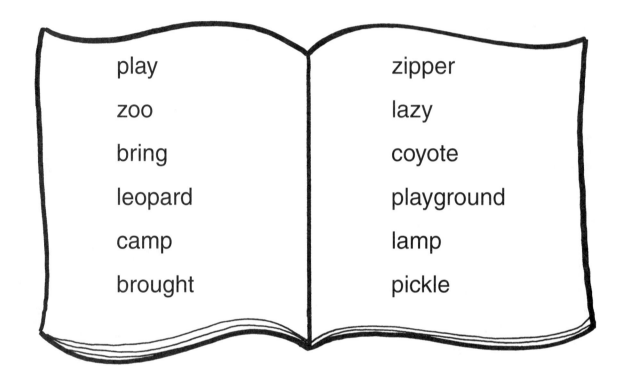

play

zoo

bring

leopard

camp

brought

zipper

lazy

coyote

playground

lamp

pickle

1._____

2._____

3._____

4._____

5._____

6._____

7._____

8._____

9._____

10._____

11._____

12._____

Lowercase

Write the lowercase letter for each uppercase letter.

A ____ B ____ C ____ D ____

E ____ F ____ G ____ H ____

I ____ J ____ K ____ L ____

M ____ N ____ O ____ P ____

Q ____ R ____ S ____ T ____

U ____ V ____ W ____ X ____

Y ____ Z ____

Uppercase

Write the uppercase letter for each lowercase letter.

a _____ b _____ c _____ d _____

e _____ f _____ g _____ h _____

i _____ j _____ k _____ l _____

m _____ n _____ o _____ p _____

q _____ r _____ s _____ t _____

u _____ v _____ w _____ x _____

y _____ z _____

Pairs

Color the item in each row that makes a pair with the first item.

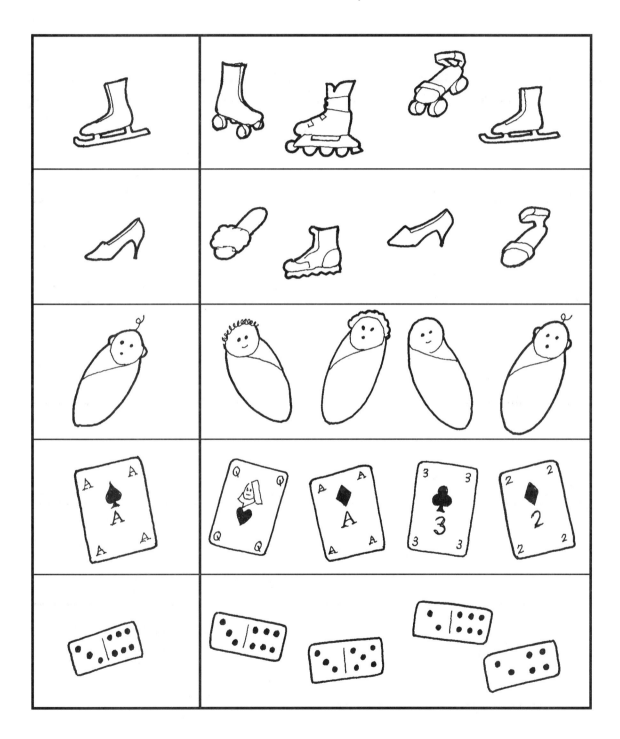

Make a Set

Match the things that go together. Color the pictures.

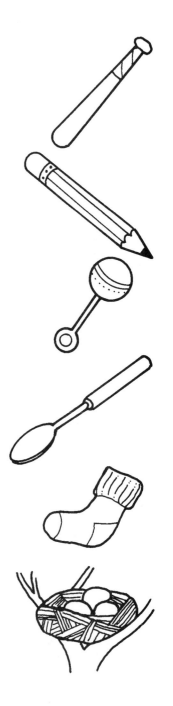

What Goes Together?

Match the things that go together. Color the pictures.

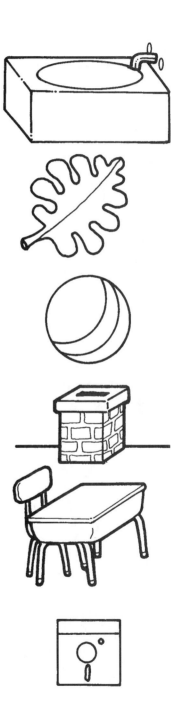

"Mirror, Mirror, on the Wall"

Match the fairy tale figures that go together. Color the pictures.

Hooves and Paws

Match the animal faces and feet. Color the pictures.

1.

A.

2.

B.

3.

C.

4.

D.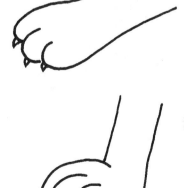

5.

E.

It Doesn't Belong

Circle everything in the picture that does not belong. Color the picture.

Two by Two

Color everything that comes in twos.

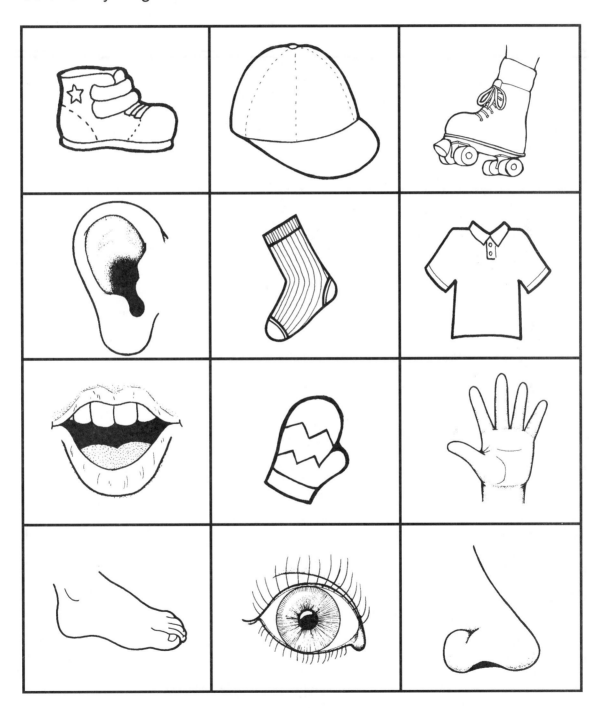

What Do We Wear?

Color everything that a person might wear.

Whose Baby?

Which baby goes to which parent? Find the things in common, and you will know.

A.

Baby #_____

B.

Baby #_____

C.

Baby #_____

D.

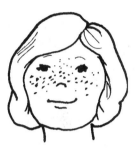

Baby #_____

1

2

3

4

Whose Is It?

Can you use the clues in the pictures to figure out what item belongs to each child? **Hint:** Think of the *number* of things. Write what each child owns on the line under his or her picture.

Mindy owns a _____ .   Pam owns a _____ .

Simon owns a _____ .

tricycle

skateboard

bicycle

A Present for Everyone

Can you match each present to each child? **Hint:** The ones that go together have something in common. Write the present on the line under each child.

Dawn   Bill   Emily   Sue   Ken

_____   _____   _____   _____   _____

bicycle

kite

doll

earrings

skates

Package Math

Complete the problem on each package. The answer will be a clue to the present inside. Write the present on the line under each package.

More Package Math

Complete the problem on each package. The answer will be a clue to the present inside. Write the present on the line under each package.

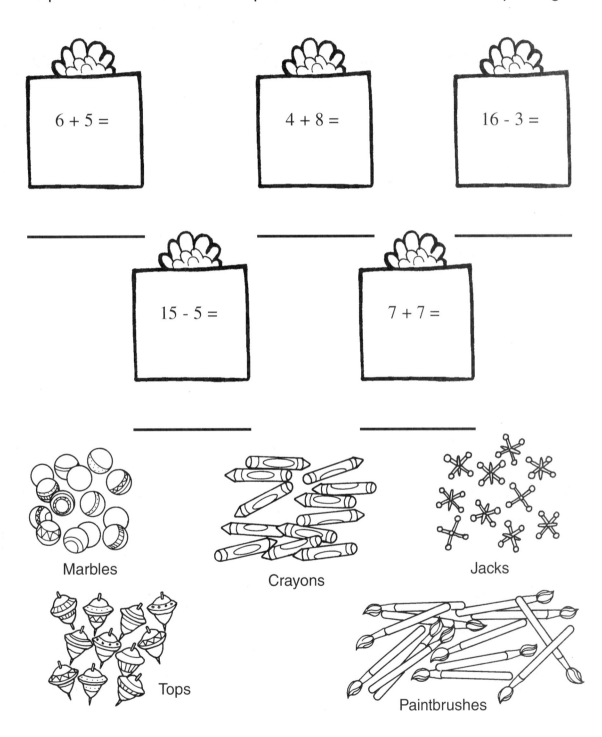

6 + 5 =

4 + 8 =

16 - 3 =

15 - 5 =

7 + 7 =

Marbles

Crayons

Jacks

Tops

Paintbrushes

Favorite Sports

Three friends, Tran, Henry, and Maya, each enjoy a different sport. When they play together, they take turns choosing the game they will play. Use the clues below to figure out each child's favorite sport. Draw a line to connect each child to his or her favorite sport.

1. Tran's favorite sport uses a bat.
2. Henry's favorite sport uses a hoop.
3. Maya's favorite sport does not use a bat or a hoop.

Tran

Henry

Maya

soccer

baseball

basketball

64

How Old Are They?

There are three children, Susie, Jimmy, and Katie. They are each different ages. One child is 6, another is 7, and the third is 8-years-old. Can you use the clues below to figure out the age of each child? Draw a line to each child's correct age.

1. Susie is two years older than Jimmy.
2. Katie is in the middle.
3. Jimmy is the youngest.

Susie

6

Jimmy

7

Katie

8

Which Is Different?

One picture in each row is different. Color the picture that is different.

Whose Balloon?

Follow the strings to see who is connected to which balloon. Write the number of the balloon below each child. Color the pictures.

Balloon # _____ **Balloon #** _____ **Balloon #** _____ **Balloon #** _____ **Balloon #** _____

Dog Day

What a tangle! Can you figure out which dog goes to which owner?
Write the number of each dog above each owner. Color the pictures.

Dog # _____   **Dog #** _____   **Dog #** _____   **Dog #** _____   **Dog #** _____

How Many Circles?

How many circles are in the picture? Count them and then color the picture.

There are _____ circles.

How Many Squares?

How many squares are in the picture? Count them and then color the picture.

There are _____ squares.

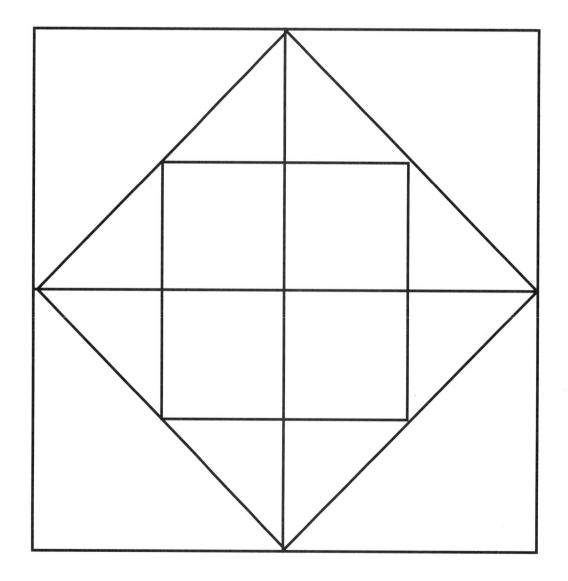

How Many Triangles?

How many triangles are in the picture? Count them and then color the picture.

There are _____ triangles.

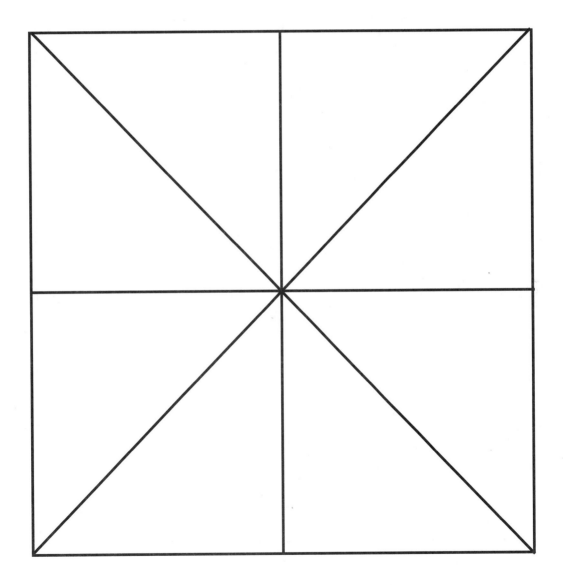

Football

Answer the questions. Color the picture.

1. How many footballs are there? _____

2. How many legs are there? _____

3. How many players are there? _____

4. How many shoes are there? _____

5. What else can you count? _____

Outer Space

Answer the questions. Color the picture.

1. How many planets are there? _____

2. How many stars are there? _____

3. How many space ships are there? _____

4. How many rings around planets are there? _____

5. What else can you count? _____

Ballet

Answer the questions. Color the picture.

1. How many people are there? _____

2. How many tutus are there? _____

3. How many roses are there? _____

4. How many ballet slippers are there? _____

5. What else can you count? _____

Sets of Five

Color every set of five items.

Sets of Ten

Complete each set to make a set of ten items. Color the pictures.

Find the Dozen

Look at the picture below. Find the animal that comes in a set of twelve. Then, color the picture.

There are 12 _____ .

Missing Word

What word is missing from each set of words?

1. _____ Bo Peep

   _____ Boy Blue

   _____ Red Riding Hood

2. The _____ Little Pigs

   The _____ Bears

   The _____ Billy Goats Gruff

3. Rockabye _____

   Bye Bye _____ Bunting

   Hush, Little _____

4. _____ Mother Hubbard

   This _____ Man

   The _____ Woman in the Shoe

Missing Letters

Fill in the missing letter to complete each word.

1. co___d

2. hap___y

3. fun___y

4. c___w

5. cro___

6. mo___her

7. rabbi___

8. jac___et

9. m___uth

10. ___ise

11. s___reet

12. ho___se

13. monke___

14. ___lamp

15. pock___t

More Missing Letters

Fill in the missing letter to complete each word.

1. s__ring

2. bac__

3. __ix

4. hai__

5. poli__e

6. e__bow

7. s__eet

8. stomac__

9. flo__r

10. co__ch

11. __lanket

12. __cout

13. chan__e

14. fin__er

15. p__ease

80

What's Missing?

Draw in the missing part of each picture.

bird

cat

zebra

dog

kangaroo

fish

Complete the Picture

Draw in the missing part of each picture.

face

slide

clock

car

sailboat

umbrella

Mother Goose

Fill in the missing words in the Mother Goose rhymes.

1. Jack be _____ ,

   Jack be _____ ,

   Jack _____ over the candlestick.

2. Mary, Mary, quite _____

   How does your _____ grow?

3. Diddle, diddle, dumpling, my _____ John

   Went to _____ with his trousers on.

4. Jack and _____

   Went up the _____

   To fetch a _____ of water.

   Jack _____ down

   And _____ his crown,

   And Jill came _____ after.

5. Little Miss Muffet _____ on her tuffet

   _____ her curds and whey.

   Along came a _____ who sat down beside her

   And frightened Miss Muffet _____ .

Fairy Tales

Fill in the missing words from the fairy tale titles.

1. The Three Little _____

2. Goldilocks and the Three _____

3. The Three _____ Goats Gruff

4. _____ White and the _____ Dwarfs

5. The _____ Mermaid

6. Beauty and the _____

7. Aladdin and the Magic _____

8. _____ and the Beanstalk

9. The _____ That Laid the Golden _____

10. The Bremen _____ Musicians

11. _____ Beauty

12. The _____ Princess

13. The Steadfast _____ Soldier

14. The Tale of Peter _____

Rhymes

Write four words that rhyme with each word below.

ten

_____

_____

_____

_____

bee

_____

_____

_____

_____

do

_____

_____

_____

_____

top

_____

_____

_____

_____

bat

_____

_____

_____

peep

_____

_____

_____

#3670 Brain Games

Opposites

List the opposites.

1. hot _____
2. dark _____
3. off _____
4. over _____
5. high _____
6. in _____
7. far _____
8. curly _____
9. up _____
10. empty _____
11. happy _____
12. wet _____
13. soft _____
14. tall _____
15. clean _____

Days of the Week

Write the day that falls between the two days given.

1. Sunday   _____ Tuesday

2. Thursday   _____ Saturday

3. Monday   _____ Wednesday

4. Friday   _____ Sunday

5. Wednesday _____ Friday

6. Tuesday   _____ Thursday

7. Saturday   _____ Monday

Months of the Year

Write the month that falls between the two months given.

1. January   _____   March

2. June   _____   August

3. October   _____   December

4. February   _____   April

5. July   _____   September

6. September   _____   November

7. March   _____   May

8. August   _____   October

9. April   _____   June

10. November   _____   January

11. May   _____   July

12. December   _____   February

Name Something

1. Name something red.   _____

2. Name something tall.   _____

3. Name something round.   _____

4. Name something thin.   _____

5. Name something fast.   _____

6. Name something loud.   _____

7. Name something blue.   _____

8. Name something small.   _____

9. Name something heavy.   _____

10. Name something quiet.   _____

11. Name something beautiful.   _____

12. Name something large.   _____

13. Name something hot.   _____

14. Name something cold.   _____

15. Name something happy.   _____

Sun Word Search

Find and circle the words.

```
j s u m g u n o p
u t u b l a s f u
s u n o n e p l m
t n u t u r u n p
a o b u n a n u t
n r u b i n f u n
```

gun   **sun**   **bun**   **nun**

fun   **run**   **spun**   **stun**

Bug Word Search

Find and circle the words.

```
s  p  u  n  o  m  u  g
u  l  n  d  u  g  r  u
b  u  g  a  g  s  u  m
u  g  b  y  h  u  g  e
n  s  i  s  t  n  j  e
r  a  t  u  g  h  u  t
a  d  e  n  o  t  g  o
```

bug	dug	hug
rug	jug	plug
tug	mug	

Fish Word Search

Find and circle the words.

```
t o s p i n i b
h e a t t i n y
i f g r i n g p
n o p i n o f i
g r i p o w i n
o c h i n a n g
f r o g e y e s
```

fin **win** **chin** **grin**

pin **tin** **spin** **thin**

Ship Word Search

Find and circle the words.

```
z z i p p e r y t i n
i o s u m m e r r s o
n o t f d o s h i p d
g i r l i p t i p o o
e m h i p l a r i p s
r i m p e l y l m e e
```

ship   **dip**   **flip**   **zip**

rip   **hip**   **trip**   **lip**

Pizza Word Search

Find and circle the words.

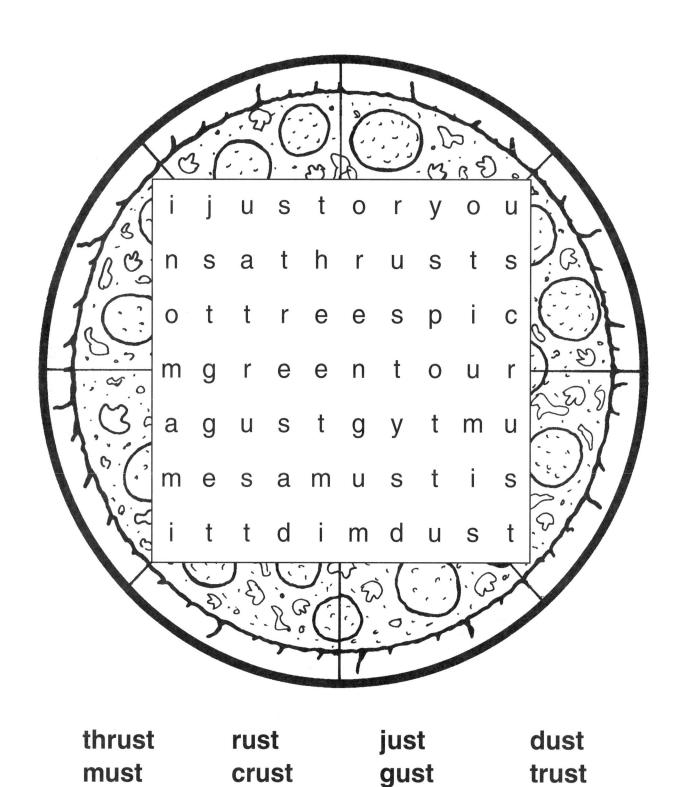

```
i  j  u  s  t  o  r  y  o  u
n  s  a  t  h  r  u  s  t  s
o  t  t  r  e  e  s  p  i  c
m  g  r  e  e  n  t  o  u  r
a  g  u  s  t  g  y  t  m  u
m  e  s  a  m  u  s  t  i  s
i  t  t  d  i  m  d  u  s  t
```

thrust   **rust**   **just**   **dust**

must   **crust**   **gust**   **trust**

Hippo Word Search

Find and circle the words.

```
s p o t b k m
w i t h e i r
n t o e s t i
s l i t s t i
g s f i t e p
i b a s i t p
h i t l i t e
e t r o b e d
```

fit   **sit**   **bit**   **kit**

pit   **lit**   **hit**   **slit**

Lock Word Search

Find and circle the words.

```
s  u  m  m  e  r  d  a  y  l
h  k  n  o  c  k  o  n  n  o
o  s  o  r  e  p  o  d  i  c
c  a  p  e  s  i  r  o  c  k
k  i  c  l  o  c  k  c  k  l
s  l  o  u  c  h  i  k  e  n
b  l  o  c  k  e  c  o  l  g
```

block   **rock**   **shock**   **dock**
clock   **lock**   **knock**   **sock**

Dog Word Search

Find and circle the words.

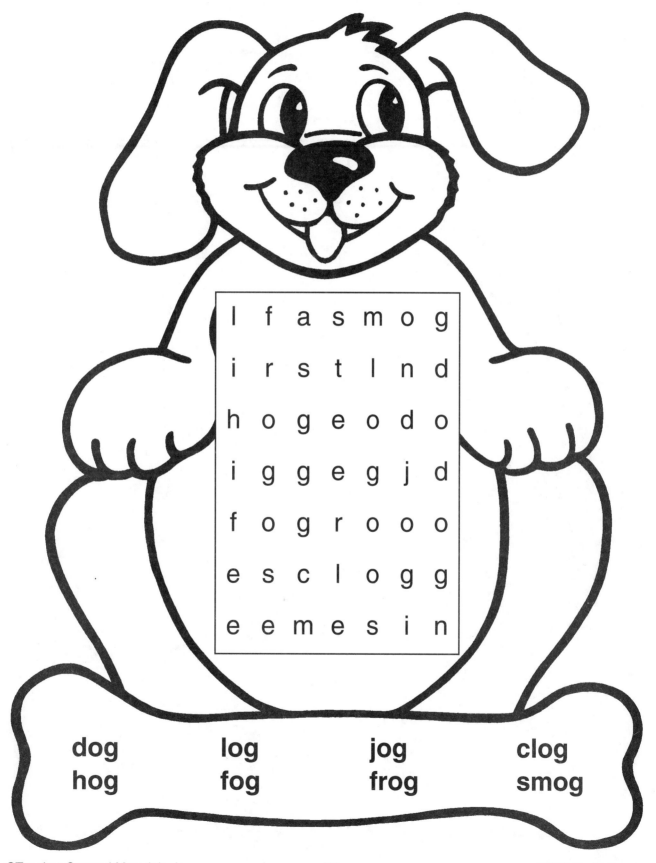

```
l  f  a  s  m  o  g
i  r  s  t  l  n  d
h  o  g  e  o  d  o
i  g  g  e  g  j  d
f  o  g  r  o  o  o
e  s  c  l  o  g  g
e  e  m  e  s  i  n
```

| **dog** | **log** | **jog** | **clog** |
| **hog** | **fog** | **frog** | **smog** |

Flying Word Search

Find and circle the words.

s	o	g	g	y	o	w	e	t
t	g	o	p	e	n	u	p	h
o	e	t	e	s	e	t	b	e
r	t	o	t	h	e	j	e	t
m	e	t	m	e	l	e	t	y

jet	let	met	set
wet	pet	get	bet

Test Word Search

Find and circle the words.

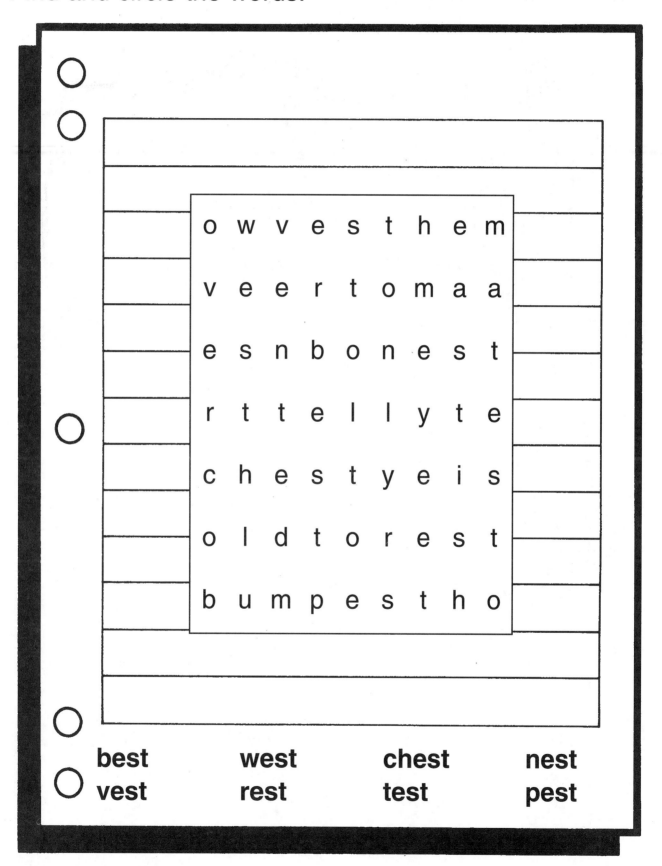

```
o w v e s t h e m
v e e r t o m a a
e s n b o n e s t
r t t e l l y t e
c h e s t y e i s
o l d t o r e s t
b u m p e s t h o
```

best	west	chest	nest
vest	rest	test	pest

Well Word Search

Find and circle the words.

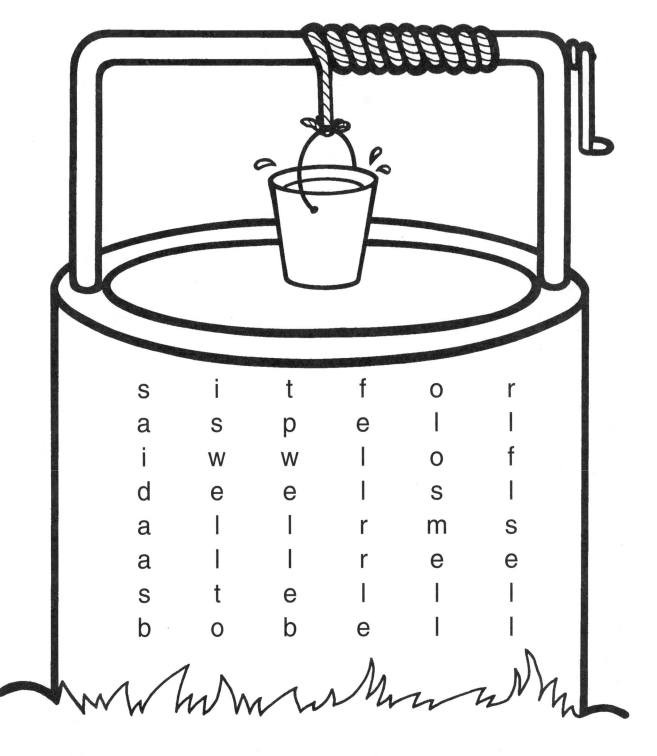

s	i	t	f	o	r
a	s	p	e	l	l
i	w	w	l	o	f
d	e	e	l	s	l
a	l	l	r	m	s
a	t	l	r	e	e
s	o	e	l	l	l
b	o	b	e	l	l

bell **well** **fell** **smell**
tell **sell** **spell** **swell**

Pot Word Search

Find and circle the words.

```
o n t o t r o t o
t u g u h o t o s
s p o t e a s p t
d i t h r e w o i
o n a l o t s t e
t o p s n o t e s
```

trot	hot	lot	dot
spot	got	not	pot

Fan Word Search

Find and circle the words.

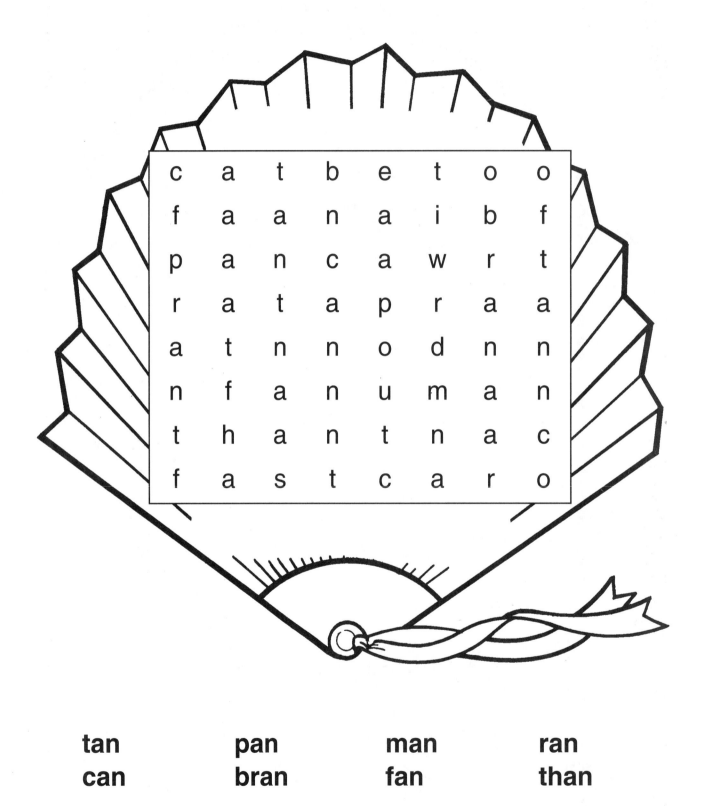

c	a	t	b	e	t	o	o
f	a	a	n	a	i	b	f
p	a	n	c	a	w	r	t
r	a	t	a	p	r	a	a
a	t	n	n	o	d	n	n
n	f	a	n	u	m	a	n
t	h	a	n	t	n	a	c
f	a	s	t	c	a	r	o

tan   **pan**   **man**   **ran**

can   **bran**   **fan**   **than**

Cap Word Search

Find and circle the words.

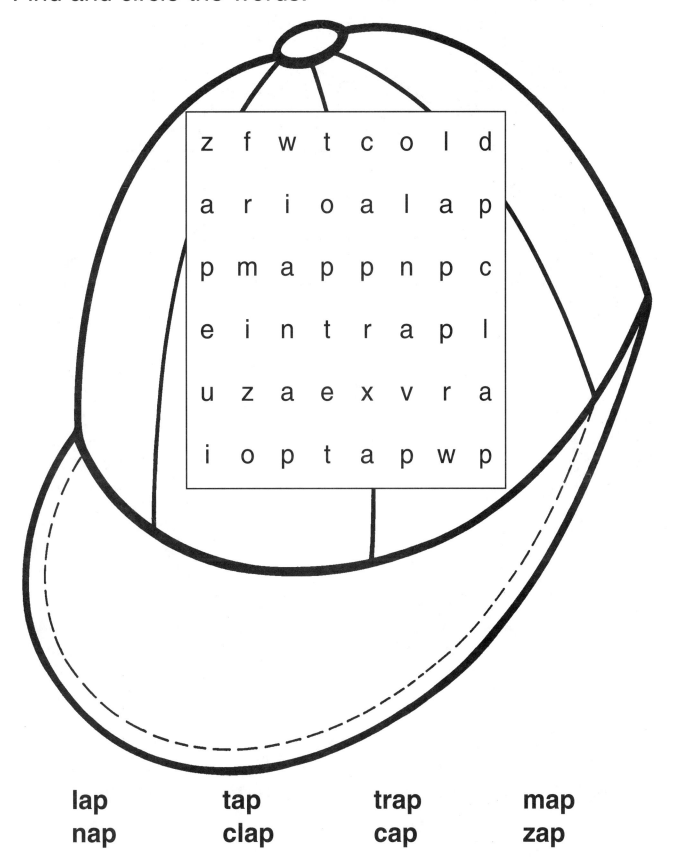

```
z f w t c o l d
a r i o a l a p
p m a p p n p c
e i n t r a p l
u z a e x v r a
i o p t a p w p
```

lap   **tap**   **trap**   **map**

nap   **clap**   **cap**   **zap**

Decorate Your Valentine

Fill in the puzzle. Use the words at the bottom of the page. Some clues have been given to help you.

bow   **candy**   **arrow**   **ribbon**
heart   **lace**   **red**   **roses**

Our First President

Fill in the puzzle. Use the words and clues to help you.

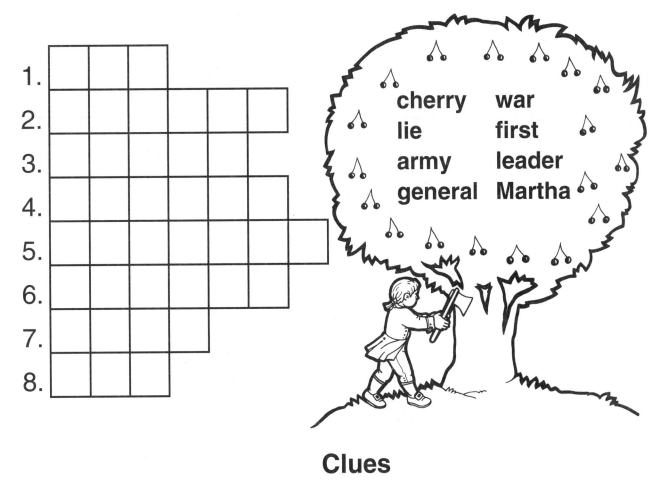

cherry   war
lie   first
army   leader
general   Martha

Clues

1. "I cannot tell a_____."

2. Washington was a great_____.

3. He was our_____president.

4. His wife's name was_____.

5. Washington was a_____in the army.

6. A kind of tree.

7. Washington led the_____.

8. America fought a_____against England.

The Rainbow's End

Fill in the puzzle. Use the words at the bottom of the page. Some clues have been given to help you.

clover   **pot**   **Irish**   **elf**   **luck**

pipe   **March**   **green**   **rainbow**   **gold**

April Fool!

Fill in the puzzle. Use the words at the bottom of the page. Some clues have been given to help you.

joke   laugh   April   prank
fool   fun   trick   first

A Holiday To Remember

Fill in the puzzle. Use the words at the bottom of the page. Some clues have been given to help you.

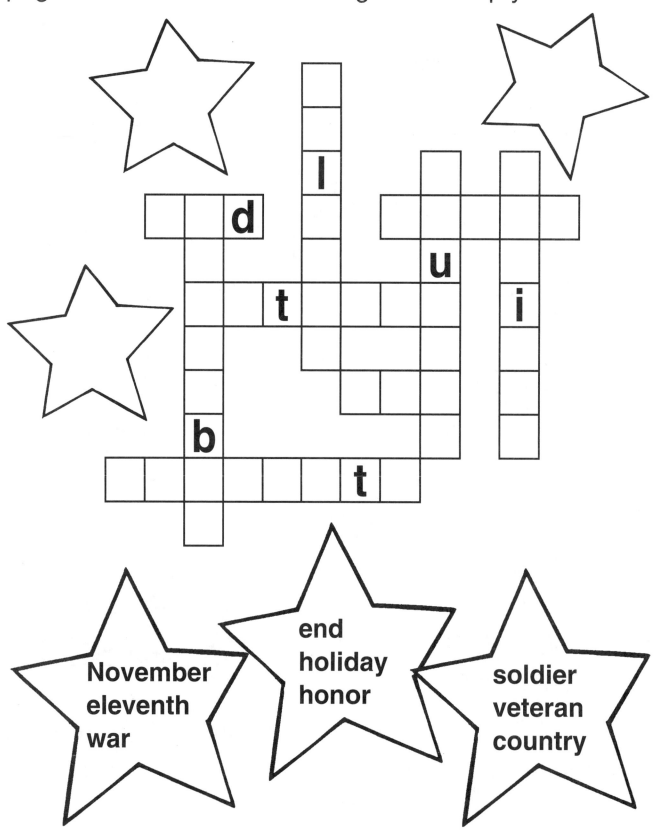

November
eleventh
war

end
holiday
honor

soldier
veteran
country

A Special Day For Dad

Fill in the puzzle. Use the words at the bottom of the page. Some clues have been given to help you.

love   honor   rest   gifts

cards   Sunday   family   June

Crazy Costumes

Fill in the puzzle. Use the words at the bottom of the
page. Some clues have been given to help you.

monster	pirate	cat	bat
cowboy	Indian	queen	scarecrow
princess	ghost	gypsy	

Halloween Fun

Fill in the puzzle. Use the words and clues to help you.

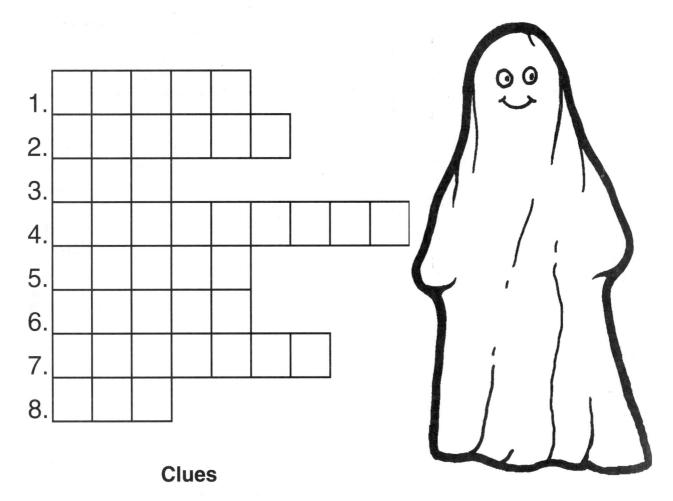

Clues

1. We trick or treat for_____.

2. We bob for_____.

3. An_____says "Whoo."

4. A scary holiday!

5. A_____says "Boo!"

6. Bats are this color.

7. We carve a face on this.

8. A_____says "Meow."

owl
ghost
pumpkin
cat
black
Halloween
candy
apples

A Day To Honor our Soldiers

Fill in the puzzle. Use the words at the bottom of the page. Some clues have been given to help you.

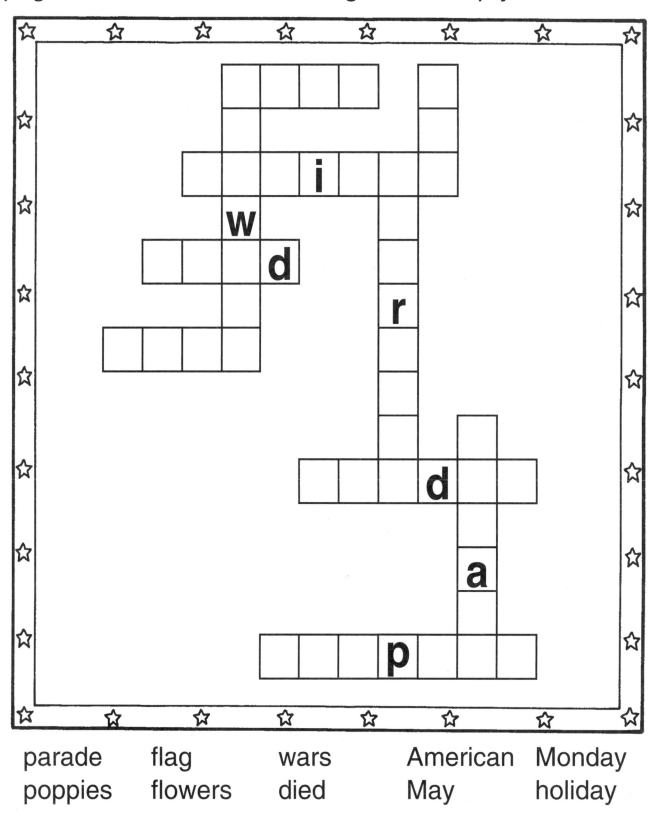

parade   flag   wars   American   Monday

poppies   flowers   died   May   holiday

Hanukkah Crossword

Fill in the puzzle. Use the words at the bottom of the page. Some clues have been given to help you.

temple   Hebrew
dreidel   eight
latkes   shalom
Hanukkah

Reindeer Round-Up

Fill in the puzzle. Use the words at the bottom of the page. Some clues have been given to help you.

| Comet | Prancer | Cupid | Blitzen |
| Dasher | Donner | Vixen | Dancer |

Under The Christmas Tree

Fill in the puzzle. Use the words at the bottom of the page. Some clues have been given to help you.

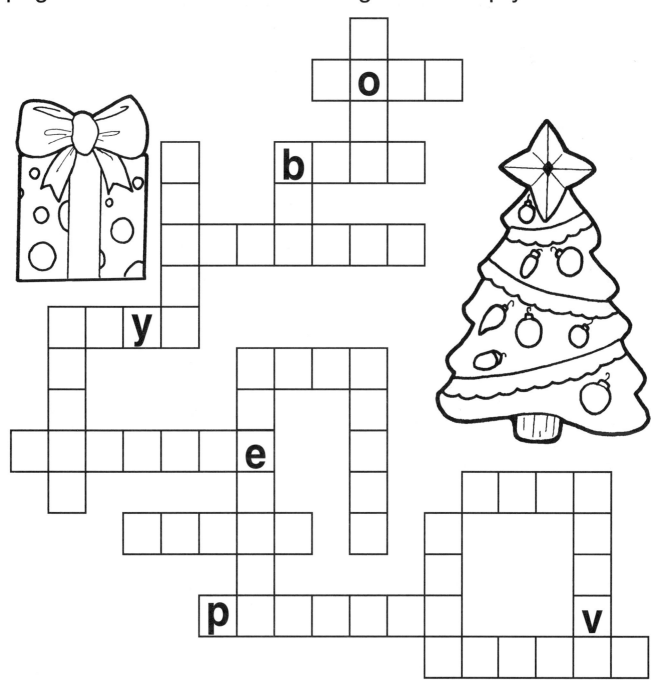

Across

book	present
ball	ring
pants	skates
bicycle	toys
mittens	sled

Down

train	doll
dress	bat
hats	glove
sweater	games

Farmyard Friends

Fill in the puzzle. Use the words and clues to help you.

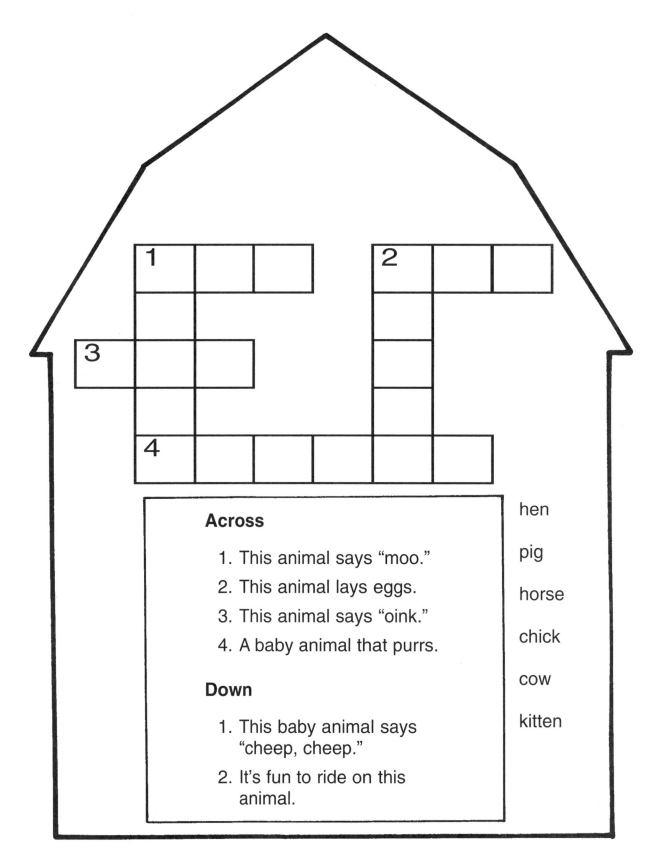

Across

1. This animal says "moo."

2. This animal lays eggs.

3. This animal says "oink."

4. A baby animal that purrs.

Down

1. This baby animal says "cheep, cheep."

2. It's fun to ride on this animal.

hen

pig

horse

chick

cow

kitten

Happy Birthday!

Fill in the puzzle. Use the clues at the bottom of the page.

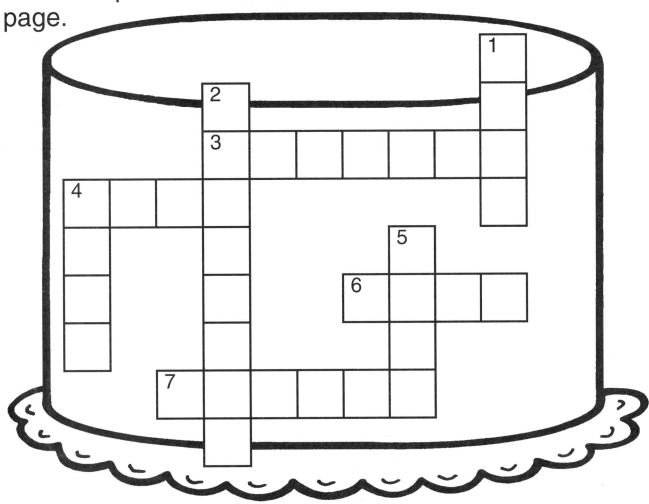

Across

3.

4.

6.

7.

card

cake

hats

wish

ice cream

favors

game

candles

Down

1.

2.

4.

5.

Backwards ABC

Follow the letters of the alphabet backwards to find the picture. Color the picture.

How Amazing!

Follow the maze to get the car in the garage.

Reading Scramble

Unscramble the letters to find words about books and reading.

1. ookb _____

2. brayrli _____

3. eard _____

4. sodrw _____

5. ictreup _____

6. tnpri _____

7. epga _____

8. rutaho _____

9. trtsai _____

10. etpy _____

11. ytrso _____

12. ptol _____

13. rcveo _____

14. cahatrcre _____

15. lusitariotnl _____

Secret Code

Crack the code to figure out the message.

A	B	C	D	E	F	G	H	I	J	K	L	M
○	▢	♥	✳	▲	❄	✦	➜	☆	✪	⇨	♣	▼

N	O	P	Q	R	S	T	U	V	W	X	Y	Z
🐦	☛	✂	✈	❖	◗	■	✏	✍	✚	★	⊘	❀

R E A D I N G

I S   L O T S   O F

F U N !

What Comes Next?

Draw the next thing in each series.

#	Series	
1.	○ □ □ ○ □ □ ○ □	
2.	♡ △ △ ♡ △ △ ♡ △	
3.	○ ☆ ○ ☆ ○ ☆ ○ ☆	
4.	□ □ □ D D D ♡ ♡	
5.	○ △ ○ ▽ ○ △ ○ ▽	
6.	≡ ☆ □ ≡ ☆ □ ≡ ☆	
7.	□ △ △ ♡ ♡ ♡ D D D	
8.	△ △ ○ ○ △ △ □ □ △	
9.	♡ ♡ ☆ ♡ ♡ □ ♡ ♡ ☆ ♡	
10.	□ ▭ □ ▭ □ ▭ □ ▭ □	

Number Series

Write the next number in each series.

a. 1 2 3 4 5 6 7 8 _____

b. 2 4 6 8 10 12 14 16 _____

c. 5 10 15 20 25 30 _____

d. 2 3 4 6 7 8 10 11 _____

e. 2 2 3 3 4 4 5 5 _____

f. 1 3 1 4 1 5 1 6 1 _____

g. 8 7 6 5 4 3 2 _____

h. 3 2 6 4 9 6 12 8 _____

i. 1 5 9 13 17 21 25 _____

j. 10 20 30 40 50 60 70 80 _____

k. 20 18 16 14 12 10 8 _____

l. 0 1 0 2 0 3 0 4 _____

m. 6 5 4 3 2 1 6 5 4 _____

n. 3 6 9 12 9 6 3 6 _____

Letter Series

Write the next letter in each series.

1. A B C D E F _____

2. B D F H J L _____

3. Z Z Y Y X X _____

4. A B C X Y _____

5. Z X V T R P _____

6. Z Y A B X W _____

7. A C B C C C _____

8. B C C B C C _____

9. A M N A M N _____

10. M M D D M M _____

11. Z A Y B X C _____

12. M N O P Q R _____

13. A C E G I K M _____

14. O Q S U W _____

15. A E I O U A E _____

Alphabetical Order

Put the words in ABC order.

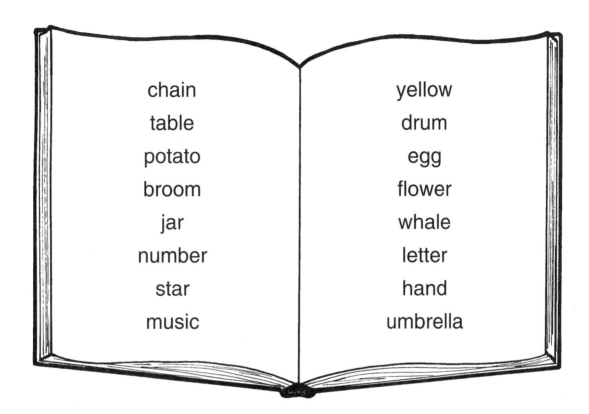

chain	yellow
table	drum
potato	egg
broom	flower
jar	whale
number	letter
star	hand
music	umbrella

1. _____

2. _____

3. _____

4. _____

5. _____

6. _____

7. _____

8. _____

9. _____

10. _____

11. _____

12. _____

13. _____

14. _____

15. _____

16. _____

Match the Pairs

Match the things that go together. Color the pictures.

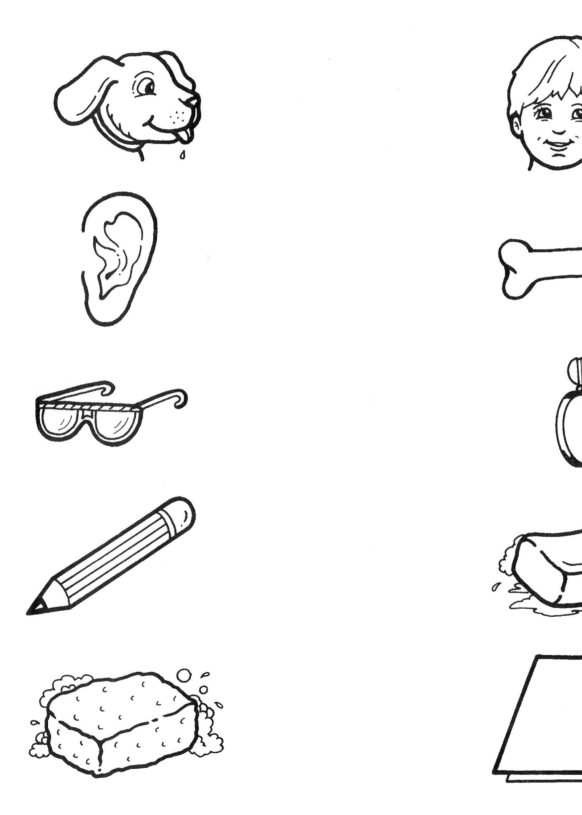

Go Togethers

Match the things that go together. Color the pictures.

Fairy Tale Match

Match the fairy tale figures that go together. Color the pictures.

128

Cookie Jar Math

Complete the problem on each cookie jar. The answer will be the number of cookies inside the cookie jar. Write the number of cookies on the line under each cookie jar. Draw lines to show which type of cookies are in each jar.

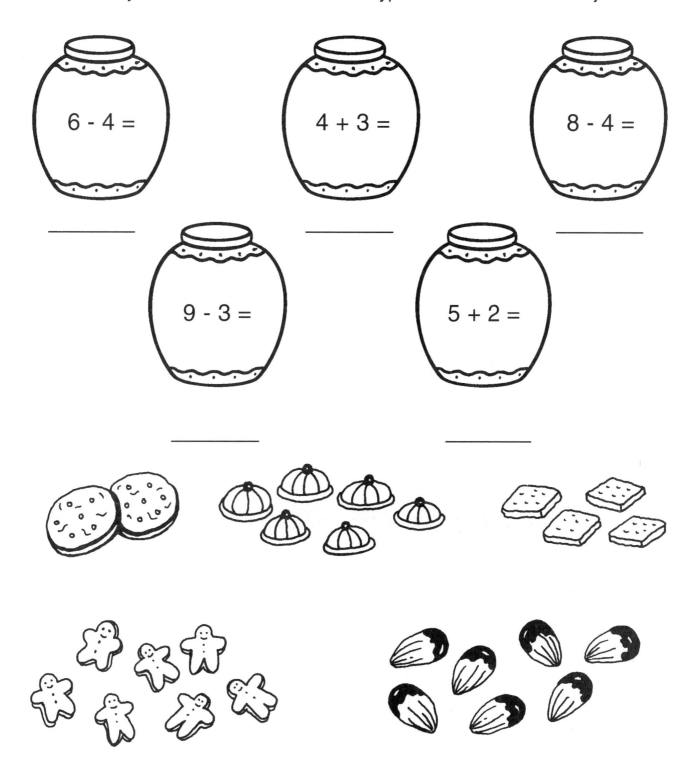

What's the Sign?

Fill in the missing + (addition) or - (subtraction).

1. $2 \boxed{} 4 = 6$

2. $5 \boxed{} 2 = 3$

3. $7 \boxed{} 2 = 9$

4. $3 \boxed{} 2 = 1$

5. $4 \boxed{} 1 = 5$

6. $3 \boxed{} 4 = 7$

7. $7 \boxed{} 2 = 9$

8. $4 \boxed{} 1 = 5$

9. $8 \boxed{} 5 = 3$

10. $12 \boxed{} 6 = 6$

11. $15 \boxed{} 1 = 14$

12. $4 \boxed{} 8 = 12$

Homes

Three children live on the same street. Each of their houses is a different color.
Can you use the clues to match each child to his or her house? Draw a line
between each child and home. Color the houses when you are through.

1. Marla's house is the color of cotton candy.

2. Pepper's house is the color of some apples.

3. Rosa's house is the color of corn on the cob.

Marla

Red House

Pepper

Yellow House

Rosa

Pink House

Which Is Different?

One picture in each row is different. Color the picture that is different.

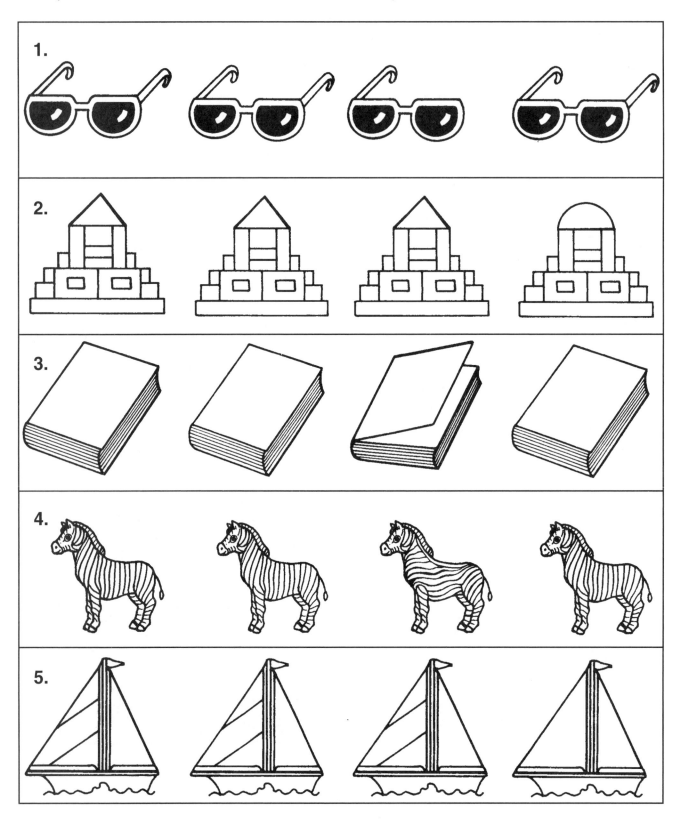

132

Whose Jump Rope?

Follow the strings to see who is connected to which jump rope. Write the number of the jump rope below each child. Color the pictures.

#1   #2   #3   #4   #5

Rope # _____   Rope # _____   Rope # _____   Rope # _____   Rope # _____

How Many Circles?

How many circles are in the picture? Count them and then color the picture.

There are _____ circles.

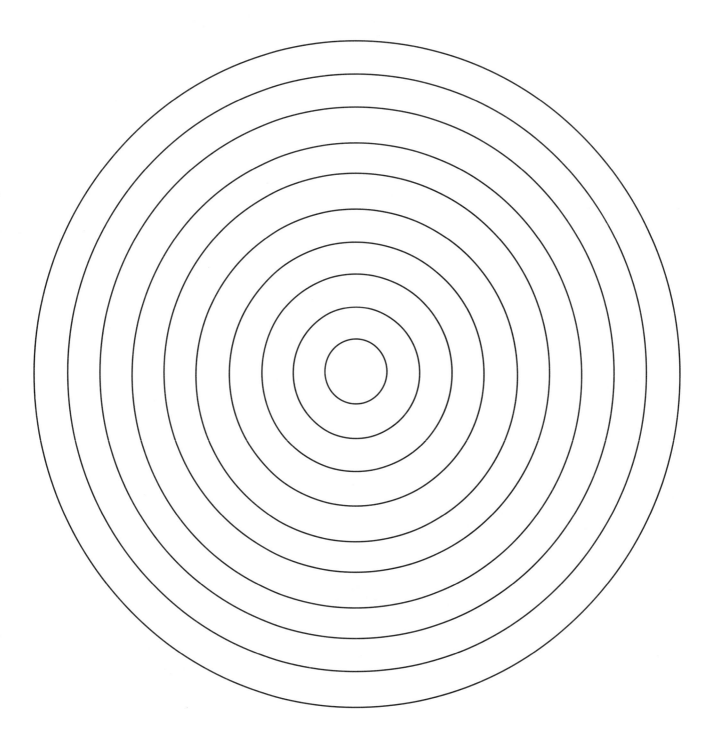

How Many Triangles?

How many triangles are in the picture? Count them and then color the picture.

There are _____ triangles.

Picture Shapes

Find the triangles and circles in the picture. Color the picture.

These things have △s :

These things have ◯s :

Missing Parts

Draw in the missing part of each picture. Color the pictures.

Ice skate

Clock

Guitar

Cat

Rabbit

Car

Rhyme Time

Write four words that rhyme with each word below.

tree

_____

_____

_____

_____

rope

_____

_____

_____

_____

dad

_____

_____

_____

_____

feet

_____

_____

_____

_____

pop

_____

_____

_____

_____

fan

_____

_____

_____

_____

138

Similes

Choose the best word from the Word Box to complete each simile.

1. As silly as a _____

2. As sharp as a _____

3. As free as a _____

4. As big as a _____

5. As cold as _____

6. As smooth as _____

7. As old as _____

8. As pretty as a _____

9. As happy as a _____

10. As busy as a _____

Word Box	
bee	silk
goose	goat
bird	time
tack	ice
house	clam

Opposites

List the opposites.

1. fix   _____

2. in   _____

3. play   _____

4. back   _____

5. old   _____

6. dark   _____

7. before   _____

8. over   _____

9. near   _____

10. no   _____

11. add   _____

12. day   _____

13. loud   _____

14. lost   _____

15. stop   _____

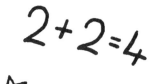

Name Something

1. Name something round. _____

2. Name something rough. _____

3. Name something hot. _____

4. Name something cuddly. _____

5. Name something light. _____

6. Name something dark. _____

7. Name something loud. _____

8. Name something wet. _____

9. Name something funny. _____

10. Name something silly. _____

11. Name something small. _____

12. Name something square. _____

13. Name something orange. _____

14. Name something soft. _____

15. Name something big. _____

Dot to Dot

Follow the numbers to find the picture. Color the picture.

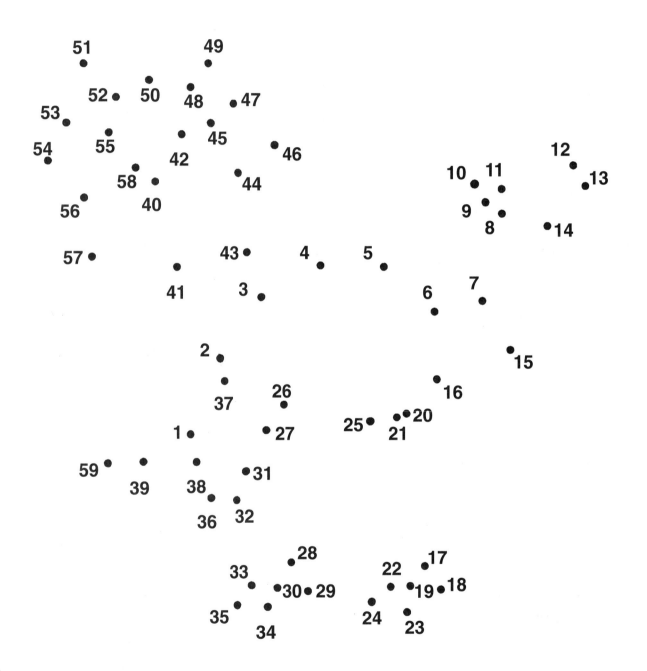

Follow the Dots

Follow the numbers to find the picture. Color the picture.

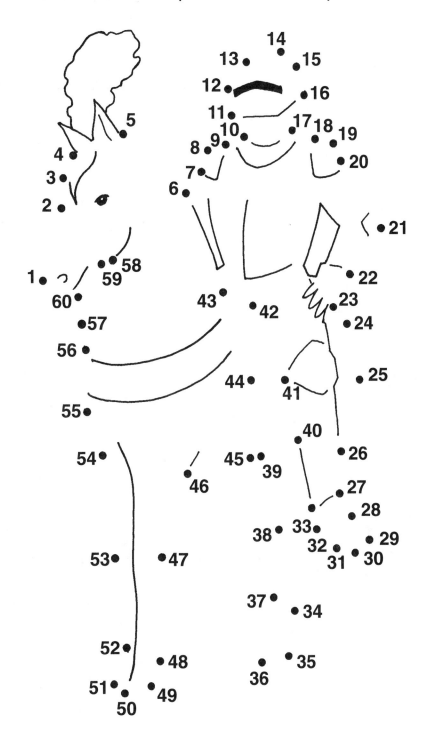

Follow the ABC's

Follow the letters of the alphabet to find the picture. Color the picture.

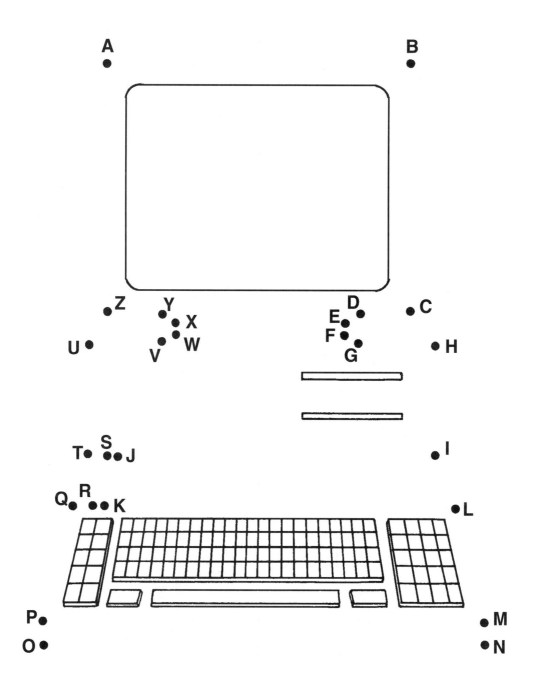

Backwards ABC

Follow the letters of the alphabet backwards to find the picture. Color the picture.

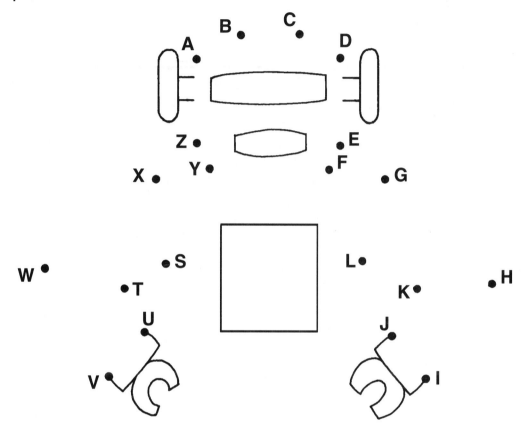

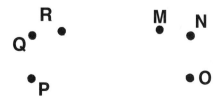

Proverb Dot to Dot

Follow the letters to spell out a famous proverb. Color the picture.
Start at the star.

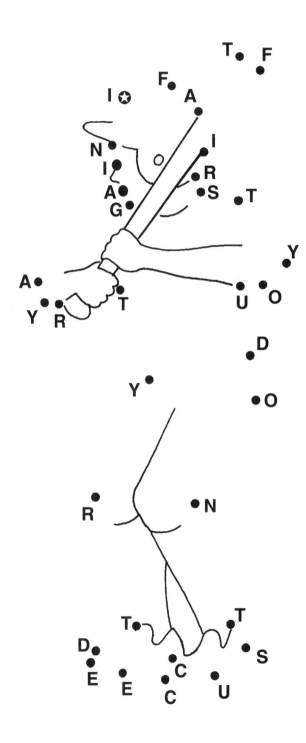

How Amazing!

Follow the maze to get the feet to the shoes.

A Maze of Letters

Follow the whole alphabet through the maze to get the mouse to the cheese.

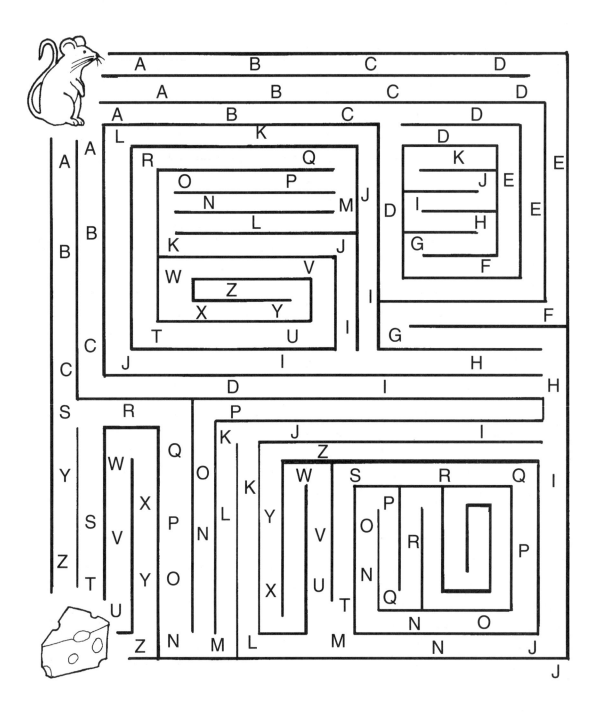

A Maze of Numbers

Follow the numbers 1 through 20 to get the butterfly to a flower.

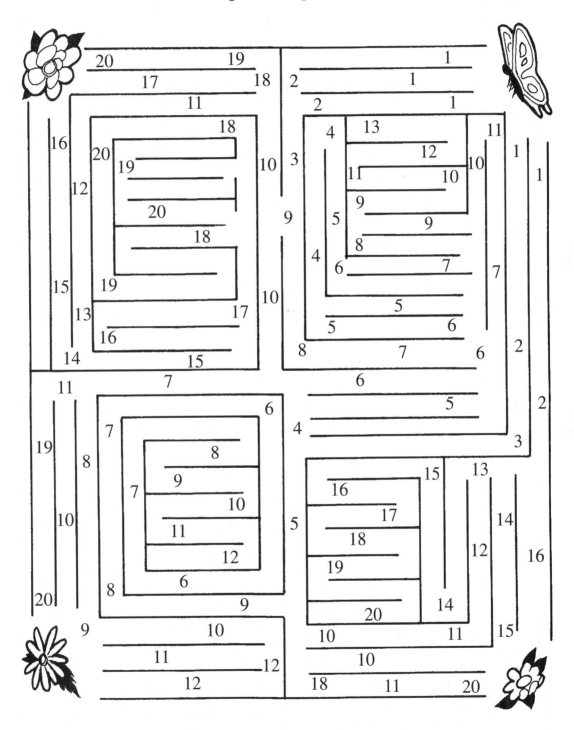

You Wear It Well

Find the items of clothing from the Word Box in the word search puzzle. The words can be found down, across, or diagonally.

```
N V L R T F C D S W N F S X P N L D Q S V D F
X B C C S N M M H C H C M H T D J E B H A D L D
L W H T R B P B N A J I V O J S T G C R N S G J
D X J P V W C R D R H N R R X B K G K O D Y W C
X Z N T W H D J B F M I T T E N S I Y H A T G R
S Q J J T D H X L G P S V S S Z H N R N L T C N
F J P Q R W J V O K C O N B H J G G C T S H N L
B A T H I N G S U I T C X E O V N S Y J D E L Q
C C N T M G J S S J N K L L E G J G S U R A X B
B K Z T V S H S E T L S M T S K L P X M E D P Z
T E M R S Y W T W P L Z B Z M Q M P W P S B C N
X T Z J J J B G S F V M Z Q J Y G Y D E S A C B
Q X F J C S Q H P N N P M L X D P G W R X N W W
P X L X S T H B R P C N S K N W Y T P M J D F G
Z O M L R G B R Y K Q Z V Y B Q B Z H W H W B T
P A N T S P S X P P D R W M Q Z B W N V V Y W S
T I G H T S D H Y M J N Q X Z J S F Z T K L W V
```

Word Box

dress	skirt	tights	jumper
shoes	blouse	mittens	leggings
socks	sandals	scarf	bathing suit
pants	jacket	coat	headband
shirt	shorts	hat	belt

What a Character!

Find all the characters from the Word Box in the word search puzzle.
The words can be found down, across, or diagonally.

```
Q R G L R V T V S S P B C F J S F Y Z K G G F L
R G O G W T W Z E Y Q K F H S D N L K K A U L K
Y P O L I V E O Y L B A T M A N S U P E R M A N
H L F P F N E Z J V M T M O Q R O X K X F B M Z
L U Y D R X T T E E P E C I M B L O P M I Y K J
X T S V A T Y Y R S O M R W C B B I P H E Q K P
F O M L B F V C R T P J D F N K U G E Y L D C M
X H H I Y N F N Y E E Q O N U N E G K B D S G G
X W M R N X B Y S R Y C N M Q D X Y S L R W J K
T C H F D N D B D D E X A C B M D C M B H O D L
D Z V N C J I V R U J D L J C Y B F Y O U L W X
S J W V F G P E W Y C D D Z W K D C T R U N F N
Q H P C Q C W S M V V K D X R R X P M N H S N F
L S R L K B Y M L O F B U P Y D G P Q H Q G E Y
Z Z D K B L N H P P U Z C C F Y R N Q Z N B W C
X F W W S V N B M H P S K P B P S H Z N F F Y X
J D W S H G V F P R C P E T V S D T K K B L B Z
```

Word Box

Mickey Mouse	Bugs Bunny	Sylvester	Superman
Goofy	Tweety	Pluto	Batman
Snoopy	Tom	Minnie Mouse	Olive Oyl
Garfield	Jerry	Charlie Brown	Popeye
Donald Duck	Daffy Duck	Elmer Fudd	Gumby

                                       #3670 Brain Games

Oh, Baby!

Find the "baby" words from the Word Box in the word search puzzle. The words can be found down, across, or diagonally.

```
K F K X W H W D C N F G P X Q J J Y Q L S A B Z
F Y N C D H M Z F C Y S Z W B C S H C U C P N Y
G C G T L D F T L O Q G L R M N P Q D L F P F H
D B D S W R C J L O F R V E J F O J H L S L P L
C T Y V S C T E W K B Z W W E Q W X C A F E J K
L R W V G K L B R I G D K N G P D D K B G S M J
D A K D G I G G L E C C R A D L E C T Y N A P H
C T J R P F B X V Y A K K P Y Y R R R L P U C T
M T Q N L O Y O B T K L Q A M C R Y P A K C V M
T L J Z A R Q W T S B K D C N F R D F B W E Z B
R E R D Y M T D J T F Y W I G J U I C E B L K K
B J Q P S U H Q X Q L L G F F T C A B N L W W D
J W J P U L N B T W D E J I H R L P D N A N K P
L H M W I A M Q L N B P N E R W M E C W N F T J
L Y K P T K X J W Z L Y P R G J J R M L K J H M
Z C P H J V Z B W C H Z S D D X H D Q S E W Z K
C N S P Y R L L N P D F B S Z P V R R C T B M S
```

Word Box

cradle	bottle	formula	cry
blanket	diaper	applesauce	giggle
crib	pacifier	nap	lullaby
rattle	powder	playsuit	crawl
juice	cereal	sleeper	cookie

Feelings

Find the "feeling" words from the Word Box in the word search puzzle. The words can be found down, across, or diagonally.

```
H F M Y J S B F J H J P Y L S K F L B R X V G W
S W X Q O M S M S Q S P Z D L I X S B T D S B N
Z C N B Y P P N Q N C X B C J M L N D Y Y L N B
Y S C W F H Z P H B R T M R B D J L B K Z Z D G
R C H C U Y W W D X C D F N Q N M X Y T X P Q W
D P R B L P D C J N C C F H S F B L S F S X V P
L B T G R W Y R T R J R W M B Z W K K G X Q S B
Y C Z H G D Z Z D C F W D H K H X L K H L J G J
B T F X W M Q X D P J B G W Y L L L Y Y V B L B
P Q R M W Q R Y Y H L T G H Q P K O F B P K A B
E D Z Q F X D L T L T X Q P A Q R N L K N V N Q
A G Y Z K M L S F B B P R M W P G E S Q H J G M
C X L F R L L C B G P S M B W F P L G A Q T R X
E N P C C N C A F V R P B G K P P Y P V D B Y W
F J J A X J M R H L O B L H F V W H X L P M L J
U X W L P H Z E D G U Y N X N X Z B C R N L D H
L M L M R Z L D F C D Q F H S K N K C S H M G F
```

Word Box

happy	sad	angry
scared	lonely	joyful
peaceful	silly	calm
	proud	

Two for T

Find the "T" words from the Word Box in the word search puzzle. The words can be found down, across, or diagonally.

```
Y B C H F Q T L Z Z Z F V B S L Y B Q Z T A P W
L V Z F T M Z R M Y J Y Q S T E A C U P B B T Y
Z W Q S W Y V F I D C K G T E J J N C W G T J J
H V P K D D G B J A N Z T T E X T C W H H S Z V
        X N F D C N L B A P C W G H
        T G H Z L K G V B E B I B H
        W F Z Z N G R L L E B S Z T
        O V W T O N G U E J B T A K
        J Y Q O F H G D Y X C A E V
        P F S P C H N B H C B C Y E
        C B V G F P S M V T A K E T
        T Q L Z G R M B W K F J R R
        C W B R L J Y L D T L T X D
        W D E N C M F Q N C D W G X
        Y T F L H F Z T L P B F V W
        K V M F V G M B Z D W B F K
        D H N N W E X S Y H R V Q G
```

Word Box

table	teacup	tongue
top	twist	teepee
twelve	triangle	tap
tack	take	two

154

Word Scrambles

Unscramble the letters to find the sports.

1. llbseaba   _____

2. tblfooal   _____

3. bfotslla   _____

4. skeblbatal   _____

5. ninnrug   _____

6. kcyeho   _____

7. llorer stngkai   _____

8. lngiias   _____

9. yccbingli   _____

10. inksig   _____

11. tbrdingksaeoa   _____

12. cei stngkai   _____

13. nisnet   _____

14. eylvlbaoll   _____

15. mnticsgyas   _____

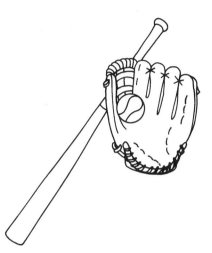

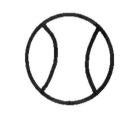

More Word Scrambles

Unscramble the letters to find the things having to do with the seasons.

1. mwnsona   _____

2. ngiloobm   _____

3. vaeles   _____

4. iarn   _____

5. neriwt   _____

6. lcdo   _____

7. ndwi   _____

8. nwos   _____

9. prngis   _____

10. toh   _____

11. nus   _____

12. umersm   _____

13. wfsolnkea   _____

14. wlfoesr   _____

15. uumnta   _____

Decoding

Match each number to the letter in the code to find the career names.

A	B	C	D	E	F	G	H	I	J	K	L	M
1	2	3	4	5	6	7	8	9	10	11	12	13

N	O	P	Q	R	S	T	U	V	W	X	Y	Z
14	15	16	17	18	19	20	21	22	23	24	25	26

1. 6 1 18 13 5 18 _____

2. 2 1 14 11 5 18 _____

3. 12 1 23 25 5 18 _____

4. 20 5 1 3 8 5 18 _____

5. 4 15 3 20 15 18 _____

6. 23 18 9 20 5 18 _____

7. 19 5 3 18 5 20 1 18 25 _____

8. 4 5 20 5 3 20 9 22 5 _____

9. 12 9 2 18 1 18 9 1 14 _____

10. 19 3 9 5 14 20 9 19 20 _____

11. 13 21 19 9 3 9 1 14 _____

12. 1 3 20 15 18 _____

13. 5 4 9 20 15 18 _____

14. 3 15 15 11 _____

15. 6 9 18 5 6 9 7 8 20 5 18 _____

More Decoding

Match each number to the letter in the code to find the wilderness animals.

<u>A</u>	<u>B</u>	<u>C</u>	<u>D</u>	<u>E</u>	<u>F</u>	<u>G</u>	<u>H</u>	<u>I</u>	<u>J</u>	<u>K</u>	<u>L</u>	<u>M</u>
1	2	3	4	5	6	7	8	9	10	11	12	13

<u>N</u>	<u>O</u>	P	<u>Q</u>	<u>R</u>	<u>S</u>	<u>T</u>	<u>U</u>	<u>V</u>	<u>W</u>	<u>X</u>	<u>Y</u>	<u>Z</u>
14	15	16	17	18	19	20	21	22	23	24	25	26

1. 18 1 3 3 15 15 14 _____

2. 2 5 1 18 _____

3. 4 5 5 18 _____

4. 18 1 2 2 9 20 _____

5. 19 11 21 14 11 _____

6. 16 15 19 19 21 13 _____

7. 15 23 12 _____

8. 13 15 15 19 5 _____

9. 2 5 1 22 5 18 _____

10. 2 1 4 7 5 18 _____

11. 5 12 11 _____

12. 1 14 20 5 12 15 16 5 _____

13. 2 15 1 18 _____

14. 13 21 19 11 18 1 20 _____

15. 4 21 3 11 _____

Secret Code

Crack the code to figure out the message.

A	B	C	D	E	F	G	H	I	J	K	L	M
○	□	♥	✳	▲	❄	✦	→	☆	✪	⇨	♣	▼

N	O	P	Q	R	S	T	U	V	W	X	Y	Z
🐦	☛	✂	✈	❖	◗	■	✏	✍	✚	★	⊙	❀

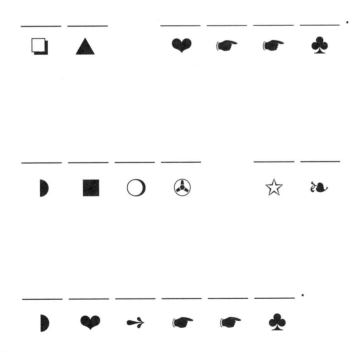

More Secret Code

Crack the code to figure out the message.

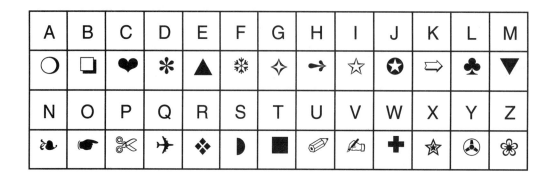

Crack the Code

To decode the message, write the letter of the alphabet that comes after each letter given. Then, complete the message. (**Note:** "A" comes after "Z.")

H   B Z M   C N

Z M X S G H M F   H

V Z M S   S N   C N   Z M C

A D   Z M X S G H M F   H

V Z M S   S N   A D.

V G D M   H   F Q N V   T O,

H   V H K K

_____

_____

_____

_____

What Comes Next?

Draw the next thing in each series.

1. □ ▱ △ □ ▱ △ □ ▱	
2. ○ □ □ ○ □ □ ○ □	
3. △ ♡ △ ♡ △ ♡ △ ♡	
4. ◇ ◇ ◇ ○ ○ ○ □ □	
5. ♡ △ ♡ ▽ ♡ △ ♡ ▽	
6. ◇ ♡ □ ♡ ◇ ♡ □ ♡	
7. ○ ♡ ♡ △ △ △ ☆ ☆ ☆	
8. ♡ ♡ □ □ ♡ ♡ △ △ ♡	
9. △ △ ☆ △ △ ♡ △ △ ☆ △	
10. □ ▭ □ ▭ □ ▭ □ ▭ □	

Number Series

Write the next number in each series.

1. 1 2 3 4 5 6 7 8   _____

2. 2 4 6 8 10 12 14 16   _____

3. 1 3 5 7 9 11 13 15   _____

4. 1 2 3 5 6 7 9 10   _____

5. 1 1 2 2 3 3 4 4   _____

6. 1 9 2 8 3 7 4 6   _____

7. 9 8 7 6 5 4 3 2   _____

8. 5 10 15 20 25 30 35 40   _____

9. 1 4 7 10 13 16 19 22   _____

10. 10 20 30 40 50 60 70 80   _____

11. 18 16 14 12 10 8 6 4   _____

12. 0 1 0 2 0 3 0 4   _____

13. 5 4 3 2 1 5 4 3   _____

14. 3 1 4 5 9 14 23 37   _____

15. 3 6 9 12 9 6 3 6   _____

Letter Series

Write the next letter in each series.

1. A B C D E F _____

2. A C E G I K _____

3. B D F H J L _____

4. Z Y X W V U _____

5. Z X V T R P _____

6. A D G J M P _____

7. A A B B C C _____

8. A B C D A B _____

9. A B C B A B _____

10. A B B A B B _____

11. Z T V Z T V _____

12. M Q E Q M Q _____

13. B D K K D B _____

14. A Z B Y C X _____

15. A Z A Y A X _____

Alphabetical Order

Put the words in ABC order.

catfish	type	bounty
apron	apple	time
eagle	basket	elevator
schooner	elephant	school
cat	tip	apricot
	schoolhouse	

1. _____

2. _____

3. _____

4. _____

5. _____

6. _____

7. _____

8. _____

9. _____

10. _____

11. _____

12. _____

13. _____

14. _____

15. _____

16. _____

More Alphabetical Order

Put the words in ABC order.

angel	fried
happy	door
doorknob	happen
joyful	friendly
paper	aardvark
mouse	doorbell
friend	moose
angle	pepper

1._____   9._____

2._____   10._____

3._____   11._____

4._____   12._____

5._____   13._____

6._____   14._____

7._____   15._____

8._____   16._____

Color the Pairs

Color the two items in each row that match.

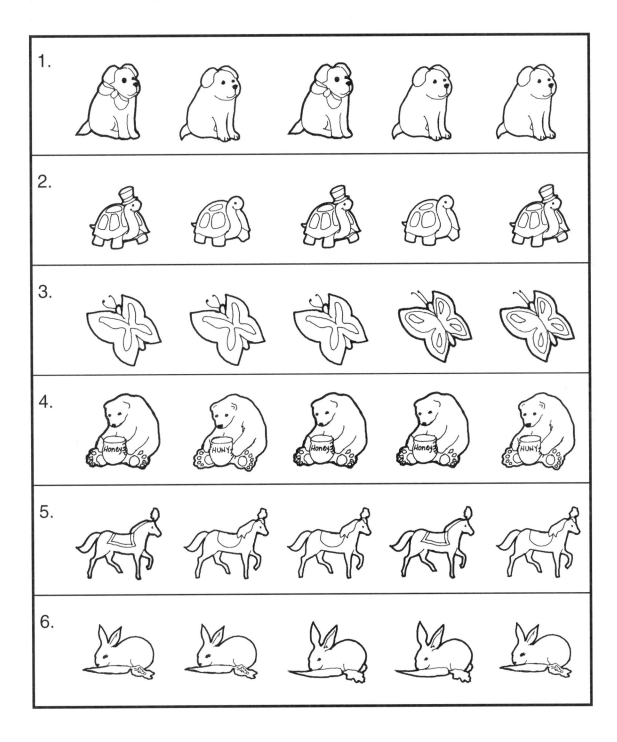

Match the Pairs

Match the things that go together. Color the pictures.

Make a Set

Match the things that go together. Color the pictures.

"Fee Fi Fo Fum"

Match the fairy tale figures that go together. Color the pictures.

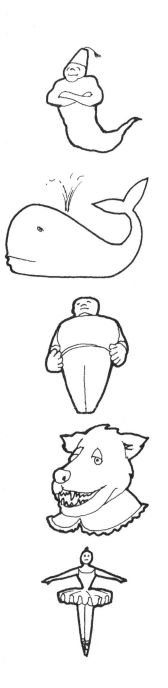

Animal Homes

Match each animal to its home. Color the pictures.

Package Surprise

Match each gift to a package. Color the pictures.

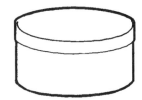

1.

2.

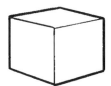

3.

4.

5.
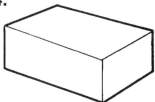

It Doesn't Fit

Circle everything in the picture that does not fit in. Color the picture.

Uni, Bi, Tri

"Uni" means *one*. "Bi" means *two*. "Tri" means *three*. Write *uni, bi,* or *tri* before each word below to complete the word.

1.

_____ cycle

2.

_____ pod

3.

_____ cycle

4.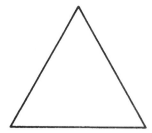

_____ angle

5.

_____ cycle

6.

_____ corn

What Can We Hear?

Color everything that makes a sound or sounds.

Friends

Each pair of friends below has something in common. Match the friends.

Kayla   Jamaal   Tran   Keisha   Danny

Will   Tamara   Nori   Lynn   Anton

Whose Is It?

Can you use the clues in the pictures to figure out what item belongs to each child? **Hint:** Think of the *number* of things. Write what each child owns on the line under his or her picture.

Kami owns_____   **Pablo** owns _____   **Maria** owns _____

wagon   **scooter**   **skates**

Whose Present Is It?

Can you match each present to each child? Look for something in common. Write the correct present on the line under each child.

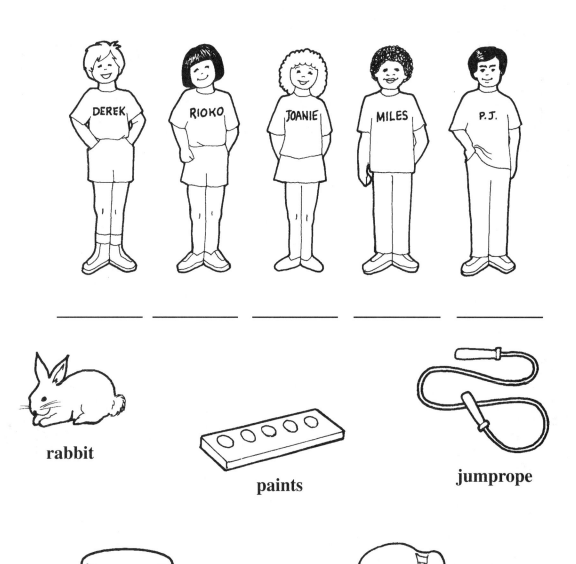

_____ _____ _____ _____ _____

rabbit

paints

jumprope

drum

mitt

Package Math

Complete the problem on each package. The answer will be a clue to the present inside. Write the present on the line under each package.

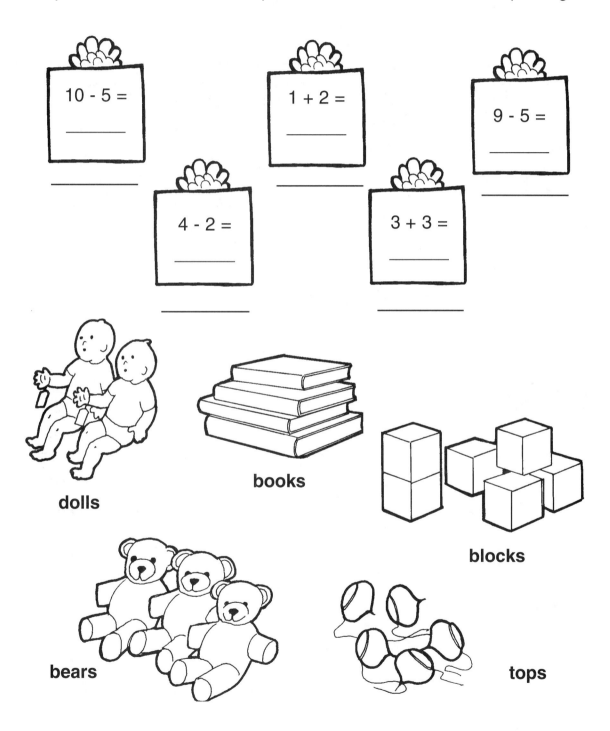

10 - 5 =

_____

1 + 2 =

_____

9 - 5 =

_____

_____

4 - 2 =

_____

3 + 3 =

_____

_____

_____

dolls

books

blocks

bears

tops

What's the Sign?

Fill in the missing +, −, or = sign.

1. $3 \square 2 = 5$

2. $6 - 1 \square 5$

3. $9 \square 3 = 6$

4. $2 \square 7 = 9$

5. $1 \square 3 = 4$

6. $4 + 3 \square 7$

7. $9 \square 6 = 3$

8. $6 + 2 \square 8$

9. $10 \square 5 = 15$

10. $12 \square 6 = 6$

11. $14 \square 4 = 10$

12. $7 \square 5 = 12$

Favorite Games

Paulo, Chan, and Denzel are three friends. Each has a favorite game. Can you use the clues to figure out each friend's favorite game? Draw a line to connect each child to a game.

1. In Chan's favorite game, someone has to count.
2. In Denzel's favorite game, someone gives directions.
3. In Paulo's favorite game, everyone runs.

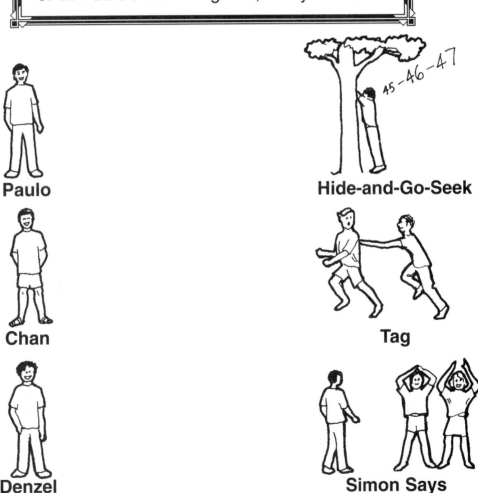

Paulo

Chan

Denzel

Hide-and-Go-Seek

Tag

Simon Says

Homes

Three children live on the same street. Each of their houses is a different color. Can you use the clues to match each child to his or her house? Draw a line between each child and home.

1. Bettina's house is the color of leaves in spring.
2. Carly's house is the color of some fire trucks.
3. Nikko's house is the color of the sky.

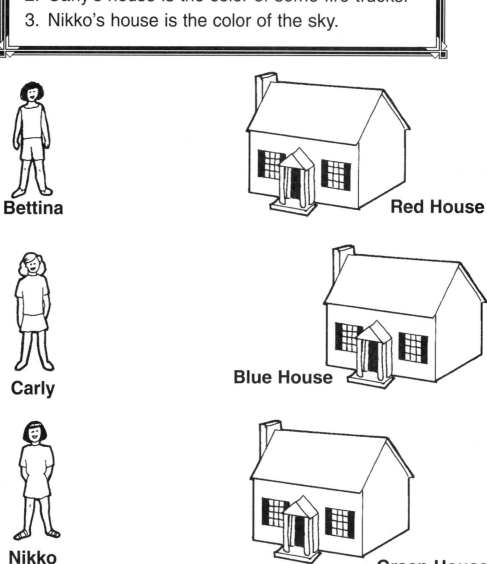

Bettina

Red House

Carly

Blue House

Nikko

Green House

Which Is Different?

One picture in each row is different. Color the picture that is different.

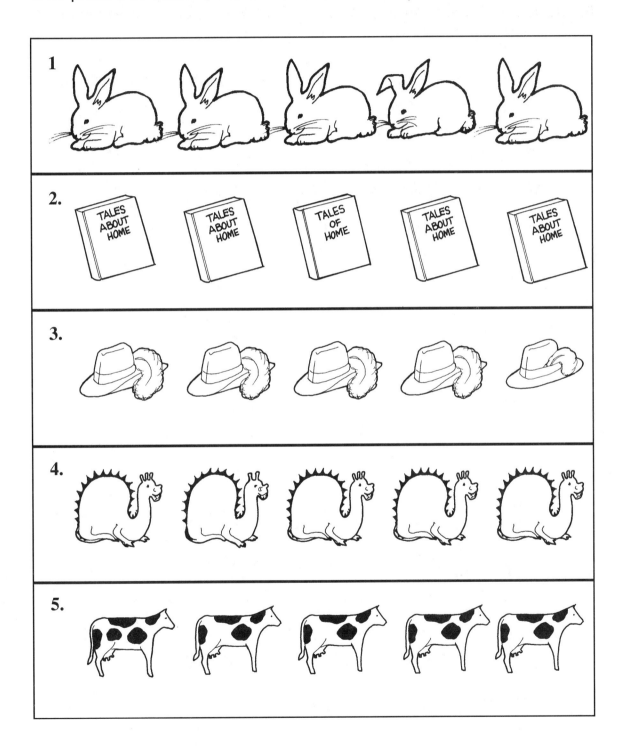

Whose Kite?

Follow the strings to see who is connected to which kite. Write the number of the kite below each child. Color the pictures.

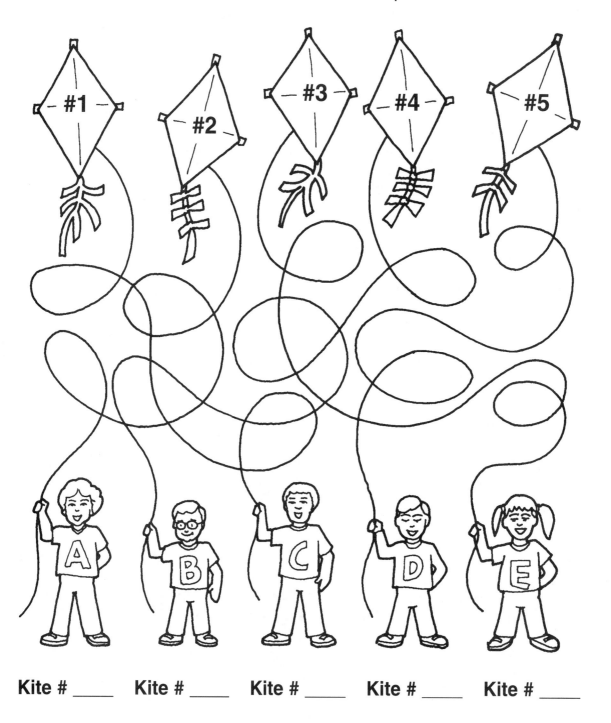

Kite # ____   Kite # ____   Kite # ____   Kite # ____   Kite # ____

Kittens and String

Follow the string to see which kitten is playing with which ball of string. Write the number of each ball of string below each kitten. Color the pictures.

String #____   **String #____**   **String #____**   **String #____**   **String #____**

How Many Circles?

How many circles are in the picture? Count them and then color the picture.

There are _____ circles.

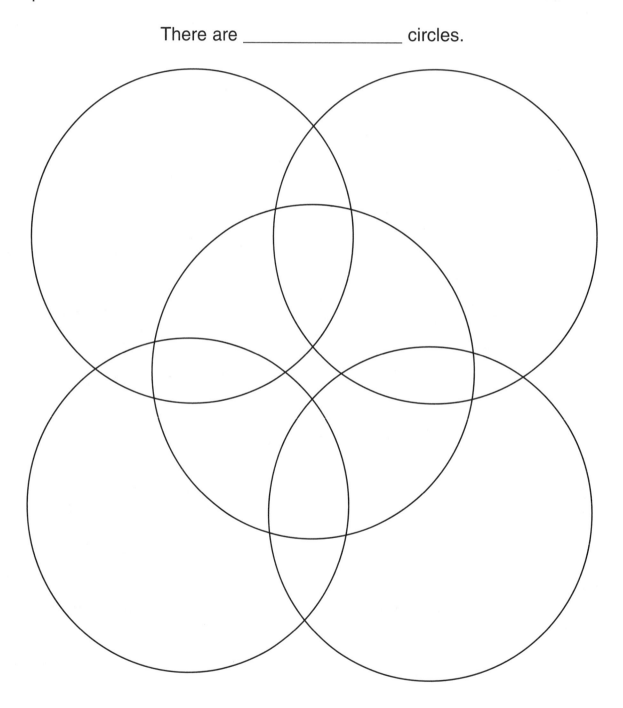

How Many Squares?

How many squares are in the picture? Count them and then color the picture.

There are _____ squares.

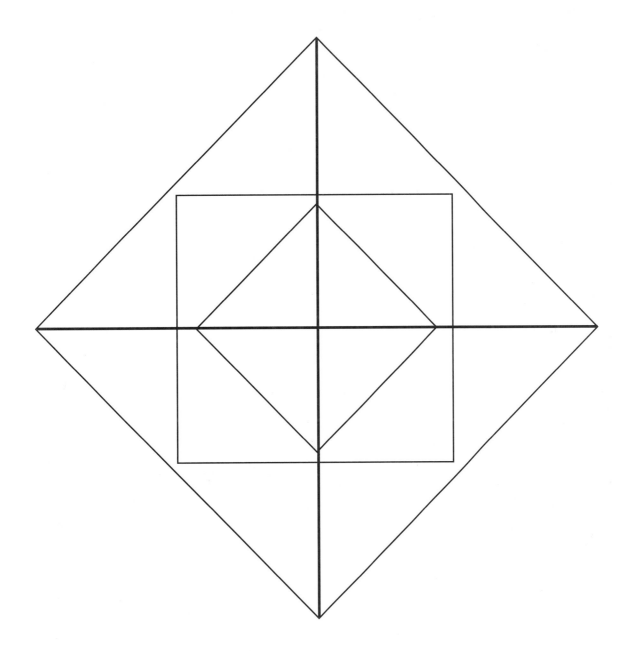

How Many Triangles?

How many triangles are in the picture? Count them and then color the picture.

There are _____ triangles.

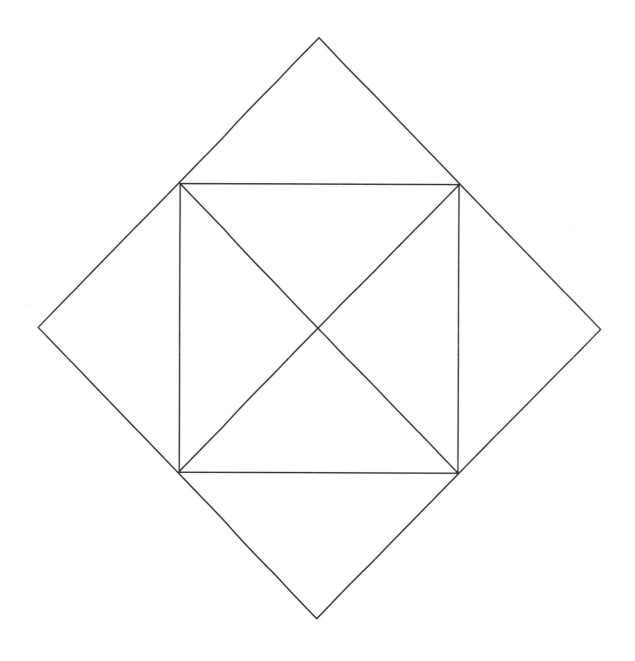

Picture Shapes

Find the triangles and circles in the picture. Color the picture.

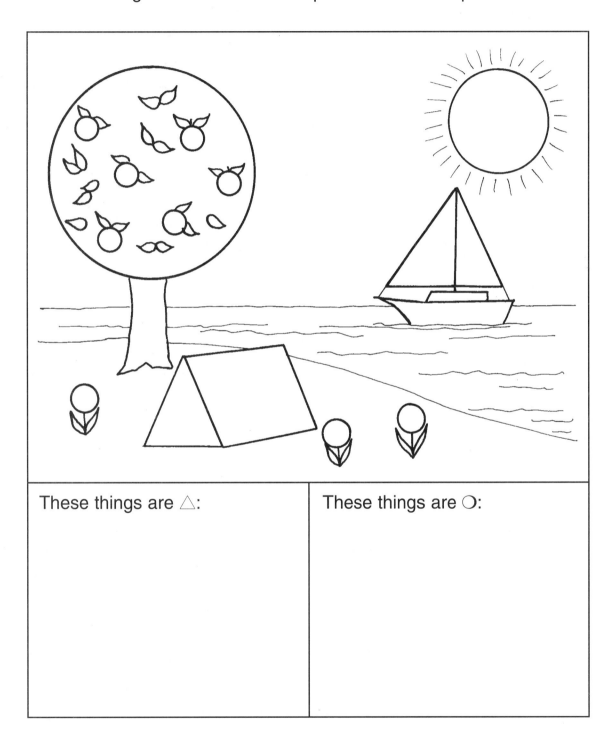

These things are △:	These things are ○:

Baseball

Answer the questions. Color the picture.

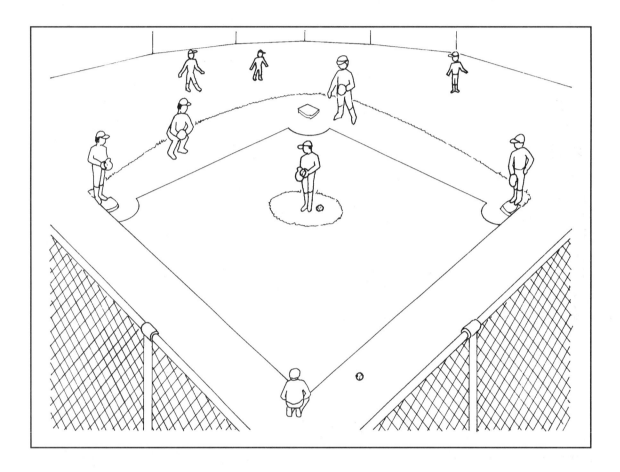

1. How many baseballs are there?   _____

2. How many players are there?   _____

3. How many caps are there?   _____

4. How many arms are there?   _____

5. How many gloves are there?   _____

Cowboys and Cowgirls

Answer the questions. Color the picture.

1. How many cowboys are there? _____

2. How many cowgirls are there? _____

3. How many horses are there? _____

4. How many cows are there? _____

5. How many legs are there? _____

The Circus

Answer the questions. Color the picture.

1. How many clowns are there?   _____

2. How many elephants are there?   _____

3. How many horses are there?   _____

4. How many saddles are there?   _____

5. How many shoes are there?   _____

On the Farm

Draw a picture of a farm with the following:

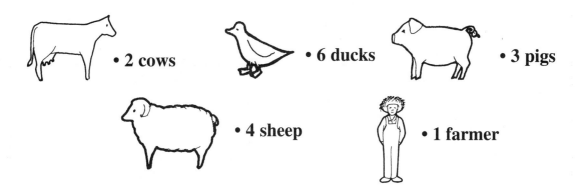

- 2 cows
- 6 ducks
- 3 pigs
- 4 sheep
- 1 farmer

In My Room

Draw a picture of a bedroom with the following:

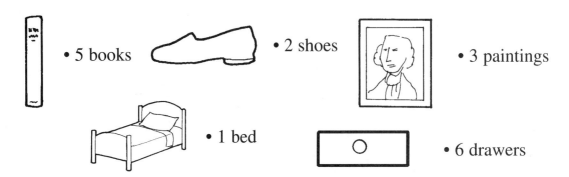

• 5 books   • 2 shoes   • 3 paintings

• 1 bed   • 6 drawers

Missing Word

What word is missing from each set of words?

1. _____ and Roll

   Between a _____ and a hard place

   _____et ship

2. *I'll Love _____ Forever*

   Between _____ and me

   _____ are my sunshine.

3. The _____ takes the cheese.

   The _____ ran up the clock.

   If You Give a _____ a Cookie

4. _____ button

   _____ broom

   _____ and pull

Terrific Child

Use the letters from the following phrase to spell other words. You may only spell words whose letters are in the phrase. You may also use your dictionary.

"I Am a Terrific Child!"

_____   _____

_____   _____

_____   _____

_____   _____

_____   _____

_____   _____

_____   _____

_____   _____

_____   _____

_____   _____

_____   _____

Feelings

Fill in the blank in the phrase below. Then, use the letters from the phrase to spell other words. You may only spell words whose letters are in the phrase. You may also use your dictionary.

"I Feel _____ Today."

_____   _____

_____   _____

_____   _____

_____   _____

_____   _____

_____   _____

_____   _____

_____   _____

_____   _____

_____   _____

Spell a Word

Use letters from each set to spell a word. You will not use all the letters. Repeat letters if you like.

1. A B C D E F G H _____

2. I J K L M N O P _____

3. O R S T U Y M A _____

4. A C E G I K M O _____

5. B D F H N A O I _____

6. E U T R L D S Y _____

7. A F G M P R E O _____

8. I B D K E H L U _____

9. G I C O M L N A _____

10. K I A B G S L C _____

11. E L A G T O N F _____

12. S E G C M H B O _____

13. T A O E M L N R _____

14. R I T S L N M E _____

15. Y E B D G F O I _____

Missing Parts

Draw in the missing part of each picture. Color the pictures.

tree

chair

bicycle

mouse

witch

birthday cake

Common Phrases

Fill in the missing words in the common phrases. Use the words from the Word Box.

1. A _____ in the hand is worth two in the bush.

2. A stitch in _____ saves nine.

3. Early to _____ and early to _____ makes a man healthy, wealthy, and wise.

4. Do unto others as you would have them do unto _____.

5. Do not put off until _____ what you can do _____.

6. Home is where the _____ is.

7. If life gives you _____, make lemonade.

8. Every _____ has a silver lining.

9. A _____ in need is a friend indeed.

10. He who _____ last, laughs best.

Word Box			
bed	rise	today	cloud
bird	tomorrow	you	laughs
heart	time	lemons	friend

Similes

Choose the best word from the Word Box to complete each simile.

1. as white as a _____

2. as strong as an _____

3. as quiet as a _____

4. as free as a _____

5. as quick as a _____

6. as sly as a _____

7. as black as _____

8. as smart as a _____

9. as happy as a _____

10. as playful as a _____

Word Box

mouse	ghost
ox	wink
night	lark
kitten	whip
fox	bird

Rhymes

Write four words that rhyme with each word below.

goat

_____

_____

_____

_____

pick

_____

_____

_____

_____

true

_____

_____

_____

tie

_____

_____

_____

stamp

_____

_____

_____

line

_____

_____

_____

More Rhymes

Write four words that rhyme with each word below.

free

_____

_____

_____

_____

plan

_____

_____

_____

_____

sad

_____

_____

_____

_____

meet

_____

_____

_____

_____

hop

_____

_____

_____

dog

_____

_____

_____

Mother Goose

Fill in the missing words in the Mother Goose rhymes.

1. Mary had a little _____ , little _____ , little _____ ,

   Mary had a little _____ whose fleece was white as _____ .

2. Old King Cole was a _____ old soul,

   A _____ old soul was he.

   He called for his _____ , he called for his _____ ,

   And he called for his fiddlers _____ .

3. Hickory Dickory _____

   The _____ ran up the clock.

   The clock struck one,

   The mouse ran _____ ,

   Hickory Dickory _____ .

4. This little pig went to _____ .

   This little pig stayed _____ .

   This little pig ate roast _____ .

   This little pig had _____ .

   And this little pig went "wee-wee-wee" all the way home.

Opposites

List the opposites.

1. friend _____

2. black _____

3. big _____

4. good _____

5. early _____

6. loud _____

7. young _____

8. large _____

9. low _____

10. hard _____

11. dark _____

12. down _____

13. dry _____

14. out _____

15. fast _____

Name Something

1. Name something funny. _____

2. Name something green. _____

3. Name something shiny. _____

4. Name something pretty. _____

5. Name something big. _____

6. Name something furry. _____

7. Name something mysterious. _____

8. Name something purple. _____

9. Name something curly. _____

10. Name something slow. _____

11. Name something salty. _____

12. Name something sweet. _____

13. Name something strong. _____

14. Name something yellow. _____

15. Name something wild. _____

Winter Word Search

Circle the words across or down.

```
Y S N O W M A N S B X O
S L K F I L B C K C G R
K E P P N V F W I C E H
A D M I T T E N S B G A
T Z R G E I B F J L C T
I P G C R O N Q D B A R
N C O L D M I G L O O C
G I T O E U X W C O S O
J A N U A R Y F I T H A
C Q B D G K L E Z S J T
```

SNOWMAN
SKATING
CLOUD
BOOTS
HAT

WINTER
COAT
SLED
ICE
COLD

MITTENS
SKIS
IGLOO
JANUARY

What's Cookin' Word Search

Circle the words down, across, or diagonally.

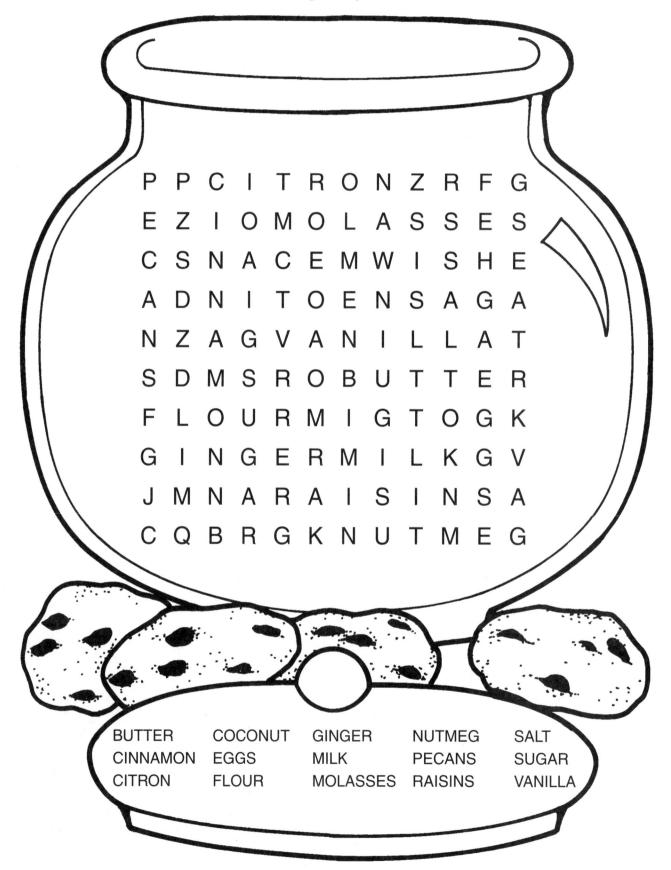

```
P P C I T R O N Z R F G
E Z I O M O L A S S E S
C S N A C E M W I S H E
A D N I T O E N S A G A
N Z A G V A N I L L A T
S D M S R O B U T T E R
F L O U R M I G T O G K
G I N G E R M I L K G V
J M N A R A I S I N S A
C Q B R G K N U T M E G
```

BUTTER	COCONUT	GINGER	NUTMEG	SALT
CINNAMON	EGGS	MILK	PECANS	SUGAR
CITRON	FLOUR	MOLASSES	RAISINS	VANILLA

Crossing the Delaware

Circle the words down, across, or diagonally.

```
W  A  S  H  I  N  G  T  O  N
A  C  R  O  S  S  I  N  G  L
M  O  R  L  P  D  W  P  N  G
A  W  R  I  V  E  R  R  B  T
Y  L  R  D  U  X  C  E  Y  B
G  V  K  A  P  R  O  S  M  I
F  B  A  Y  S  Q  U  I  N  R
O  C  Z  L  O  R  N  D  U  T
R  K  E  S  L  M  T  E  F  H
G  M  Y  E  S  E  R  N  I  D
G  E  O  R  G  E  Y  T  S  A
F  E  B  R  U  A  R  Y  G  Y
```

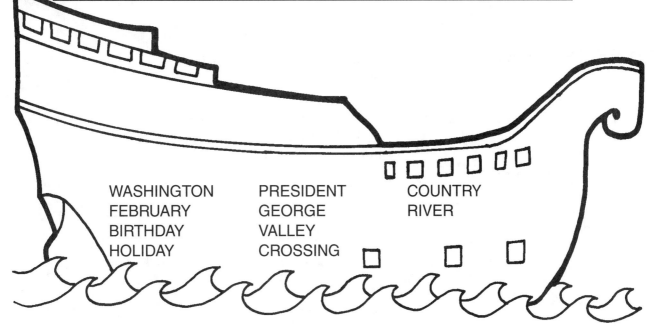

WASHINGTON   PRESIDENT   COUNTRY
FEBRUARY   GEORGE   RIVER
BIRTHDAY   VALLEY
HOLIDAY   CROSSING

Saint Patrick's Day Word Search

Circle the words across or down.

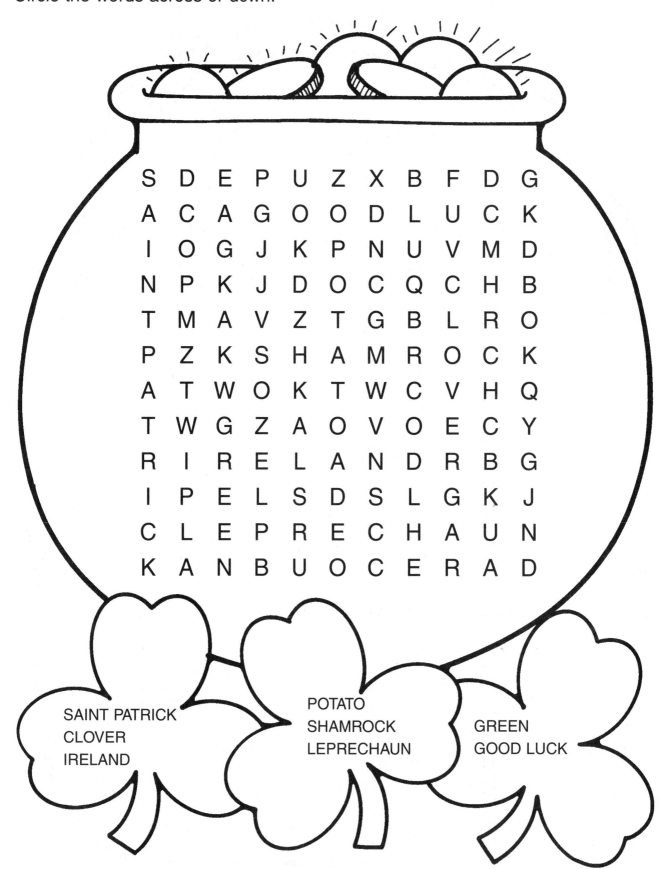

```
S  D  E  P  U  Z  X  B  F  D  G
A  C  A  G  O  O  D  L  U  C  K
I  O  G  J  K  P  N  U  V  M  D
N  P  K  J  D  O  C  Q  C  H  B
T  M  A  V  Z  T  G  B  L  R  O
P  Z  K  S  H  A  M  R  O  C  K
A  T  W  O  K  T  W  C  V  H  Q
T  W  G  Z  A  O  V  O  E  C  Y
R  I  R  E  L  A  N  D  R  B  G
I  P  E  L  S  D  S  L  G  K  J
C  L  E  P  R  E  C  H  A  U  N
K  A  N  B  U  O  C  E  R  A  D
```

SAINT PATRICK
CLOVER
IRELAND

POTATO
SHAMROCK
LEPRECHAUN

GREEN
GOOD LUCK

Easter Word Search

Circle the words across or down.

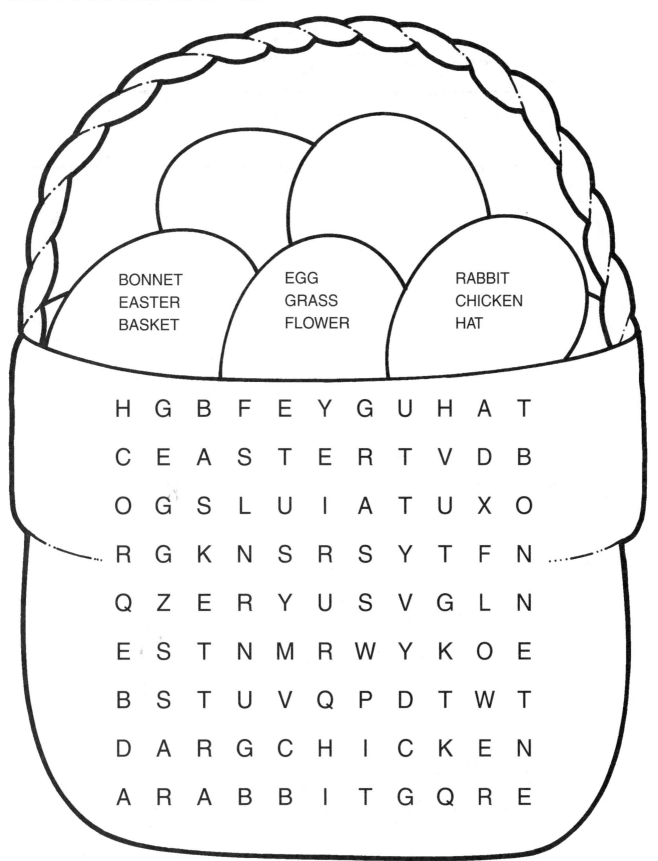

BONNET
EASTER
BASKET

EGG
GRASS
FLOWER

RABBIT
CHICKEN
HAT

H G B F E Y G U H A T
C E A S T E R T V D B
O G S L U I A T U X O
R G K N S R S Y T F N
Q Z E R Y U S V G L N
E S T N M R W Y K O E
B S T U V Q P D T W T
D A R G C H I C K E N
A R A B B I T G Q R E

Sleeping Beauty Word Search

Circle the words across, down, or diagonally.

```
X S L E E P I N G F E M
J W O R C D X M S J O B
S P K C A S T L E D Q E
W R I I R O E T G S U A
O I N N M R N B N E U
R N G T I G I S E D E T
D C D V G K N E O S N Y
X E O B Z S U T A R B N
O S M S D Q O W K I S S
N S A M P R I N C E X A
```

SLEEPING	PRINCE	CASTLE	QUEEN	PRINCESS
BEAUTY	SWORD	KING	KINGDOM	KISS

Bug Word Search

Find all the insects in the word search. Words may be written across, down, or diagonally.

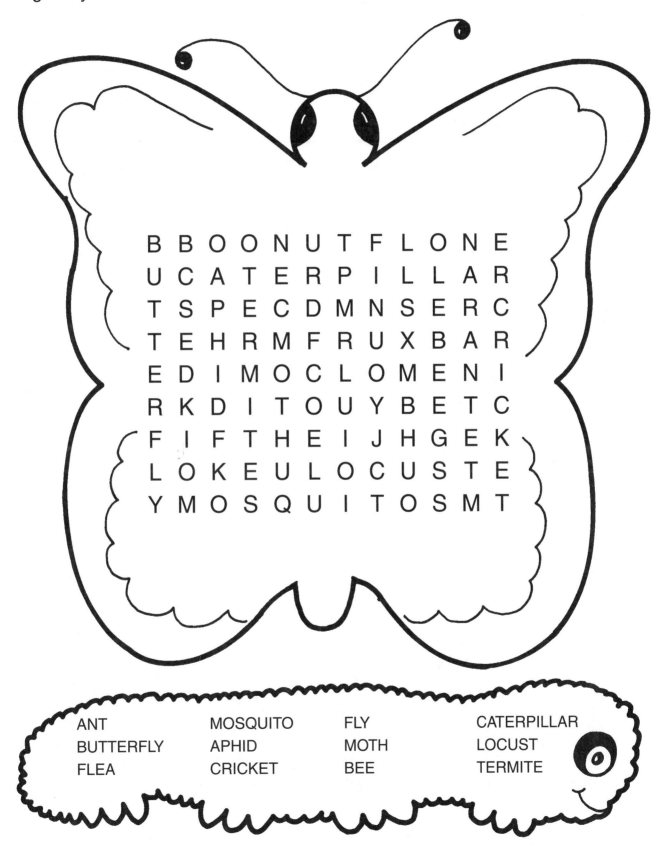

```
B B O O N U T F L O N E
U C A T E R P I L L A R
T S P E C D M N S E R C
T E H R M F R U X B A R
E D I M O C L O M E N I
R K D I T O U Y B E T C
F I F T H E I J H G E K
L O K E U L O C U S T E
Y M O S Q U I T O S M T
```

ANT   MOSQUITO   FLY   CATERPILLAR

BUTTERFLY   APHID   MOTH   LOCUST

FLEA   CRICKET   BEE   TERMITE

Splashing Fun

Circle the words across, down, or diagonally.

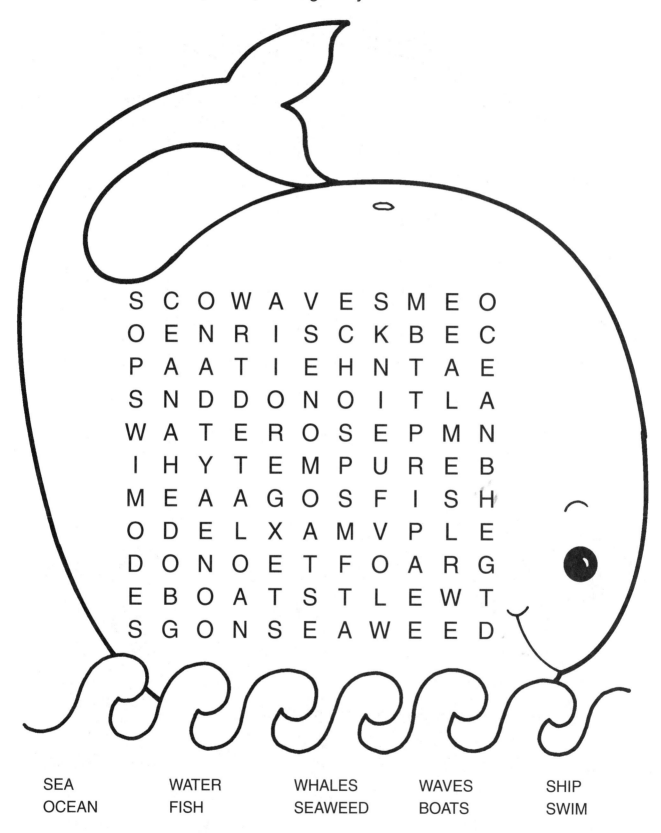

```
S C O W A V E S M E O
O E N R I S C K B E C
P A A T I E H N T A E
S N D D O N O I T L A
W A T E R O S E P M N
I H Y T E M P U R E B
M E A A G O S F I S H
O D E L X A M V P L E
D O N O E T F O A R G
E B O A T S T L E W T
S G O N S E A W E E D
```

SEA   WATER   WHALES   WAVES   SHIP

OCEAN   FISH   SEAWEED   BOATS   SWIM

Beach Bunnies Word Search

Circle the words across or down.

```
S T O D A L O T I O N
U U I S W I M S U I T
N N S D T I S G M A T
G W W O R I U L I L A
B L I E M Y R A J O N
E A M L O T F S A N D
A L O V H E I S H O T
C R A C W A N E D W W
H O A R K W G S N E S
```

SUN	SAND	LOTION	SWIMSUIT	SWIM
TAN	BEACH	HOT	GLASSES	SURFING

It's a Jungle Out There!

Circle the words across, down, or diagonally.

```
T S A F A R I F A S L
P A J V I O T K N T E
L L T L I W R H I F O
A I S I Y N E O M A P
N J U N G L E N A D A
T A N D W E S S L P R
S S R D O I R T S I D
Y R I V E R S E L O S
R M O N K E Y S G A M
```

SAFARI   TREES   ANIMALS   LEOPARDS   PLANTS

JUNGLE   VINES   TIGER   MONKEYS   RIVERS

Rainbows and Butterflies
Word Search

Circle the words across or down.

L I G H T N I N G A
P U D D L E R K T H
C L O U D E Y A L O
T U M B R E L L A N
H H I N F L O W E R
U E U F E R B U G A
N H K R S P R I N G
D C B R A I N B O W
E M R A I N C O A T
R B U T T E R F L Y

RAINBOW	FLOWER	PUDDLE	LIGHTNING
BUTTERFLY	UMBRELLA	RAINCOAT	CLOUD
SPRING	BUG	THUNDER	

Baseball Word Search

Circle the words across or down.

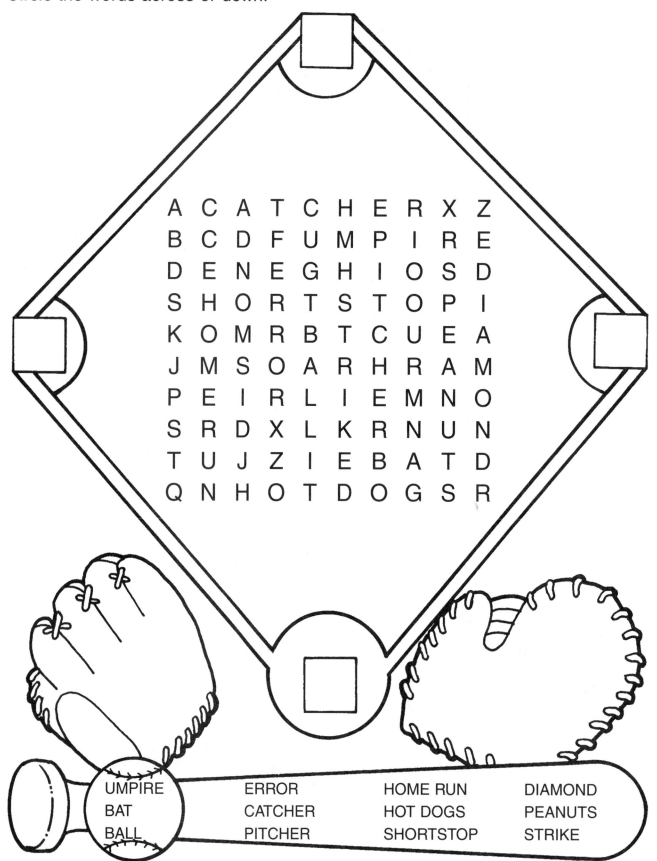

```
A C A T C H E R X Z
B C D F U M P I R E
D E N E G H I O S D
S H O R T S T O P I
K O M R B T C U E A
J M S O A R H R A M
P E I R L I E M N O
S R D X L K R N U N
T U J Z I E B A T D
Q N H O T D O G S R
```

UMPIRE	ERROR	HOME RUN	DIAMOND
BAT	CATCHER	HOT DOGS	PEANUTS
BALL	PITCHER	SHORTSTOP	STRIKE

Farm Word Search

Circle the words across or down.

```
T P L A N T R A N B
R C C O W G E P K A
A L E C O O O M S R
C S F E N C E S O L
T H A R V E S T I E
O P S I L O M C L Y
R H W H E A T O O L
P L O W I S D R I O
B A R N U L R N M O
```

COW
TRACTOR
HARVEST
PLOW
SOIL
PLANT
BARN
SILO
FENCE
WHEAT
BARLEY
CORN

Down on the Farm

Circle the words across or down.

```
P I G S P F A R M E R
S G S T E I G C Y A C
C R C T R E M R L P O
A O H L C L E O U M W
R W I B A D E P I T C
E I C U Q S H S U R O
C A K H C D I C O A D
R N E B A R N P O C O
O H N C K C S C I T R
W A S N A N O O C O A
E L X I D M R Q L R Y
```

COW   CHICKENS   FIELDS   TRACTOR   GROW
FARMER   BARN   PIGS   CROPS   SCARECROW

A Sale at The Pet Shop

Circle the words across, down, or diagonally.

```
D F O O D I C A G E S
M O Y F N O M E B T R
E I G I S E N R A I Q
V E C S H A C C O N Y
K P Y H O B I R D S V
I I U V O C N S O E E
T L M P T O A T E L C
T A L I P F O T N T P
E A I A M I T W S R E
N T Y S E V E E N V T
S T U R T L E S E T S
```

PETS	CATS	PUPPIES	BIRDS	CAGES
DOGS	KITTENS	FISH	FOOD	TURTLES

New Year's Day

Fill in the crossword puzzle. Use words from the Word List.

Word List

ring	greet	happy
Year	Father	new

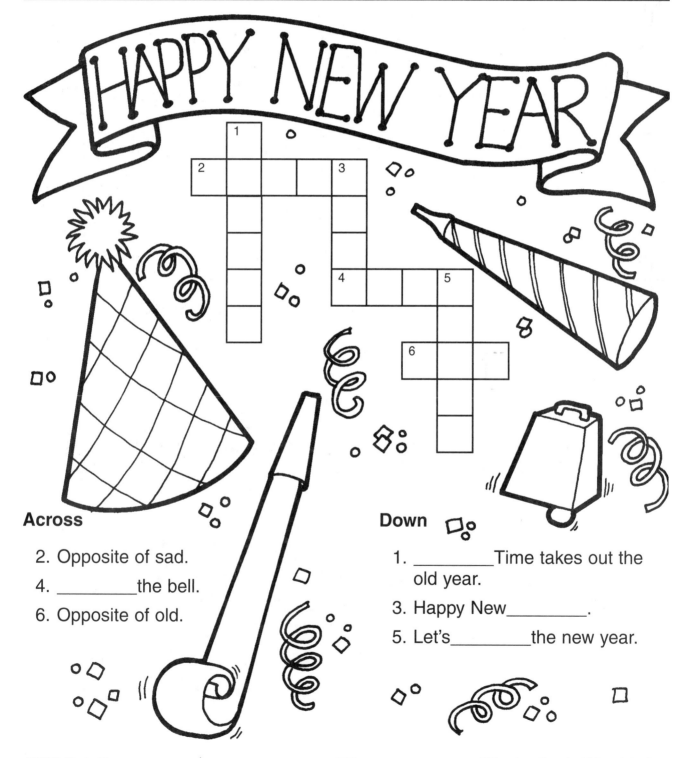

Across

2. Opposite of sad.
4. _____the bell.
6. Opposite of old.

Down

1. _____Time takes out the old year.
3. Happy New_____.
5. Let's_____the new year.

222

I Am a Citizen

Fill in the spaces in the puzzle below with words from the Word List. Some clues have been given to help you.

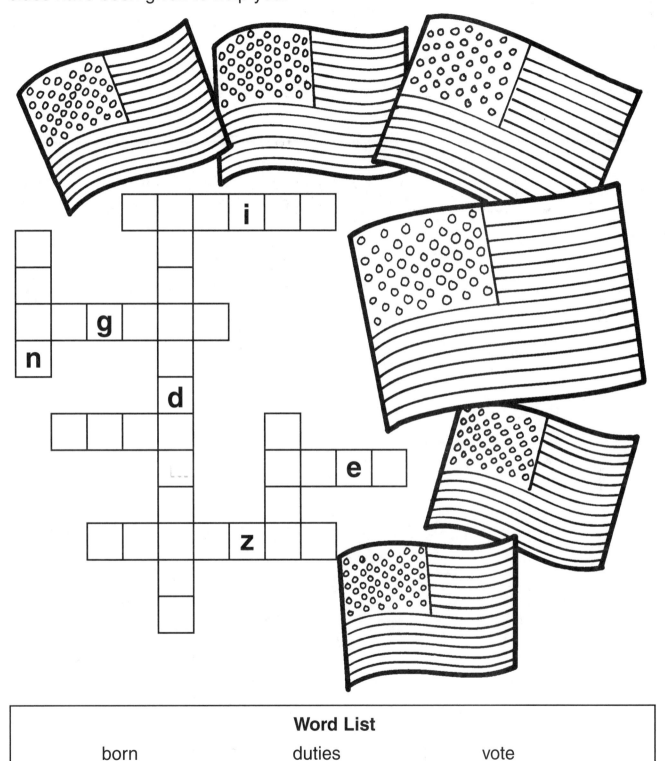

Word List

born	duties	vote
United States	obey	citizen
rights	laws	

Sports Galore!

Fill in the puzzle. Use words from the Word List.

Word List

bowling	football	volleyball	basketball
tennis	soccer	diving	squash
sailing	golf	baseball	cycling
surfing	fencing	rugby	

 ©Teacher Created Materials, Inc.

Where Do I Live?

Fill in the puzzle with the name of the home for each. Use words from the Word List.

Word List

pond	hive	nest
water	tree	house

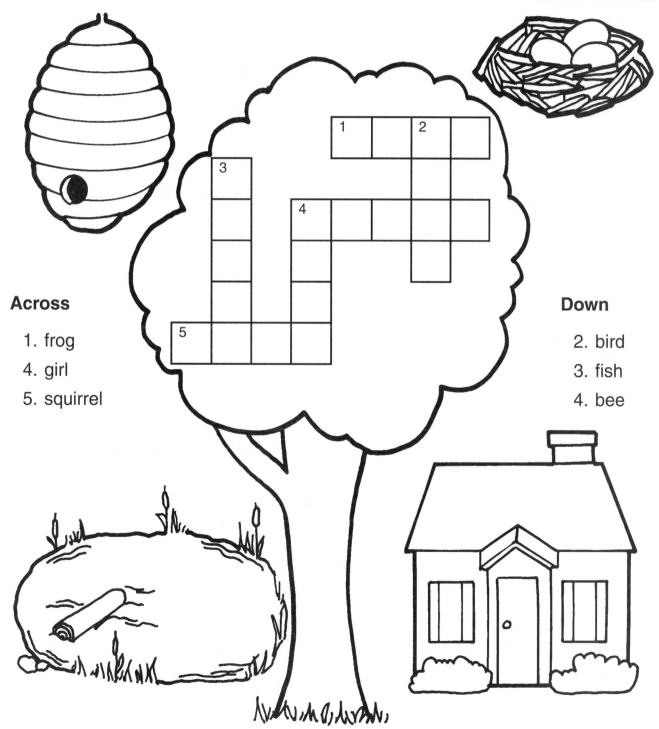

Across

1. frog
4. girl
5. squirrel

Down

2. bird
3. fish
4. bee

The Seashore

Fill in the puzzle by matching the picture clue with the word in the Word List.

Word List		
sand	seaweed	ocean
pail	clam	shovel
beach	shell	bird

Across

1.
4.
2.
5.
6.

Down

1.
4.
3.
6.

A Snowy Day

Complete this puzzle by selecting the word from the Word List which matches the picture clue.

Word List		
sled	skate	snowflake
scarf	hat	snowman

Across

1.

3.

4.

Down

1.

2.

3.

#3670 Brain Games

Which Month Am I?

Fill in the crossword puzzle. Use words from the Word List.

Across

2. The month before July.

4. A cold winter month.

5. _____showers bring May flowers.

Down

1. A month for Valentines!

3. A warm summer month.

Word List				
January	February	July	April	June

Mixed-Up Months

Fill in this puzzle. Use the words in the Word List.

Word List

JANUARY	MAY	SEPTEMBER
FEBRUARY	JUNE	OCTOBER
MARCH	JULY	NOVEMBER
APRIL	AUGUST	DECEMBER

Which Holiday Am I?

Fill in the puzzle. Use the Sentence Clues and the Word List.

Word List			
THANKSGIVING	CHRISTMAS	MOTHER'S	ST. PATRICK'S
VALENTINE'S	FATHER'S	HALLOWEEN	

1.   T   E   '
2.   W   E
3.   A   N   '
4.   R   K '
5.   H   K   I
6.   O   R '
7.   R   M

Sentence Clues

1. Dads are honored on_____Day.

2. We dress in costumes on_____.

3. Pretty cards are given on_____Day.

4. Wear green on_____Day.

5. We eat turkey on_____Day.

6. Let Mom rest on_____Day.

7. Santa brings gifts on_____.

What's My Rhyme?

Write a word that rhymes with each picture. Use words from the Word List.

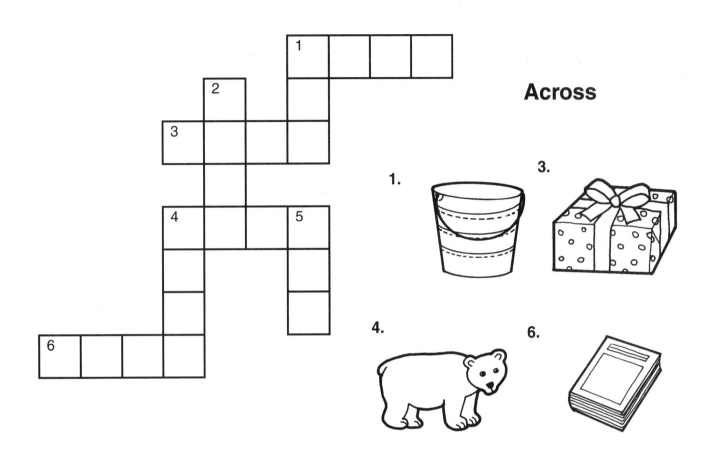

Across

1.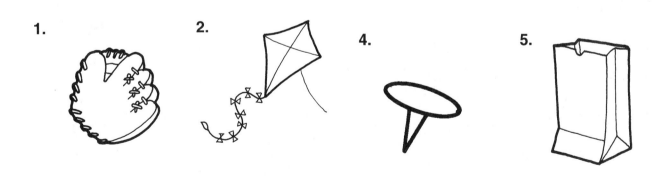

3.

4.

6.

Down

1.

2.

4.

5.

Word List			
pear	lift	sit	took
bite	pack	rag	sail

What Pet Am I?

Fill in the puzzle. Use words from the Word List.

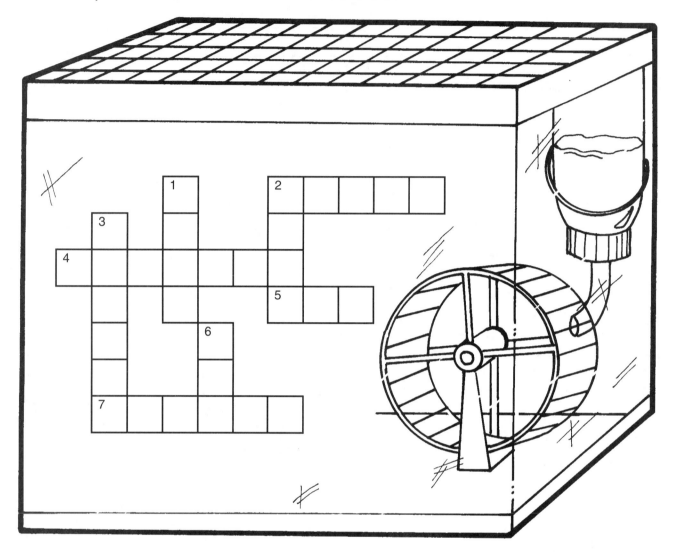

Across

2. I have long ears and a cotton tail.

4. I am small and brown. I love to burrow in my cage.

5. I wag my tail and bark.

7. I walk slowly. I carry my house on my back.

Down

1. Swimming is what I love to do!

2. I love to sit on my perch and sing.

3. My feathers are brightly colored. I come from the jungle.

6. I'm soft and I love to purr.

Word List

fish
cat
bunny
bird
dog
hamster
parrot
turtle

What's My Shape?

Fill in this puzzle by matching the picture clue with its name from the Word List.

Across

1.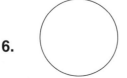

5.

4.

6.

Down

2.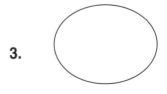

3.

Name Game

Fill in this puzzle. Use words from the Word List.

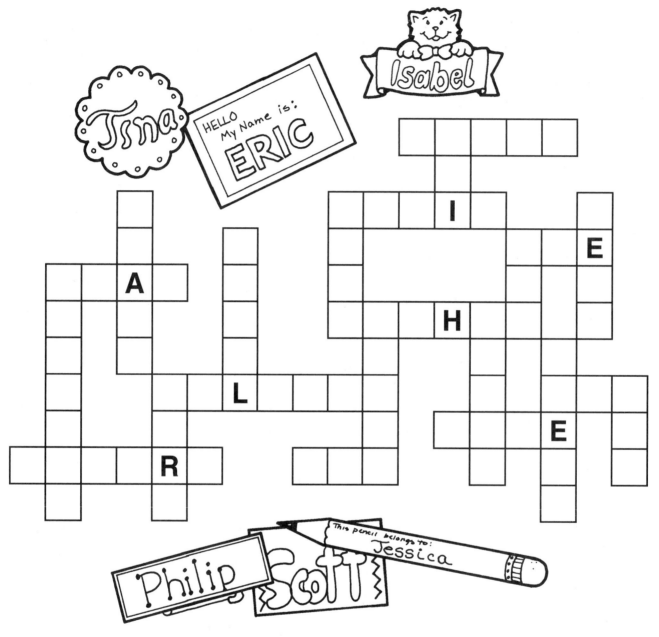

Word List

MALCOLM	DAVID	QUANG	MAX
MARK	ABDUL	HAI	JOE
RAMON	RICHARD	JIM	DON
GRAHAM	AARON	CHRIS	TEDA
ARTURO	RYAN	TIM	
DOUG	JOSE	STEVE	

Football Word Search

Find and circle the words from the Word List. Words may be across, down, or diagonal.

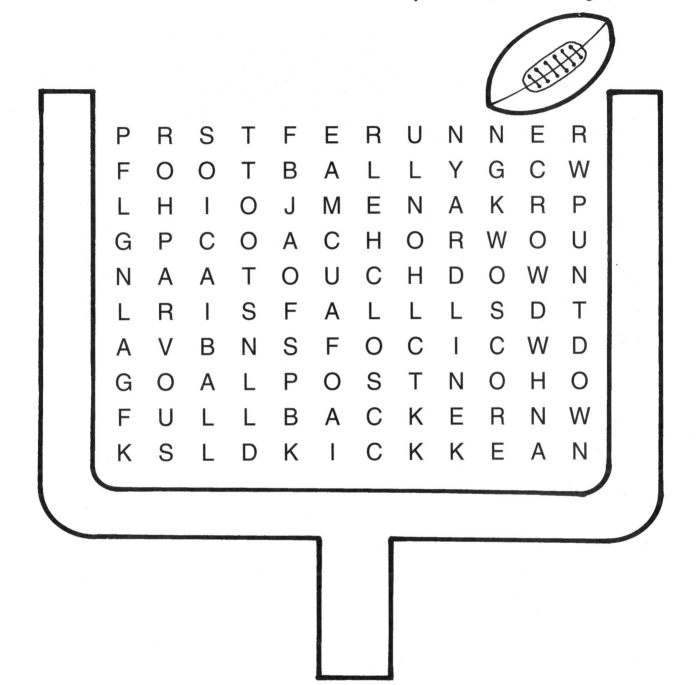

```
P R S T F E R U N N E R
F O O T B A L L Y G C W
L H I O J M E N A K R P
G P C O A C H O R W O U
N A A T O U C H D O W N
L R I S F A L L L S D T
A V B N S F O C I C W D
G O A L P O S T N O H O
F U L L B A C K E R N W
K S L D K I C K K E A N
```

Word List

football	kick	pass	score
gain	fullback	touchdown	fall
crowd	yardline	goalpost	down
runner	coach	punt	ball

Martin Luther King, Jr. Word Search

Find and circle words from the Word List. Words may be across, down, diagonal, or backwards.

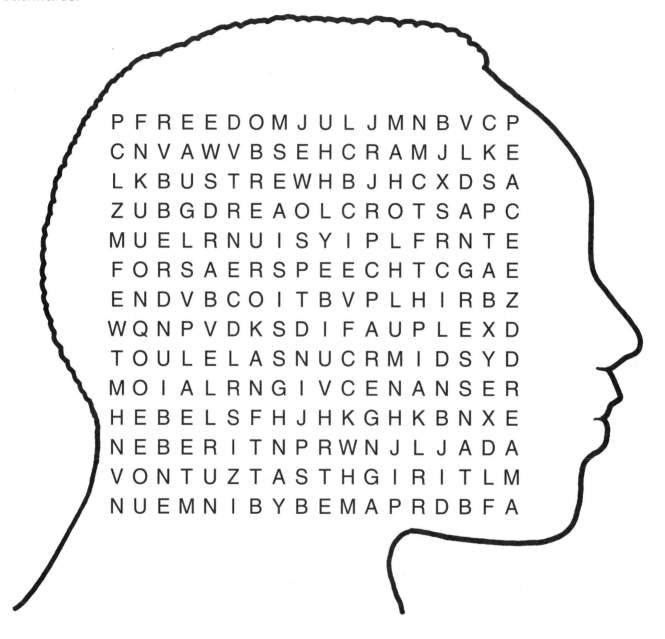

```
P F R E E D O M J U L J M N B V C P
C N V A W V B S E H C R A M J L K E
L K B U S T R E W H B J H C X D S A
Z U B G D R E A O L C R O T S A P C
M U E L R N U I S Y I P L F R N T E
F O R S A E R S P E E C H T C G A E
E N D V B C O I T B V P L H I R B Z
W Q N P V D K S D I F A U P L E X D
T O U L E L A S N U C R M I D S Y D
M O I A L R N G I V C E N A N S E R
H E B E L S F H J H K G H K B N X E
N E B E R I T N P R W N J L J A D A
V O N T U Z T A S T H G I R I T L M
N U E M N I B Y B E M A P R D B F A
```

Word List

blacks	bus	rights
pastor	marches	peace
church	equality	dream
speech	Nobel	choir
freedom	Alabama	

Valentine Word Search

Find and circle the 14 words about Valentine's Day. They can be across, down, diagonal, or backwards.

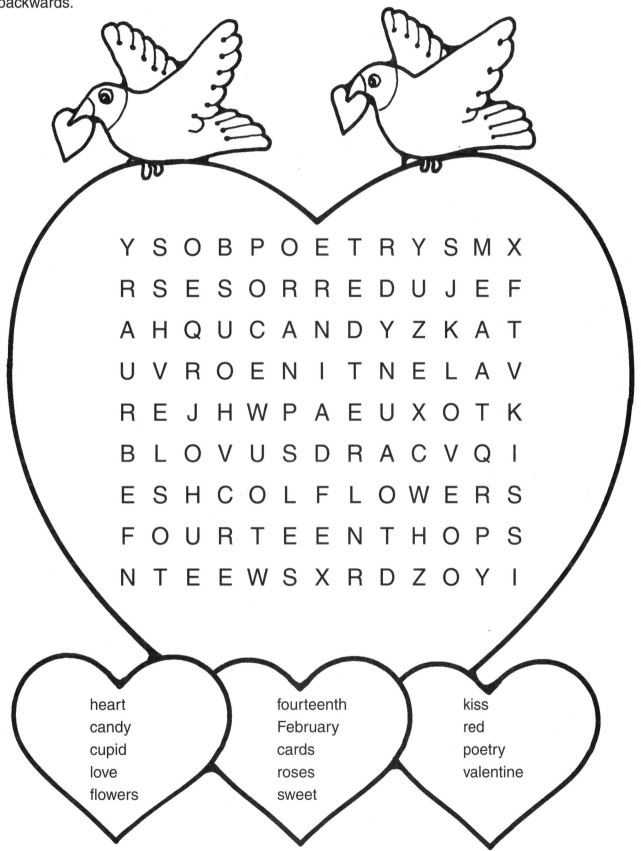

```
Y S O B P O E T R Y S M X
R S E S O R R E D U J E F
A H Q U C A N D Y Z K A T
U V R O E N I T N E L A V
R E J H W P A E U X O T K
B L O V U S D R A C V Q I
E S H C O L F L O W E R S
F O U R T E E N T H O P S
N T E E W S X R D Z O Y I
```

heart
candy
cupid
love
flowers

fourteenth
February
cards
roses
sweet

kiss
red
poetry
valentine

President Washington

Read the story. Find the underlined words in the word search. Words may be down, across, diagonal, or backwards.

The first <u>president</u> of the United States was George <u>Washington</u>. As a young boy, he liked to study <u>math</u>. A story says that George never lied. He told his father he was the one who chopped down the <u>cherry</u> tree. George led America's fight with <u>England</u>. He is called the "<u>Father</u> of Our <u>Country</u>."

```
I T R E S P Y R T L U O C F R M O U E
F C N V A W V B H J U R M M A T H J N
A X Q E S R F G J L O P N I G E C G G
T C I T S I M R A I R W Q D L R O W L
H D U E Y R R C H E R R Y I F E N T A
E F O R A O E T S D S E E T H G A N N
R C A D E I O I T R U C E Z I R E D D
W C N C O U N T R Y R N O O L E S D D
T O S L E L S H N U C U E I D S Y P N
M O I O P I R G I V A E N R N S E T T
T P R E S I D E N T U K G H K M N X R
R N E T R E S T H P V C S X M J U D C
Q P L K J H X S D E O B N A B E T C Z
I W A S H I N G T O N J L K T R D A S
```

George Washington Word Search

Circle the words down, across, or diagonally.

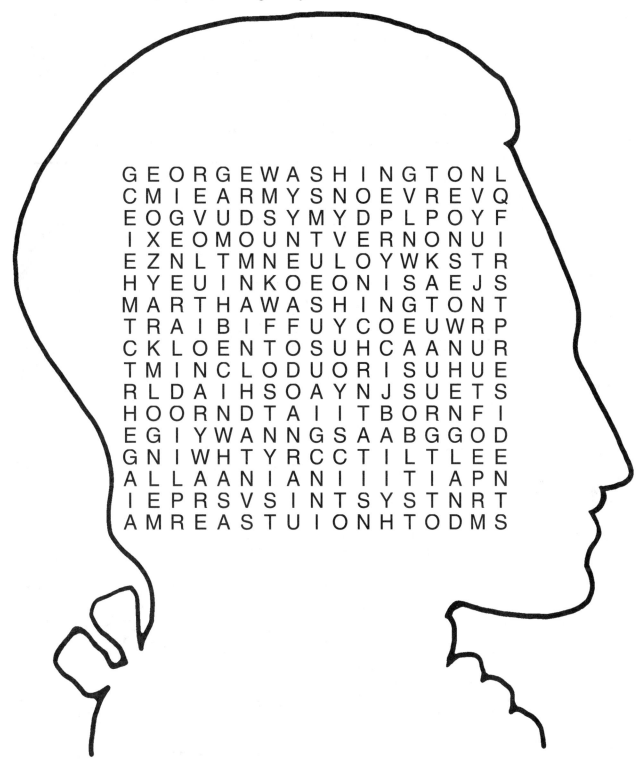

```
G E O R G E W A S H I N G T O N L
C M I E A R M Y S N O E V R E V Q
E O G V U D S Y M Y D P L P O Y F
I X E O M O U N T V E R N O N U I
E Z N L T M N E U L O Y W K S T R
H Y E U I N K O E O N I S A E J S
M A R T H A W A S H I N G T O N T
T R A I B I F F U Y C O E U W R P
C K L O E N T O S U H C A A N U R
T M I N C L O D U O R I S U H U E
R L D A I H S O A Y N J S U E T S
H O O R N D T A I I T B O R N F I
E G I Y W A N N G S A A B G G O D
G N I W H T Y R C C T I L T L E E
A L L A A N I A N I I I T I A P N
I E P R S V S I N T S Y S T N R T
A M R E A S T U I O N H T O D M S
```

George Washington	Revolutionary War	Martha Washington
Mount Vernon	General	Virginia
First President	England	

Abraham Lincoln Word Search

Circle the words across or down.

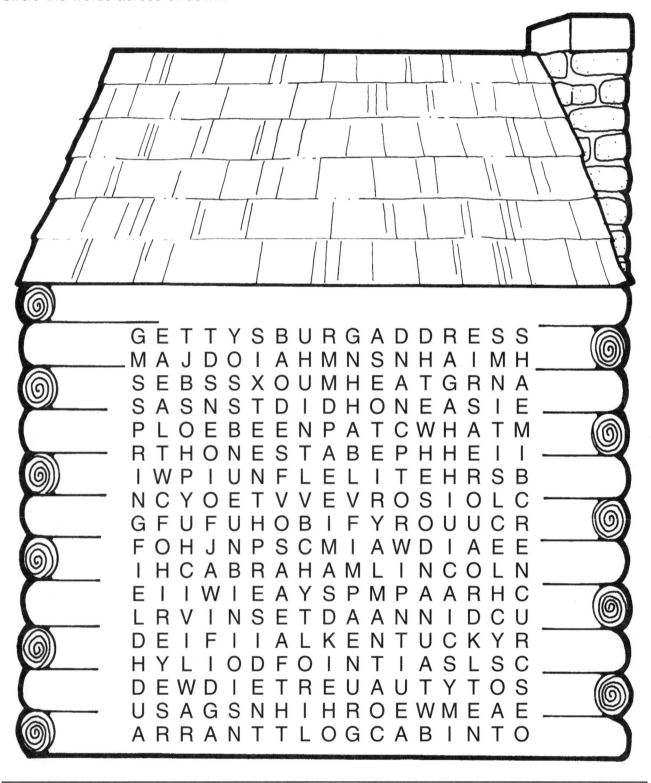

```
G E T T Y S B U R G A D D R E S S
M A J D O I A H M N S N H A I M H
S E B S S X O U M H E A T G R N A
S A S N S T D I D H O N E A S I E
P L O E B E E N P A T C W H A T M
R T H O N E S T A B E P H H E I I
I W P I U N F L E L I T E H R S B
N C Y O E T V V E V R O S I O L C
G F U F U H O B I F Y R O U U C R
F O H J N P S C M I A W D I A E E
I H C A B R A H A M L I N C O L N
E I I W I E A Y S P M P A A R H C
L R V I N S E T D A A N N I D C U
D E I F I I A L K E N T U C K Y R
H Y L I O D F O I N T I A S L S C
D E W D I E T R E U A U T Y T O S
U S A G S N H I H R O E W M E A E
A R R A N T T L O G C A B I N T O
```

Kentucky	Log Cabin	Civil War
Honest Abe	Gettysburg Address	Abraham Lincoln
Springfield	Sixteenth President	

Our Sixteenth President

Find and circle the words from the Word List in the puzzle below. Words may be across, down, diagonal, or backwards.

```
H P U L N E B A T S E N O H W P B
Y R H O S M N N P C W T F V U K L
T E I U O U O X I O R E K A E P S
E S F G U R I V I B G S X V Y H S
W I K H T I I K H R A U E P R D I
T D Y H H L O R U G X C S C E H X
U E W A W D E B A T E S G B V L T
G N I A R S D Q X K L N M O A X E
X T R Y K Y F E C R E Y W A L Z E
K O I N T M Y V B M E N P A S I N
K E N T U C K Y L I O P N C Z F T
D E E R F B L H F I I U D C W S H
R G T Y H K C O N F E D E R A T E
T O H S I W S U Z S D F B U V N C
```

Word List

president	sixteenth	Gettysburg	speaker
lawyer	Kentucky	North	Honest Abe
log cabin	slavery	South	debates
Civil War	freed	Union	Confederate

We Celebrate Memorial Day

Read the paragraph below. Find and circle the underlined words in the word search. Words may be across, down, diagonal, or backwards.

 Memorial Day, also known as <u>Decoration</u> Day, is a <u>patriotic</u> <u>holiday</u> in the <u>United States</u>. On the last <u>Monday</u> of <u>May</u>, we honor those <u>Americans</u> who have died in all the wars since the <u>Civil War</u>. People traditionally place <u>flowers</u> and <u>flags</u> on the <u>graves</u> of those who gave their lives for our <u>country</u>. <u>Memorial</u> Day is sometimes called Poppy Day because small, red artificial <u>poppies</u> are sold to help disabled <u>veterans</u>.

```
H O Y J N B G F V R A W L I V I C C W
O T A J F R W A Z X C V G H J I O L O
L G D N L I U Y C I T O I R T A P V S
I H N C O S P L K J S Z A R T U N E S
D H O E W I N B C O U N T R Y O T C V
A P M T E B T A C I J H B D F A T E E
Y L B S R N O A C R T Q U L T I O S T
A A Y E S R I V R I U B A S W E Q X E
L I U I D A V I E O R Y D H B S X J R
S R V P G R A V E S C E A M E M F F A
O O P P E X R Z V T T E M Y E D L L N
K M O O T E W X C I O P D A L K E A S
T E M P F E S T N V C F S U L P J G S
I M Y U I O P U P J K L F C M A Y S O
```

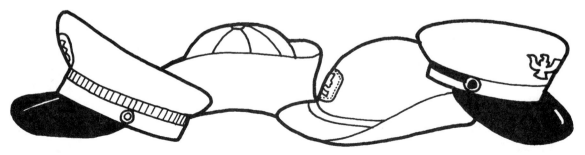

It's a Grand Old Flag!

Read the story below. Find all the underlined words in the word search. Words may be down, across, diagonal, or backwards.

On <u>June</u> 14, 1777, the Stars and Stripes was <u>adopted</u> as the <u>official</u> flag of the <u>United</u> <u>States</u>. Every year on this day businesses, public buildings and homes <u>display</u> the flag. Today's <u>flag</u> has <u>thirteen</u> alternating <u>red</u> and <u>white</u> <u>stripes</u> that stand for the <u>original</u> thirteen <u>colonies</u>. A <u>blue</u> background contains <u>fifty</u> white <u>stars</u>, one for each <u>state</u>.

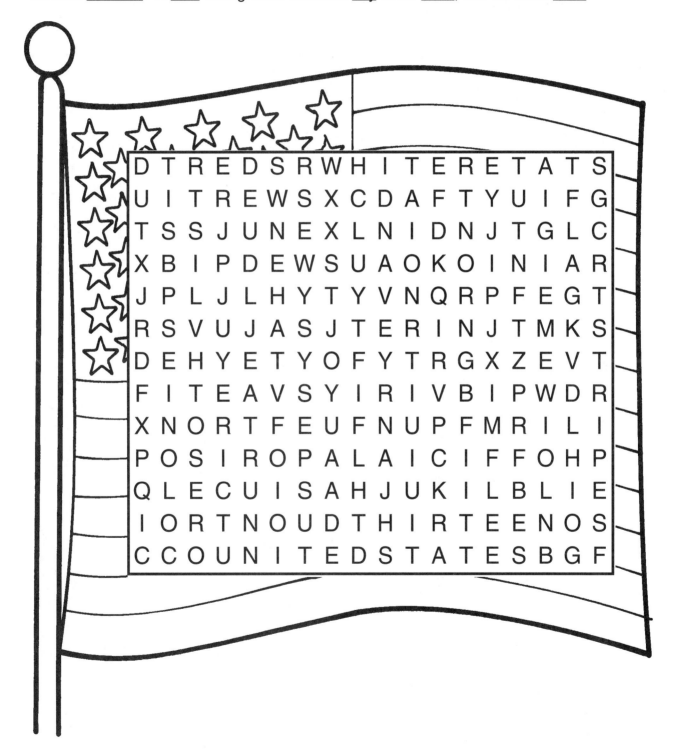

D T R E D S R W H I T E R E T A T S
U I T R E W S X C D A F T Y U I F G
T S S J U N E X L N I D N J T G L C
X B I P D E W S U A O K O I N I A R
J P L J L H Y T V N Q R P F E G T
R S V U J A S J T E R I N J T M K S
D E H Y E T Y O F Y T R G X Z E V T
F I T E A V S Y I R I V B I P W D R
X N O R T F E U F N U P F M R I L I
P O S I R O P A L A I C I F F O H P
Q L E C U I S A H J U K I L B L I E
I O R T N O U D T H I R T E E N O S
C C O U N I T E D S T A T E S B G F

A Patriotic Holiday

Read the following story. Find the underlined words in the word search. Words may be down, across, diagonal, or backwards.

The <u>Fourth</u> of July, also known as <u>Independence</u> Day, is the <u>anniversary</u> of the signing of the <u>Declaration</u> of Independence. It is the <u>birthday</u> of our <u>country</u>. Independence Day was first <u>observed</u> in <u>Philadelphia</u>, Pennsylvania, in 1776, with a <u>parade</u> and ringing church bells. Today, people <u>celebrate</u> the Fourth of <u>July</u> by having <u>picnics</u> and watching <u>fireworks</u>.

U Y A D H T R I B H Y U I H F U Y T R
P Y T V G E M T F D C N G I J M I F T
H E T A R B E L E C O N R U H N J H S
I G N I N G I S K I G E N H D H G R A
L N G F C L C S T U W N F E V C S W Q
A G F R T I M A S O G T P J H B X S D
D S C P N U R G R F C E P A R A D E E
E V F C U A S K N B N R B O P W E S V
L B I Y L F S U H D U J P M Y E L A R
P P O C V G T F E F R T Y U J L G R E
H I E C U A N N I V E R S A R Y U O S
I D R T R E C H U I O L M N B V O J B
A D R T G E N B V G F T Y H U I O L O
F O U R T H N J K C O U N T R Y N G Q

Reindeer Word Search

Can you find the names of Santa's reindeer listed on the bottom of this page? Circle the words down, across, or diagonally.

```
A Q T R A Y Z K L T N E E S U
V X W B C O M E T D V D M O T
V B E T U H C C I R A A S S C
S O R R P U E V E R E S H A M
U F R L I A O S A L D H C C H
Q B E C D O N N E R R E M I A
S M E V E H R E M L E R R T H
R U D O L P H L A W K I S H P
A Y V O U E O R N Y I B B E D
D A N C E R H E C E H O L I D
D O R I I N X K I R L I I R E
L W C D E I U Z L D U D T Y A
T C H D V A T D W O H Z Z U E
X Y O B U Q L P R A N C E R L
N E O T U E B E P Y P N N B S
```

Word List

Comet	Vixen	Blitzen
Cupid	Prancer	Dancer
Donner	Rudolph	Dasher

Sports Word Search

Circle the words across, down, or diagonally.

```
G T E N N I S R A L
F Y H O C K E Y L B
O S M C H E L A R A
O O L N E A B G U L
T C N P A T K O G L
B C O N E S K L B E
A E E K V I T F Y T
L R S W I M M I N G
L A T R A C K N C O
B A S E B A L L J S
```

Word List

baseball	soccer	golf
football	basketball	hockey
tennis	track	swimming
rugby	gymnastics	ballet

Circus Word Search

Circle the words across, down, diagonally, or backwards.

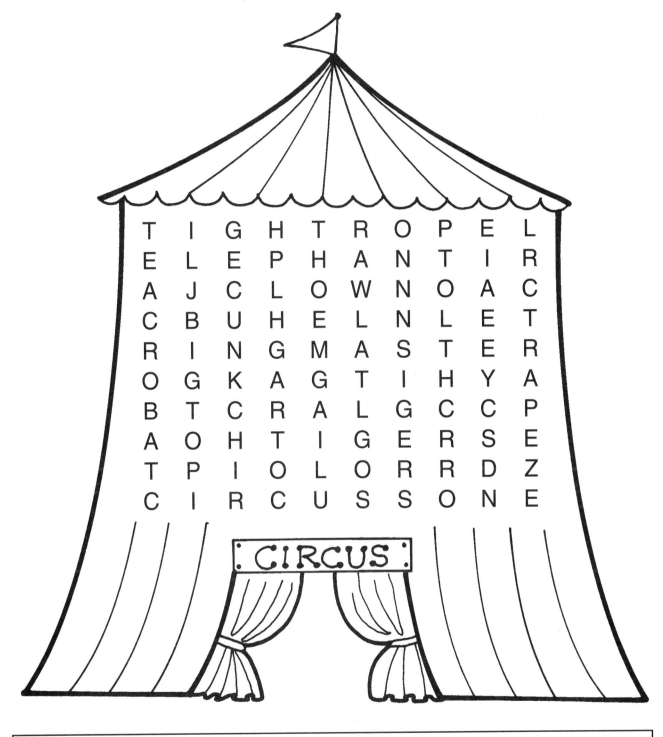

```
T I G H T R O P E L
E L E P H A N T I R
A J C L O W N N O A C
C B U H E L N L E T
R I N G M A S T I R A
O G K A G T I H Y R P
B T C R A L G C C E
A O H T I G E R S D Z
T P I O L O R R D N E
C I R C U S S S O N
```

Word List

tightrope	juggler	trapeze
clown	acrobat	lion
circus	ringmaster	tigers
elephant	big top	

Space Word Search

Circle the words across, down, diagonally, or backwards.

```
B L A C K H O L E D
X Z S H U T T L E E
G O P L A N E T P E
A Z C B O M I C K S
L S O O T A N O N R
A T M O S P H E R E
X A E H U S O M E V
Y R T A N O X B O I
R G R A V I T Y X N
S P A C E S H I P U
```

Word List

star	spaceship	gravity
planet	shuttle	galaxy
sun	comet	atmosphere
moon	universe	black hole

Monster Word Search

Circle the words across, down, diagonally, or backwards.

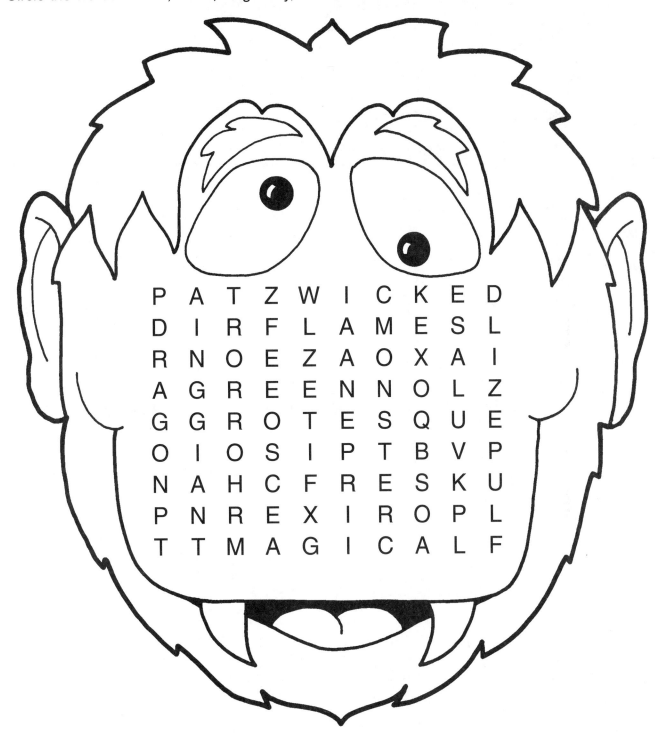

```
P A T Z W I C K E D
D I R F L A M E S L
R N O E Z A O X A I
A G R E E N O L Z Z
G G R O T E S Q U E
O I O S I P T B V P
N A H C F R E S K U
P N R E X I R O P L
T T M A G I C A L F
```

Word List

ogre	dragon	wicked
green	giant	horror
monster	grotesque	magical

The Rim Runner

Moving along the rim of the word field below, list the words you "run" across as you make your way around the field. There are many words that can be formed following the direction of the arrows. Words may only be used once and must have 2 or more letters. No proper nouns such as Andrew or Kate can be counted. Can you find 25? 35? 45?

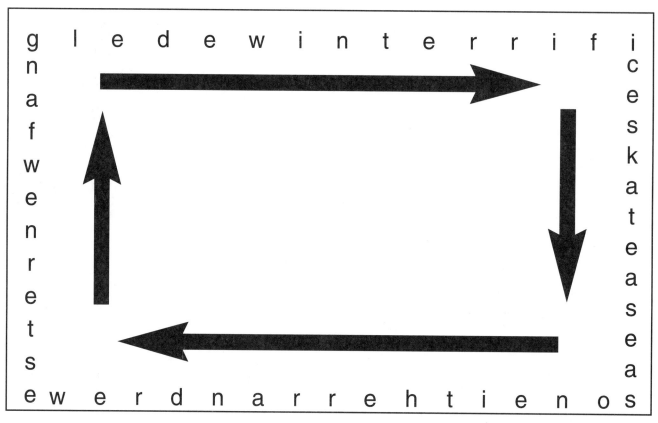

Write your words here:

_____ _____ _____ _____ _____

_____ _____ _____ _____ _____

_____ _____ _____ _____ _____

_____ _____ _____ _____ _____

_____ _____ _____ _____ _____

_____ _____ _____ _____ _____

_____ _____ _____ _____ _____

Name the Month

Write the name of the month in which these holidays occur.

Across

3. Thanksgiving
6. Mother's Day
7. Christmas
8. New Year's

Down

1. Valentine's Day
2. St. Patrick's Day
4. Halloween
5. Father's Day

Special Signs

Fill in the puzzle by matching the clue with the word in the Word List.

Word List

maypole	turkey	pumpkin	clock
heart	bunny	cake	tree

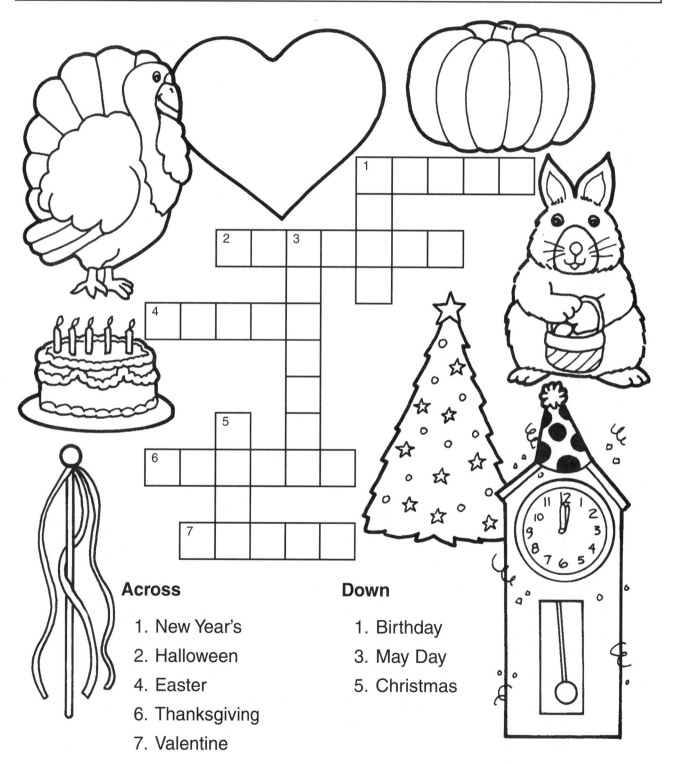

Across

1. New Year's
2. Halloween
4. Easter
6. Thanksgiving
7. Valentine

Down

1. Birthday
3. May Day
5. Christmas

Three in a Row

Add the three numbers in each problem below. Use the Word List to write the word name for each answer in the crossword puzzle.

Word List				
six	fifteen	twelve	ten	nine
eleven	eight	fourteen	thirteen	seven

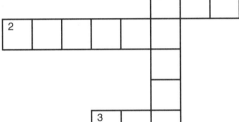
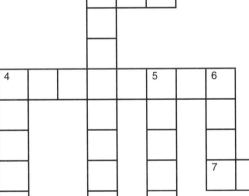

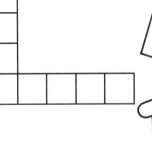

Across

1. 2 + 3 + 1
2. 6 + 4 + 2
3. 4 + 3 + 3
4. 8 + 1 + 5
7. 2 + 5 + 1

Down

1. 3 + 1 + 3
3. 5 + 6 + 2
4. 9 + 2 + 4
5. 3 + 6 + 2
6. 2 + 0 + 7

Mystery Math

Fill in the puzzle by solving the addition problems. Use the Word List at the bottom of the page and the clues in the footprints below.

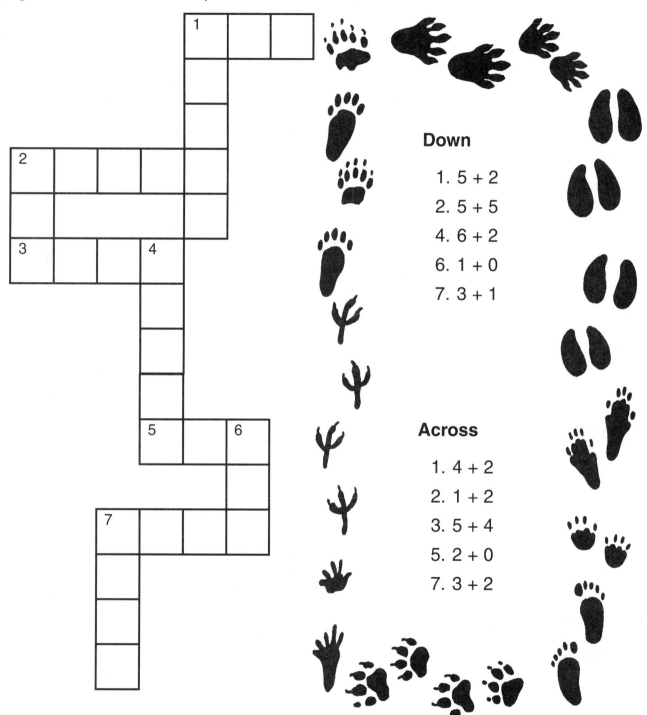

Down

1. 5 + 2
2. 5 + 5
4. 6 + 2
6. 1 + 0
7. 3 + 1

Across

1. 4 + 2
2. 1 + 2
3. 5 + 4
5. 2 + 0
7. 3 + 2

Word List				
one	three	five	seven	nine
two	four	six	eight	ten

Feathered Friends

Fill in the puzzle. Use words from the Word List.

Word List

stork	wren	ostrich	gull
cardinal	owl	canary	hawk
jay	falcon	lark	eagle
robin	oriole	kingbird	kiwi
hummingbird	duck	pelican	

Land, Ho!

Fill in the puzzle. Use words from the Word List.

Word List

spices	queen	Spain	boat
small	ocean	land	

Across

1. Columbus looked for_____.
3. The_____was very big.
4. One_____was the *Santa Maria*.
5. The Spanish_____sent Columbus.
6. He finally saw_____.

Down

1. Columbus sailed from_____.
2. His ship was_____in size.

Our Flag

Fill in the puzzle. Use words from the Word List.

Word List

red	blue	stripes	parades
white	stars	July	flag

1. Some stripes are_____.
2. Everyone loves_____.
3. The_____are red and white.
4. Some stripes are_____.
5. Our_____is red, white and blue.
6. The flag's birthday is in_____.
7. The stars are on a_____field.
8. The_____are white.

May Day

Fill in the puzzle. Use words from the Word List.

Word List

ribbon	sun	daisy	grass
flowers	spring	rain	

Across

1. May Day is in the_____.

3. _____helps the flowers grow.

5. _____bloom in the spring.

6. A_____is a spring flower.

Down

1. The_____is yellow.

2. Let's put a_____on the Maypole.

4. The_____is green.

Fourth of July Fun

Fill in the puzzle. Use words from the Word List.

Word List

picnic	July	holiday	fireworks
birthday	parade	flag	

Across

2. These light up the sky.
3. A band marches in this.
5. Happy_____, America!

Down

1. A special kind of day.
2. This flies on a pole.
3. A special basket for carrying food.
4. This month comes after June.

Pick a Name

Fill in the puzzle. Use words from the Word List.

Word List

BRENDA	INEZ	SARAH	ANNE
JUANITA	TIFFANY	SUE	FIONA
ROSA	MARIA	ADA	THANH
BARBARA	MOLLY	NELL	THI
HILLARY	YOLANDA	LISA	BETH
YVONNE	KATE	JEAN	

Subtraction Solutions

Fill in the puzzle by solving the subtraction problems. Use the word names in the Word List.

Word List

eleven	thirteen	fifteen	seventeen	nineteen
twelve	fourteen	sixteen	eighteen	twenty

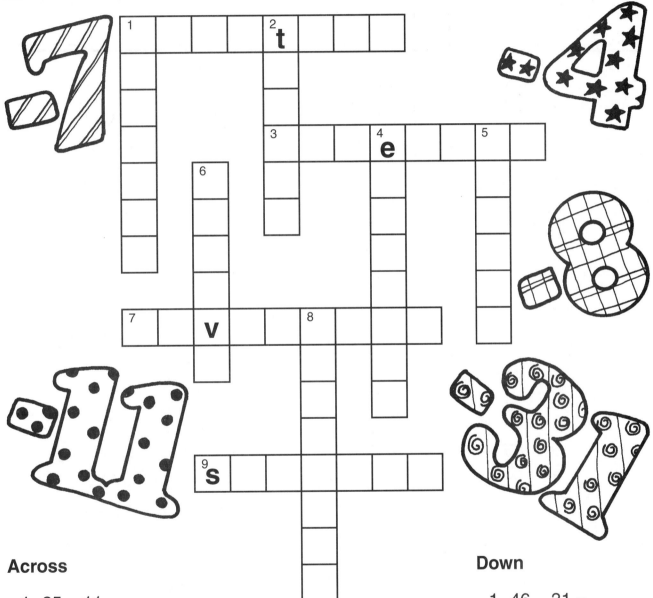

Across

1. 25 − 11 =

3. 40 − 21 =

7. 33 − 16 =

9. 51 − 35 =

Down

1. 46 − 31 =

2. 27 − 7 =

4. 22 − 4 =

5. 19 − 8 =

6. 44 − 32 =

8. 38 − 25 =

#3670 Brain Games

Puzzling Endings

A *verb* is a word that shows action. *Fill* and *enjoy* are verbs. A verb in the past tense shows action that has already happened and ends in the suffix "ed." *Filled* and *enjoyed* are actions that have already happened. To complete the crossword puzzle below, use the past tense verb for the underlined word in each clue. Sometimes the spelling is varied.

Across

1. John <u>talks</u> too much.
3. Did you <u>discover</u> the treasure?
4. Ann <u>whispers</u> to her friend.
5. Christopher <u>explores</u> the cave.
10. She <u>dips</u> the pen in ink.

Down

1. Did you ever <u>travel</u> to Europe?
2. Rover <u>barks</u> very loudly.
6. Betty <u>watches</u> TV every night.
7. <u>Peel</u> some potatoes.
8. She <u>dries</u> her clothes on the line.
9. Jeff <u>dances</u> well.

Presto Change-o Anagrams

An *anagram* is a word which is made from another word by changing the positions of the letters. Find the anagrams in the bold words below. Write them on the spaces provided.

1. Turn **STEW** into a cardinal direction. _____

2. Turn **LIVES** into a rock and roll star. _____

3. Turn **LAST** into a food seasoning. _____

4. Turn **LUMP** into a fruit. _____

5. Turn **SENT** into a home for birds. _____

6. Turn **RAIN** into a country. _____

7. Turn **LATE** into a story. _____

8. Turn **TUNA** into a relative. _____

9. Turn **MARS** into parts of the body. _____

10. Turn **FLOG** into a game. _____

Now, try making up 10 anagram puzzles of your own, using different words.

My Anagram Puzzles	My Answers
1. Turn_____ into _____	_____
2. Turn_____ into _____	_____
3. Turn_____ into _____	_____
4. Turn_____ into _____	_____
5. Turn_____ into _____	_____
6. Turn_____ into _____	_____
7. Turn_____ into _____	_____
8. Turn_____ into _____	_____
9. Turn_____ into _____	_____
10. Turn_____ into _____	_____

Compound Word Puzzle

Use the letters below each puzzle and the clue to form two words that make a compound word. The first one has been done for you.

1. **AALSTLEK**
   (a sport)

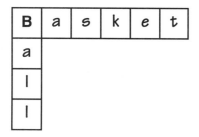

2. **EGDHUS**
   (where Fido sleeps)

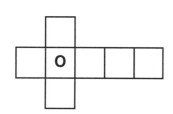

3. **MDBTI**
   (Good night!)

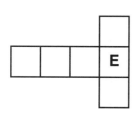

4. **OEAHRE**
   (where Sally sells shells)

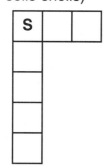

5. **YRREEUL**
   (a fruit)

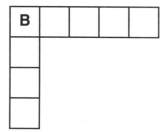

6. **TREVCA**
   (worn in cold weather)

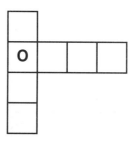

7. **RCDDROB**
   (what cartons are made of)

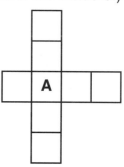

8. **RRCSSDW**
   (a puzzle)

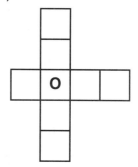

Contraction Word Search

Hidden in the box below are 10 pairs of words that can be made into contractions. Write the words in the spaces below, and next to the words write the contractions that can be made.

Example:

Word Pair	**Contraction**
are not	aren't

L	M	E	W	I	H	S	T	O	W	R	P
W	I	L	L	N	O	T	H	U	H	S	Q
L	D	O	B	E	W	O	E	R	O	H	R
E	I	W	I	M	I	N	Y	T	W	E	B
T	S	W	T	A	S	E	H	H	O	W	I
U	N	A	I	L	E	R	A	R	U	I	N
S	O	B	S	L	L	A	V	E	L	L	E
D	T	T	O	I	L	R	E	A	D	L	E
V	E	R	S	H	O	U	L	D	N	O	T

Word Pair　　　　　　　　　　　　　　**Contraction**

1. _____　　_____
2. _____　　_____
3. _____　　_____
4. _____　　_____
5. _____　　_____
6. _____　　_____
7. _____　　_____
8. _____　　_____
9. _____　　_____
10. _____　　_____

Say What?

Complete the famous saying:

1. A fool and his money are soon _____.

2. A bird in the hand is worth _____.

3. He who laughs last _____.

4. A stitch in time _____.

5. Actions speak louder than _____.

6. Absence makes the heart _____.

7. Look before you _____.

8. Early to bed, early to rise, makes a man _____.

9. An ounce of prevention is worth _____.

10. People who live in glass houses _____.

11. Two may keep a secret if _____.

12. It is better to have loved and lost than _____.

13. The grass is always greener _____.

14. A watched pot _____.

15. Two's company, _____.

Analogies

An *analogy* is a way of comparing two things. For example, "big is to little as hot is to cold" is an analogy because *big* and *little* are opposites, or antonyms, and so are *hot* and *cold*. To solve these analogies, you must first decide how the first two items are related and then decide how the missing word should be related to the third word. In analogies, the symbol **:** means "is to" and the symbol **::** means "as." So the example above would be written *big* **:** *little* **::** *hot* **:** *cold*.

1. USA : North America :: Spain :_____

2. nose : smell :: eyes :_____

3. train : track :: car :_____

4. in : out :: up :_____

5. dog : bark :: cat :_____

6. lemon : sour :: sugar :_____

7. wind : blow :: sun :_____

8. near : far :: thin :_____

9. summer : hot :: winter :_____

10. hat : head :: sock :_____

11. story : author :: symphony :_____

12. mother : daughter :: father :_____

13. cow : milk :: chicken :_____

14. Detroit : Michigan :: Chicago :_____

15. sky : blue :: grass :_____

Break the Code!

In this puzzle, the letters stand for other letters. Can you figure out what letters the code letters stand for? The fifth word, *venetian*, has been decoded for you. Look at the first letter, "V." It is over the "Y." That means "Y" stands for "V" in the code. At the bottom of your page, write "Y" under the letter "V" on your decoder. Follow these steps for each letter in *venetian*. Then start trying to figure out some of the other missing letters in the puzzle.

Decoded Line:									'	
Coded Line:	E	B	E	W	Z	C	U	C	K'	W

Decoded Line:			
Coded Line:	B	L	U

Decoded Line:	V	E	N	E	T	I	A	N
Coded Line:	Y	C	K	C	W	E	J	K

Decoded Line:						,		
Coded Line:	I	O	E	K	G	V,	E	W

Decoded Line:						
Coded Line:	Z	L	X	O	G	I	C

Decoded Line:									
Coded Line:	H	X	U	W	J	E	K	V	B	L	U

Decoded Line:							!
Coded Line:	J	O	O	L	B	X	V!

Decoder

Alphabet–	A	B	C	D	E	F	G	H	I	J	K	L	M
Code–	(J)	_	_	_	(C)	_	_	_	(E)	_	_	_	_
Alphabet–	N	O	P	Q	R	S	T	U	V	W	X	Y	Z
Code–	(K)	_	_	_	_	_	(W)	_	(Y)	_	_	_	_

Calculated Story

To complete this story, solve the math problems on a calculator and then turn the calculator upside down to read the word. Write the word in the blank.

Once upon a time, a girl named _____ broke her _____ when she
$(45{,}678 - 14{,}105)$ $(123 + 814)$

fell down a _____. Her friend _____ came over to say
$(38{,}570 \div 5)$ $(9 \times 33 + 40)$

"_____." _____ brought _____ an
$(2 + 2 + 10)$ $(9 \times 33 + 40)$ $(45{,}678 - 14{,}105)$

_____. But when _____ saw _____ quickly
$(2979 \div 3)$ $(9 \times 33 + 40)$ $(45{,}678 - 14{,}105)$

_____ it down, she broke into
$(300{,}000 + 70{,}000 + 8{,}800 + 9)$

_____. _____ told _____,
$(5 \times 1{,}000{,}000 + 379{,}919)$ $(9 \times 33 + 40)$ $(45{,}678 - 14{,}105)$

"_____! You're not supposed to eat the _____!"
(9×501) $(386{,}725 \div 5)$

Now, try to find some new calculator words.

Number	Word
_____	_____
_____	_____
_____	_____
_____	_____
_____	_____
_____	_____
_____	_____

Riddle Math

How Do You Make a Hot Dog Stand?

The answer to this riddle is written in a special code at the bottom of this page. Each pair of numbers stands for a point on the graph . Write the letter shown at the point near the intersection of each pair of numbers. Read numbers across and then up. The letters will spell out the answer to the riddle.

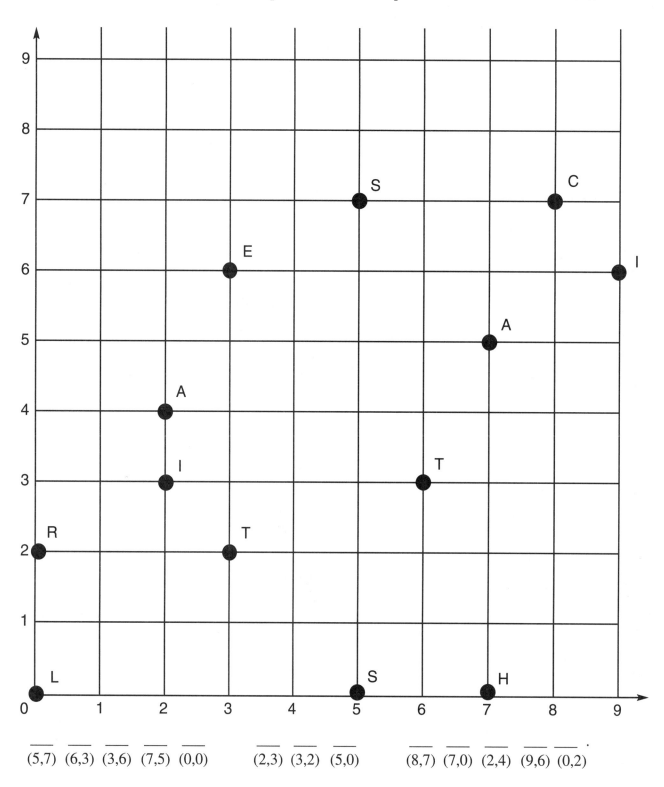

$\overline{}$ $\overline{}$ $\overline{}$ $\overline{}$ $\overline{}$ $\overline{}$ $\overline{}$ $\overline{}$ $\overline{}$ $\overline{}$ $\overline{}$ $\overline{}$ $\overline{}$.
(5,7) (6,3) (3,6) (7,5) (0,0)   (2,3) (3,2) (5,0)   (8,7) (7,0) (2,4) (9,6) (0,2)

I've Been Framed!

Each number in the large boxes below is written within a smaller different shape or frame. Using this as a guide, write the correct number in each shape below and solve each problem.

8	3	5
6	9	7
4	2	1

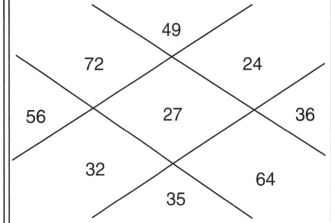

1. $(\wedge \div \lfloor\ ) \times (\diamondsuit \div \sqcup) =$

2. $(\langle\rangle \div \rceil) \times (\vee \div \square) =$

3. $(\smile \div \square) \times (\langle \div \rfloor) =$

4. $(\rangle \div \square) \times (\sqcap \div \rfloor) =$

5. $(\langle \div \rbrack) \times (\wedge \div \square) =$

Oceanography—
Sea Life Word Search

Oceans cover nearly three-fourths of the earth's surface and measure thousands of feet deep. Although it looks like a lonely place from the deck of a boat, the ocean is full of a countless variety of living things from algae to zooplankton and every letter in between.

Directions: Explore the word box below. See how many of the ocean creatures you can find. A word list is provided at the bottom of the page to assist you with your fishing trip. The hidden words may read up, down, across, diagonally, or backwards. Circle each word as you find it.

```
S  A  I  L  F  I  S  H  O  R  C  A  L  M  A

J  T  I  G  E  R  S  H  A  R  K  O  Q  T  N

E  U  A  B  Z  E  B  R  A  E  M  C  L  E  E

L  N  A  R  W  H  A  L  L  D  S  T  O  P  M

L  A  S  T  F  I  G  C  H  I  T  O  N  M  O

Y  E  L  L  O  I  A  B  D  O  L  P  H  I  N

F  L  A  G  U  N  S  E  A  S  L  U  G  L  E

I  M  M  E  R  S  E  H  O  N  E  S  T  L  Y

S  P  L  A  N  K  T  O  N  M  A  R  L  I  N

H  O  B  R  O  Y  R  O  G  E  R  D  A  L  E
```

anemone	barnacle	chiton	dolphin
eel	jellyfish	limpet	marlin
narwhal	octopus	plankton	sailfish
sea slug	starfish	tiger shark	tuna

Do Some Research: Use an encyclopedia or other library resource to determine which of the above sea creatures swims the fastest.

Baseball Word Search

Known as "America's Pastime," baseball has been played in sandlots and stadiums for over 150 years. Newspapers, magazines, radio, and television have been used to bring the excitement of baseball to fans all around the world. Professional baseball players are hired to represent one of the 28 teams that comprise the National and American Leagues. Each team will play more than 160 ball games during the regular season. Two highlights of professional baseball are the mid-season All-Star Game and the season-ending World Series.

Directions: Explore the word box below. See how many baseball terms you can find that are listed at the bottom of the page. The hidden words may read up, down, across, diagonally, or backwards. Circle each word as you find it.

```
X  S  D  M  O  U  T  H  P  I  E  C  E  D  O
Y  H  O  U  T  F  I  E  L  D  Q  A  R  I  S
D  O  U  B  L  E  P  L  A  Y  W  T  S  A  L
Z  R  B  O  S  A  C  R  I  F  I  C  E  M  O
A  T  L  L  I  T  T  E  R  H  A  D  W  O  N
I  S  E  R  R  O  R  P  Z  N  O  B  A  N  O
U  T  H  V  Y  C  E  I  N  F  I  E  L  D  R
F  O  E  G  I  B  H  T  K  N  L  H  K  A  R
G  P  A  W  C  A  T  C  H  E  R  Y  E  L  L
A  H  D  A  O  L  E  H  O  P  O  J  O  J  O
T  O  E  S  I  L  R  E  E  N  A  J  B  U  S
E  T  R  U  N  U  N  R  I  S  S  K  R  W  T
```

ball	catcher	diamond	doubleheader
double play	error	fly out	hit
infield	outfield	pitcher	run
sacrifice	shortstop	strike	walk

Basketball Word Search

Basketball was a game created in Springfield, Massachusetts, by physical education instructor Jim Naismith. The first official game was played on January 20, 1892, using a soccer ball and two peach baskets. The new game caught on immediately and today ranks as one of the most popular in existence. Teams exist at high school, collegiate, and professional levels for both men and women. It has been estimated that over 200 million people pay to watch a basketball game every year. In addition to providing entertainment, basketball is an easy sport to learn and fun to play. Whether you are practicing all alone or participating on an organized team, basketball can provide an excellent way to get your exercise!

Directions: Explore the word box below. See how many basketball terms you can find from the list at the bottom of the page. The hidden words may read up, down, across, diagonally, or backwards. Circle each word as you find it.

```
T  F  A  I  R  Y  N  B  A  P  A  S  S  A  G  E  M
D  R  I  B  B  L  E  Y  K  E  Y  A  L  M  A  K  L
S  E  A  T  O  F  T  C  I  R  I  S  K  Y  R  N  G
D  E  N  V  R  I  L  O  T  I  M  H  E  S  A  U  H
O  T  H  R  E  E  O  U  T  O  F  B  O  U  N  D  S
S  H  U  T  B  L  R  R  E  D  A  R  E  O  D  I  P
T  R  A  P  O  D  I  T  N  E  C  O  I  I  P  I  A
T  O  F  R  U  G  M  N  S  C  H  O  O  L  I  N  G
O  W  L  O  N  O  A  N  G  L  E  S  U  U  X  I  E
D  R  U  M  D  A  D  D  Y  L  O  N  G  L  E  G  S
O  Y  F  O  U  L  E  D  S  W  I  N  G  P  L  A  Y
```

court	dribble	dunk	field goal
foul	free throw	hoop	key
NBA	net	out of bounds	pass
period	rim	rebound	traveling

Hockey Crossword

Directions: Using the clues provided, complete the puzzle boxes.

Across

2. This country to the north of the U.S. is famous for its hockey.

4. This player stands in front of the goal.

7. This is made of hard black rubber.

8. This is the number of periods in a game.

9. This illegal procedure does not belong on top of birthday cakes.

10. This painful maneuver will send your opponent into the boards.

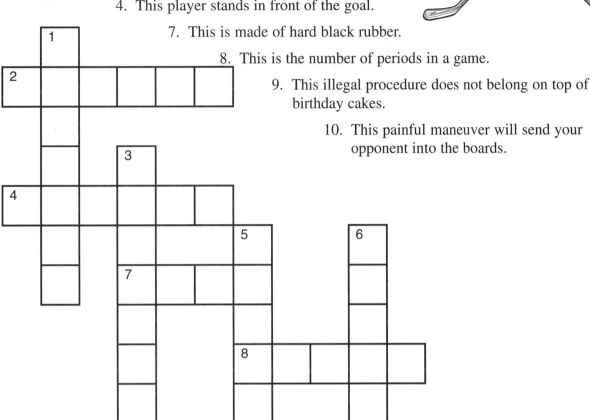

Down

1. Every game begins with this event in the center of the ice.

3. This is a forceful swing of the hockey stick used to make an attempt to score a goal.

5. To play hockey, you need these on your feet.

6. It won't make you sad to discover this colorful segment marking the distance halfway between center ice and the goal.

Exercise Your Brain: Using the words from this puzzle, write a newspaper article about last night's championship ice hockey game.

Leisure Sports Word Search

We all know the values of fitness. In order to live long healthy lives, we need to eat right and exercise two to three times per week. That is easy when we are young. School provides us with physical education class, recess breaks, and outside play time with our friends after school. Also, most of us participate in some type of organized sport or activity. As we get older, however, the opportunity to participate in group games and activities becomes more and more difficult. Our friends may move away or are too busy to join us in a game of soccer or tag. Health-conscious persons need to find fitness activities that they can do alone or in very small groups. We call these activities leisure or lifetime sports because we are able to do them for fitness and recreation our whole lives.

Directions: Explore the word box below. See how many of the listed leisure sports and fitness activities you can find. The hidden terms may read up, down, across, diagonally, or backwards. Circle each word as you find it.

```
A  R  Q  P  O  N  M  L  K  J  I  H  G  D
E  D  D  I  E  S  W  I  M  M  I  N  G  A
R  U  N  N  I  N  G  O  U  T  I  O  R  N
O  S  O  B  A  D  M  I  N  T  O  N  O  C
B  O  W  L  I  N  G  O  F  H  F  E  Z  I
I  S  T  H  A  T  A  I  J  E  E  O  S  N
C  O  H  O  R  T  L  B  O  R  N  F  K  G
S  T  E  W  C  T  S  U  G  F  C  C  I  S
F  A  R  C  H  E  R  Y  G  L  I  A  I  I
L  O  N  G  T  E  N  S  I  O  N  R  N  N
O  B  I  C  Y  C  L  I  N  G  G  L  G  N
O  E  A  H  I  K  I  N  G  R  A  S  S  E
W  A  L  K  I  N  G  R  E  E  N  B  O  T
```

aerobics	archery	badminton	bicycling
bowling	dancing	fencing	golf
hiking	jogging	running	skiing
swimming	tennis	walking	weight lifting

Playground Games Word Search

It has been said that "necessity is the mother of invention." The individual and group games that boys and girls play are born out of the environment and resources which are made available to them. For example, the old-time favorite of **kickball** requires only a field of grass or sand and a rubber ball. Other playground games like **capture the flag**, **hide and seek**, and **frozen tag** require no equipment at all.

Playground games remain popular because they provide lots of fun and exercise without complicated rules. The rules involved in the game of tag are very simple—avoid getting touched by the boy or girl who is "it." **Animal tag**, **TV tag**, **amoeba tag**, and **dog catcher** are all variations of the simple game of tag.

Spud, **four square**, and **wall ball** are all simple games involving a rubber playground ball and boys and girls numbering two to twenty-two. The only thing that limits fun on the playground is your imagination!

Directions: Have some playground game fun. Explore the word box below. Search for the words that have been boldfaced in the above text. The hidden word may read up, down, across, diagonally, or backwards. Circle each word or combination of words as you find it.

```
C  G  R  E  E  N  G  R  A  S  S  K  I  D
H  A  M  O  E  B  A  T  A  G  O  I  N  O
A  T  P  O  L  I  C  E  M  A  N  C  A  G
R  L  Y  T  S  P  U  N  O  R  T  K  B  C
L  A  S  P  U  D  A  V  I  D  V  B  I  A
I  M  O  F  F  R  O  Z  E  N  T  A  G  T
E  I  N  E  W  A  E  X  T  V  A  L  H  C
C  N  O  T  O  N  E  T  Y  E  G  L  O  H
H  A  V  I  N  G  H  O  H  G  W  X  U  E
A  H  I  D  E  A  N  D  S  E  E  K  S  R
P  E  R  A  U  Q  S  R  U  O  F  E  E  R
L  O  N  G  W  A  L  L  B  A  L  L  F  I
I  F  A  B  O  D  Y  C  A  T  C  H  A  N
N  T  H  R  O  U  G  H  T  H  E  R  R  G
```

Exercise Your Mind: Use the back of this paper to invent a playground game. Share the rules with your friends and play it.

Soccer Crossword

Directions: Using the crossword grid provided below, enter the words that best correspond with the numbered clues. *Across* words will go left to right; *down* words will go from up to down.

Across

1. Stops opposing players from scoring points.
3. Only the goalkeeper may touch the ball with these.
6. Perhaps the greatest player the sport has ever known.
7. Patrols the touchlines and assists the referee with determining possession.
10. To propel the ball with the head.
12. This competition happens every four years.
17. Enforces the rules of the game, also known as "the Law."
18. They mark the sides of the soccer field.
19. International governing body of the sport.
20. Also known as defenders.

Down

2. Maximum number of players allowed from one team on the field.
4. To control the ball with the feet.
5. Also known as midfielders.
8. Players in this position are mostly responsible for scoring the goals.
9. Purpose of the game.
11. May be found on either end of the playing field.
13. Touching the ball with your hands will result in one of these.
14. Term for guarding an opponent.
15. The world's most popular team sport.
16. Round, inflated bladder covered in leather.

Team Mascot Decoder

Every sports team has a name. The team name usually contains two parts—the place or organization the members play for and the team's chosen mascot. Most team names and mascots are chosen from the animal kingdom, like the Chicago Bears football team and Detroit Tigers baseball team. However, some team mascots are human characters representative of the team's sponsor or state. For example, the Dallas Cowboys is a professional football team that represents a city in the grand state of Texas.

Directions: Use the clues provided and unscramble the names of these professional sports teams.

1. A little red bird from Missouri is the mascot of this big-league baseball team.

   TS IULOS DIRCANSAL

   _____

2. This east coast professional basketball team is not really from Ireland.

   NBSOTO TCLSIEC

   _____

3. Despite living near the ocean, there is nothing fishy about this football team.

   MMIIA LDPOIHNS

   _____

4. This hockey team was created soon after the successful release of a children's film.

   HMAANIE GYMITH KCDUS

   _____

5. The Baltimore Blast is this Ohio indoor soccer team's greatest rival.

   EEVLCNDAL RUNCCH

   _____

Exercise Your Mind: What is your school's team mascot? Is your mascot a good representation of your school's history and character? Write a paragraph that explains why or why not.

Who Got The Gold?

(Olympic Deduction Game)

The United States Junior Olympic Team won five gold medals. Read the clues below and put your deductive reasoning skills to work. Put an X on the grid to match each athlete with the Olympic event that he or she won.

Clues

1. Brian enjoyed watching the biathlon the most.
2. Nicole never did learn how to ice-skate.
3. Madeline was surprised to see Nicole jump so far.
4. Maxine and Brian could not get tickets to watch the figure skating finals.
5. Claudia was glad she did not have to compete in cold air.

	Biathlon	Fencing	Figure Skating	Ski Jump	Luge
Claudia					
Maxine					
Brian					
Madeline					
Nicole					

Part 1 Answer Key

Page 6
1. square
2. star
3. triangle
4. square
5. rectangle

Page 7
a. 3
b. 3
c. 1
d. 4
e. 1
f. 4
g. 118
h. 14
i. 120
j. 30

Page 8
1. Q
2. Z
3. B
4. E
5. B
6. Z
7. A
8. M
9. C
10. P

Page 10
1. apple
2. book
3. cat
4. dog
5. elephant
6. jump
7. kite
8. map
9. run
10. skate
11. tree
12. zebra

Page 12
spoon-bowl
sleeping baby-crib
lunch box-sandwich
bat-ball
lamp-light bulb

Page 13
1. d - mouse
2. c - giraffe
3. a - pig
4. e - lion
5. b - dog

Page 14
lamp, couch, pig, computer,
boots, school bell, snowman, hat
and scarf, mittens, chicken, sun-
glasses on the sun

Page 15
Joanna—jump rope
Tom—truck
Helena—hat
Carol—crayons
Bob—ball

Page 16
3 + 3 = 6 carrots
10 - 6 = 4 cupcakes
8 - 6 = 2 sandwiches
5 + 2 = 7 ants
3 + 2 = 5 apples

Page 17
Jose - football
Mike - tennis
Latanya - tetherball

Page 20
1. Seven
2. One, Two
3. Three
4. Three
5. Twelve
6. Forty
7. Three
8. Six
9. One Hundred and One
10. Three

Page 22
1. empty
2. up
3. happy
4. far
5. wet
6. crooked
7. in
8. soft
9. high
10. over
11. tall/long
12. off
13. heavy/dark
14. clean
15. hot

Page 23
Answers will vary.

Page 24
Answers will vary.

Page 25
giraffe

Page 26
castle

Page 27
whale

Page 28
schoolhouse

Part 1 Answer Key *(cont.)*

Page 29

Page 30

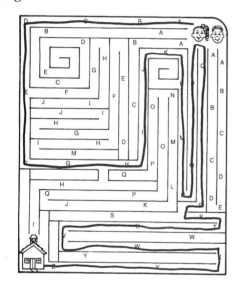

Page 31

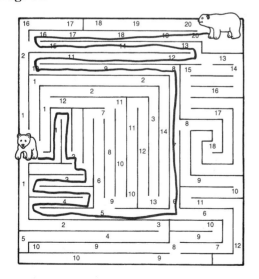

Page 32

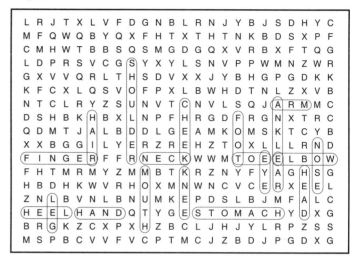

Page 33

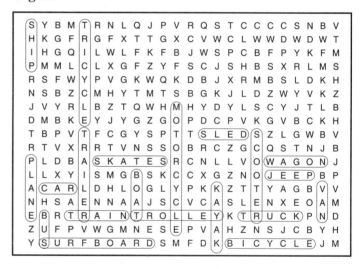

Page 34

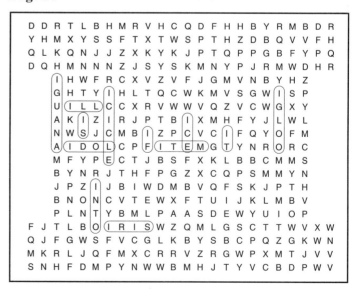

Part 1 Answer Key *(cont.)*

Page 35

```
N R N B S W S P M R N J N L R L B S H K M J R Z
X R N L G V S C P L G W N P A G I U F Q R H J K
S R M X J H B V C N G F D L R U R S I S E Y U V
M L B T L D N Z V A L F H A E U G X T L A G M S
S L O O K F P A I N T C R Y A W N H J E D Q P X
K W Y R V Q S Q P T H C F O T M T R O E N X R M
I B V L N L N X N R B H C W L Z L G P H C K J
P W R M H Q I D P V O R X O P N T D L S F W V H
C S G E X P D F F K W D H U X J H D M Z N D F
L J K K A N E R N F B Y N G W F K O H I T Y T Q
I B Q T C K X Y V D M C Y H X M H W P L Z W S B
M P N M M D Y R X G S L M Q T B X G L E D Y G C
B H W G V D C R V S V C Y G Z Z B Y H T X G S H
T V D W V C P V W R F N P Y K Y M F T H Y V F
Q J V D R L F M Z M L Y G K S T T R N W K Q S D
N S V B F P H L K S J L B M D L G Y S Y Q X G R
D K Q V L T S K Z C M Y M T L B T V S B R X F J
```

Page 36

```
W O R D Z Y T Z W O R D Q Z B W S V Q W V M H P
M T X R S R F X C Q G P L R T W O R D N Z V X T
G T S X S V C C W L T G M W H L B Q X T W O R D
K Y B G Q C V C M O K R H O T V M G J K N K C G
J V V P W W K Y T Y R J M R K D M R V K S N R W
D K V P D O V P F Q F D R D V T G R D H H P L O
Y T S J R R R V Z R Y P C Z G Y T R W O R D R
D Z W Y H D N G W Y W O R D B G O F T R G D G D
J Z O W P N W B F O L F F Y L W M G R D H J T J
W O R D D M V T J R L L Y F P Y X S V W X X H
T C D X F Y X J S R M D Q Z V C D Z Y C O P W G
H T R D N G N Y R W B P V P C Z V Y W F R M M D
T P W W Q F K K D O F J P N F M D C N H D J K S
X B L C W D D Q S R M S J T R R B V Y M T W V C
T D Y J S K K K Z D G R B F O Z X V C F F O V H
B V R S W Y C D T Q Y N G W N V W G D Z G R X R
M B B P D W O R D V B D M N R C F Q W O R D S H
T F U P K V G B M F W R T F P K V G B M F W R
V Z R P K T F D V J Y L V Z R P K T F D V J Y L
L K V T F R E S C X M N Y B J C L P S C Z X M N Y B
J C L P S C Z X M N Y B J C L P S C Z X M N Y B
K G D S A V T H J A V I K G D S A V T H J A V I
```

Page 37
1. hen
2. pig
3. horse
4. cow
5. goose
6. duck
7. rooster
8. mule
9. goat
10. cat
11. sheep
12. dog

Page 38
1. drums
2. flute
3. guitar
4. piano
5. banjo
6. violin
7. tuba
8. triangle
9. harp
10. oboe
11. cello
12. organ

Page 39
1. bed
2. lamp
3. oven
4. television
5. table
6. sink
7. glass
8. chair
9. towel
10. plate
11. tub
12. fork

Page 40
1. blue
2. red
3. purple
4. green
5. black
6. yellow
7. white
8. silver
9. orange
10. pink
11. gold
12. brown

Page 41
1. pencil
2. chalk
3. student
4. globe
5. playground
6. teacher
7. desk
8. eraser
9. crayons
10. paper
11. principal
12. ruler

Part 1 Answer Key *(cont.)*

Page 42
1. heart
2. triangle
3. heart
4. triangle
5. square

Page 43
1. 3
2. 2
3. 1
4. 3
5. 1
6. 1
7. 4
8. 1
9. 1
10. 25
11. 1
12. 64

Page 44
1. K
2. V
3. P
4. F
5. A
6. E
7. Y
8. E
9. A
10. D
11. Z
12. C

Page 45
C D F I K L N R S T V X Y

Page 46
b e f h i l m n o q s t u w x z

Page 47
1. baby
2. bath
3. dash
4. dress
5. foot
6. football
7. ice
8. igloo
9. mirror
10. monkey
11. wombat
12. wooly

Page 48
1. bring
2. brought
3. camp
4. coyote
5. lamp
6. lazy
7. leopard
8. pickle
9. play
10. playground
11. zipper
12. zoo

Page 49
Aa Bb Cc Dd Ee Ff Gg Hh Ii Jj
Kk Ll Mm Nn Oo Pp Qq Rr Ss Tt
Uu Vv Ww Xx Yy Zz

Page 50
aA bB cC dD eE fF gG hH iI jJ
kK lL mM nN oO pP qQ rR sS tT
uU vV wW xX yY zZ

Page 51
ice skate, high-heeled shoe, one-curl baby, ace, matching domino

Page 52
fork and spoon, baseball and bat, baby and rattle, bird and nest, paper and pencil, and shoe and sock

Page 53
house and chimney, rubber duck and bathtub, tree and leaf, computer and disc, school and desk, and child and ball

Page 54
pumpkin and glass slipper, wolf and basket of goodies, bear and porridge, pig and straw house, and witch and apple

Page 55
1. C
2. D
3. E
4. B
5. A

Page 56
Circled: sailboat on the grass, hippo, fish in the sky, dog in the tree, television set, and giraffe

Page 57
shoe, skate, ear, sock, mitten, hand, foot, and eye

Page 58
jacket, shoe, hat, tie, sock, scarf

Page 59
A. 3
B. 4
C. 1
D. 2

Page 60
Mindy owns a bicycle.
Simon owns a tricycle.
Pam owns a skateboard.

Page 61
Dawn = doll
Bill = bicycle
Emily = earrings
Sue = skates
Ken = kite

Page 62
3 + 2 = 5 (bears)
6 - 4 = 2 (cars)
1 + 3 = 4 (dominoes)
4 + 2 = 6 (books)
7 - 4 = 3 (dolls)

Page 63
6 + 5 = 11 (tops)
4 + 8 = 12 (crayons)
16 - 3 = 13 (paintbrushes)
15 - 5 = 10 (jacks)
7 + 7 = 14 (marbles)

Page 64
Tran likes baseball.
Henry likes basketball.
Maya likes soccer.

Page 65
Susie is 8.
Jimmy is 6.
Katie is 7.

Page 66
Different picture: third, second, first, fourth, and second

Page 67
A. 4   D. 3
B. 5   E. 1
C. 2

Part 1 Answer Key *(cont.)*

Page 68
A. 4
B. 5
C. 1
D. 2
E. 3

Page 69
There are 9 circles.

Page 70
There are 11 squares.

Page 71
There are 16 triangles.

Page 72
1. 2
2. 15
3. 8
4. 13
5. Answers will vary depending on individual examination, perception, and creativity.

Page 73
1. 7
2. 13
3. 3
4. 6
5. Answers will vary depending on individual examination, perception, and creativity.

Page 74
1. 9
2. 4
3. 7
4. 15
5. Answers will vary depending on individual examination, perception, and creativity.

Page 75
kittens, balls, dice, crayons, hot dogs, and books

Page 76
3 more birds, 4 more candles, 1 more Valentine, and 5 more hats

Page 77
There are 12 rabbits.

Page 78
1. Little
2. Three
3. Baby
4. Old

Page 79
1. cold (l)
2. happy (p)
3. funny (n)
4. cow (o)
5. crow or crop (w or p)
6. mother (t)
7. rabbit (t)
8. jacket (k)
9. mouth (o)
10. rise or wise (r or w)
11. street (t)
12. horse or house (r or u)
13. monkey (y)
14. clamp (c)
15. pocket (e)

Page 80
1. spring or string (p or t)
2. back (k)
3. six, mix, or fix (s, m, or f)
4. hair or hail (r of l)
5. polite or police (t or c)
6. elbow (l)
7. sheet, sleet, or sweet (h, l, or w)
8. stomach (h)
9. floor or flour (o or u)
10. coach or couch (a or u)
11. blanket (b)
12. scout (s)
13. change or chance (g or c)
14. finger (g)
15. please (l)

Page 81
the bird's beak, the cat's tail, the zebra's stripes, the dog's ears, the kangaroo's pouch, and the fish's fins

Page 82
the face's nose, the slide's ladder, the clock's hands, the car's wheels, the sailboat's sail, and the umbrella's handle

Page 83
1. nimble, quick, jump
2. contrary, garden
3. son, bed
4. Jill, hill, pail, fell, broke, tumbling
5. sat, eating, spider, away

Page 84
1. Pigs
2. Bears
3. Billy
4. Snow, Seven
5. Little
6. Beast
7. Lamp
8. Jack
9. Goose, Eggs
10. Town
11. Sleeping
12. Swan
13. Tin
14. Rabbit

Page 85
Answers will vary.

Page 86
1. cold
2. light
3. on
4. under
5. low
6. out
7. near
8. straight
9. down
10. full
11. sad
12. dry
13. hard
14. short
15. dirty

Page 87
1. Monday
2. Friday
3. Tuesday
4. Saturday
5. Thursday
6. Wednesday
7. Sunday

Page 88
1. February
2. July
3. November
4. March
5. August
6. October
7. April
8. September
9. May
10. December
11. June
12. January

Page 89
Answers will vary.

Part 1 Answer Key *(cont.)*

Page 90

j	s	u	m	g	u	n	o	p

gun   sun   bun   nun
fun   run   spun   stun

Page 91

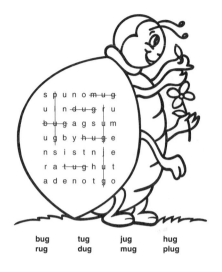

bug   tug   jug   hug
rug   dug   mug   plug

Page 92

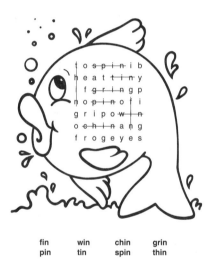

fin   win   chin   grin
pin   tin   spin   thin

Page 93

ship   dip   flip   zip
rip   hip   trip   lip

Page 94

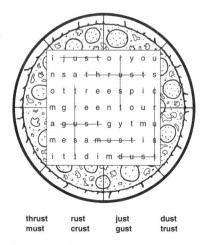

thrust   rust   just   dust
must   crust   gust   trust

Page 95

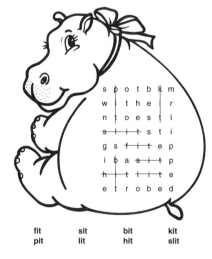

fit   sit   bit   kit
pit   lit   hit   slit

Part 1 Answer Key *(cont.)*

Page 96

block	rock	shock	dock
clock	lock	knock	sock

Page 97

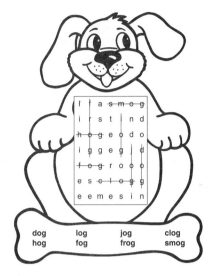

dog	log	jog	clog
hog	fog	frog	smog

Page 98

jet	let	met	set
wet	pet	get	bet

Page 99

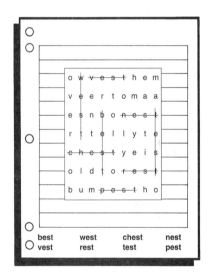

best	west	chest	nest
vest	rest	test	pest

Page 100

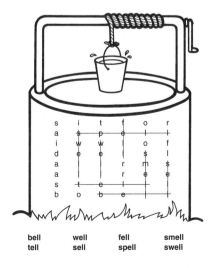

bell	well	fell	smell
tell	sell	spell	swell

Page 101

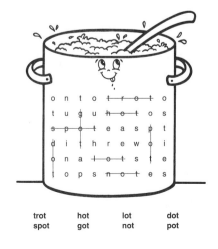

trot	hot	lot	dot
spot	got	not	pot

Part 1 Answer Key *(cont.)*

Page 102

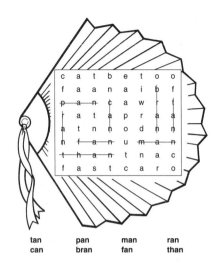

tan   pan   man   ran
can   bran   fan   than

Page 103

lap   tap   trap   map
nap   clap   cap   zap

Page 104

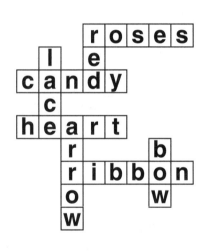

Page 105

Page 106

Page 107

Page 108

Page 109

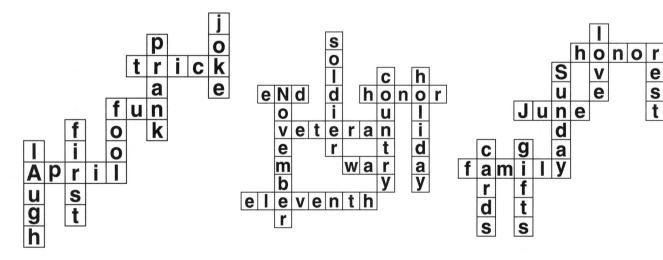

Part 1 Answer Key *(cont.)*

Page 110

Page 111

Page 112

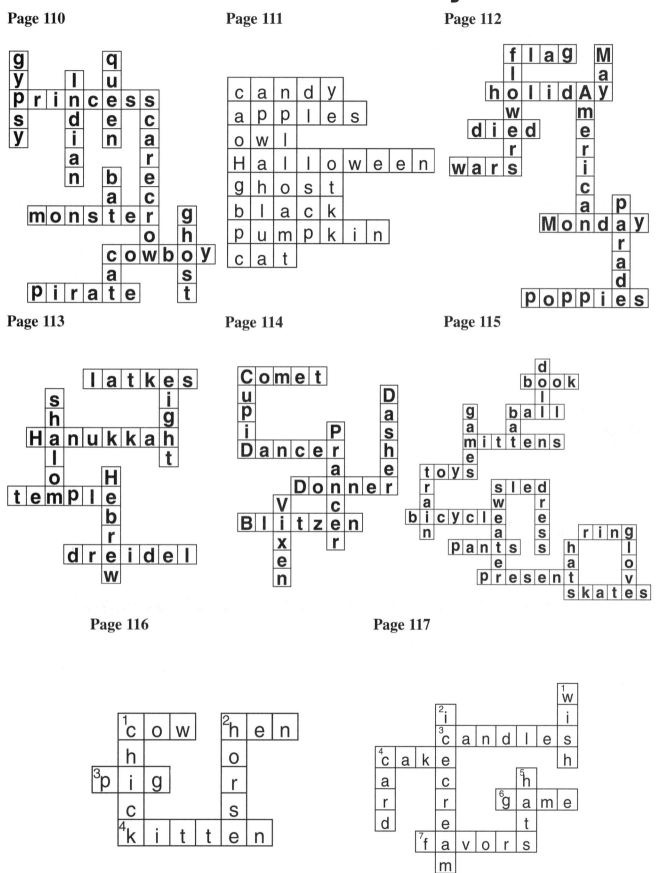

Page 113

Page 114

Page 115

Page 116

Page 117

Part 1 Answer Key (cont.)

Page 119

Page 120

1. book
2. library
3. read
4. words
5. picture
6. print
7. page
8. author
9. artist
10. type
11. story
12. plot
13. cover
14. character
15. illustration

Page 121

Reading is lots of fun!

Page 122

1. square
2. triangle
3. circle
4. heart
5. circle
6. square
7. half circle
8. triangle
9. heart
10. upper rectangle

Page 123

a. 9
b. 18
c. 35
d. 12
e. 6
f. 7
g. 1
h. 15
i. 29
j. 90
k. 6
l. 0
m. 3
n. 9

Page 124

1. G
2. N
3. W
4. Z
5. N
6. C
7. D
8. B
9. A
10. D
11. W
12. S
13. O
14. Y
15. I

Page 125

1. broom
2. chain
3. drum
4. egg
5. flower
6. hand
7. jar
8. letter
9. music
10. number
11. potato
12. star
13. table
14. umbrella
15. whale
16. yellow

Page 126

dog-dog bone
ear-earring
glasses-face with eyes
pencil-paper
sponge-soap

Page 127

horse-wagon
milk in glass - straw
umbrella-rain
battery-flashlight
bat-ball

Page 128

Cinderella-glass slipper
Red Riding Hood-basket
Rumpelstiltskin
spinning wheel
Baby Bear - porridge
Puss-boots

Page 129

6–4= 2
4+3= 7
8–4= 4
9–3= 6
5+2= 7

Page 130

1. +
2. -
3. +
4. -
5. +
6. +
7. +
8. +
9. -
10. -
11. -
12. +

Page 131

Marla - pink

Pepper - red
Rosa - yellow

Page 134

10 circles

Page 135

8 triangles

Page 136

Triangles–sun, swings, slide,
mountains, circles, table, bench
Circles–trees, sun, trees, slide, cup

Page 138

Answers will vary.

Page 139

1. goose
2. tack
3. bird
4. house
5. ice
6. silk
7. time
8. picture
9. clam
10. bee

Page 140

1. break
2. out
3. work
4. front
5. young/new
6. light
7. after
8. under
9. far
10. yes
11. subtract
12. night
13. soft
14. found
15. go

Part 1 Answer Key *(cont.)*

Page 142
camel and palm tree

Page 143
knight and horse

Page 144
computer and keyboard

Page 145
robot

Page 146
If at first you don't succeed, try, try again.
baseball player

Page 147

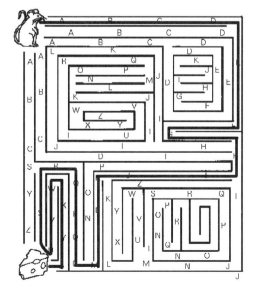

Page 148

Page 149

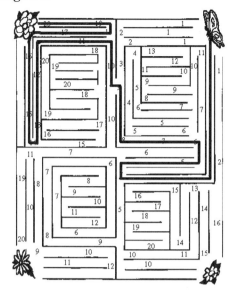
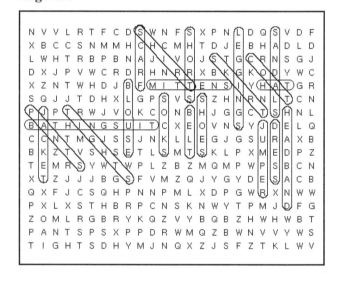

Page 150

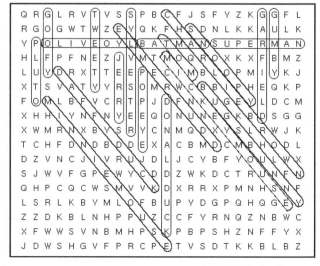

Page 151

Part 1 Answer Key *(cont.)*

Page 152

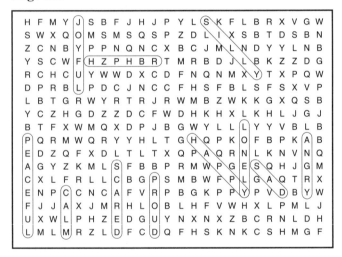

Page 153

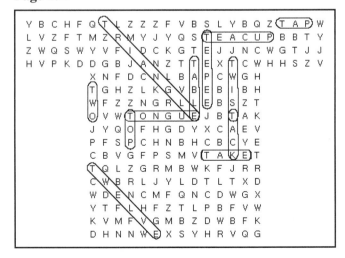

Page 154

Page 155
1. baseball
2. football
3. softball
4. basketball
5. running
6. hockey
7. roller skating
8. sailing
9. bicycling
10. skiing
11. skateboarding
12. ice skating
13. tennis
14. volleyball
15. gymnastics

Page 156
1. snowman
2. blooming
3. leaves
4. rain
5. winter
6. cold
7. wind
8. snow
9. spring
10. hot
11. sun
12. summer
13. snowflake
14. flowers
15. autumn

Page 157
1. farmer
2. banker
3. lawyer
4. teacher
5. doctor
6. writer
7. secretary
8. detective
9. librarian
10. scientist
11. musician
12. actor
13. editor
14. cook
15. fire fighter

Page 158
1. raccoon
2. bear
3. deer
4. rabbit
5. skunk
6. possum
7. owl
8. moose
9. beaver
10. badger
11. elk
12. antelope
13. boar
14. muskrat
15. duck

Page 159
Be cool. Stay in school.

Page 160
I am a special person!

Page 161
I can do anything I want to do and be anything I want to be. When I grow up, I will .

Page 162
1. triangle
2. square
3. triangle
4. square
5. heart
6. diamond
7. star
8. heart
9. triangle
10. rectangle

Page 163
1. 9
2. 18
3. 17
4. 11
5. 5
6. 5
7. 1
8. 45
9. 25
10. 90
11. 2
12. 0
13. 2
14. 60
15. 9

Part 1 Answer Key (cont.)

Page 164
1. G
2. M
3. N
4. T
5. N
6. S
7. D
8. C
9. C
10. A
11. Z
12. E
13. D
14. D
15. A

Page 165
1. apple
2. apricot
3. apron
4. basket
5. bounty
6. cat
7. catfish
8. eagle
9. elephant
10. elevator
11. school
12. schoolhouse
13. schooner
14. time
15. tip
16. type

Page 166
1. aardvark
2. angel
3. angle
4. door
5. doorbell
6. doorknob
7. fried
8. friend
9. friendly
10. happen
11. happy
12. joyful
13. moose
14. mouse
15. paper
16. pepper

Page 167
1. first and third
2. second and fourth
3. fourth and fifth
4. second and fifth
5. first and fourth
6. third and fourth

Page 168
postal carrier and letter; peanut butter and jelly; hen and egg; paintbrush and paint; hand and glove; window and curtain

Page 169
mouse and cheese; hammer and nail; train and track; cloud and rain; piggybank and coin; car and traffic light

Page 170
beanstalk and giant; princess and beast; tin soldier and ballerina; wooden boy and whale; lamp and genie

Page 171
bird and nest; bear and cave; beaver and dam; squirrel and hole in the tree; bee and hive

Page 172
1. hat
2. ball
3. umbrella
4. doll
5. guitar

Page 173
helicopter, surfer, truck, postal carrier, television set, and clown

Page 174
1. unicycle
2. tripod
3. bicycle
4. triangle
5. tricycle
6. unicorn

Page 175
tambourine, cat, radio, whistle, bird, dog, child

Page 176
Kayla and Lynn; Jamaal and Will; Tran and Anton; Keisha and Tamara; Danny and Nori

Page 177
Kami owns the skates.
Pablo owns the wagon.
Maria owns the scooter.

Page 178
Derek = drum
Rioko = rabbit
Joanie = jumprope
Miles = mitt
P.J. = paints

Page 179
10 − 5 = 5 (tops)
4 − 2 = 2 (dolls)
1 + 2 = 3 (bears)
3 + 3 = 6 (blocks)
9 − 5 = 4 (books)

Page 180
1. 3 + 2 = 5
2. 6 − 1 = 5
3. 9 − 3 = 6
4. 2 + 7 = 9
5. 1 + 3 = 4
6. 4 + 3 = 7
7. 9 − 6 = 3
8. 6 + 2 = 8
9. 10 + 5 = 15
10. 12 − 6 = 6
11. 14 − 4 = 10
12. 7 + 5 = 12

Page 181
Paulo = tag
Chan = hide-and-go-seek
Denzel = Simon says

Page 182
Bettina = green house
Carly = red house
Nikko = blue house

Page 183
1. fourth
2. third
3. fifth
4. second
5. first

Page 184
A = 2
B = 4
C = 1
D = 5
E = 3

Page 185
A = 5
B = 2
C = 4
D = 3
E = 1

Page 186
5 circles

Page 187
7 squares

Page 188
12 triangles

Page 189
triangles = tent and sail
circles = sun, flowers, tree, and apples

Part 1 Answer Key *(cont.)*

Page 190

1. 3
2. 9
3. 8
4. 16
5. 5

Page 191

1. 4
2. 3
3. 6
4. 5
5. 51

Page 192

1. 4
2. 3
3. 4
4. 6
5. 10

Page 195

1. rock
2. you
3. mouse
4. push

Page 196

Answers will vary.

Page 197

Answers will vary.

Page 198

Answers will vary.

Page 199

the tree's leaves, the bicycle's wheel, the witch's hat, the chair's leg, the mouse's tail, and the birthday cake's candles

Page 200

1. bird
2. time
3. bed, rise
4. you
5. tomorrow, today
6. heart
7. lemons
8. cloud
9. friend
10. laughs

Page 201

1. ghost
2. ox
3. mouse
4. bird
5. wink
6. fox
7. night
8. whip
9. lark
10. kitten

Page 202

Answers will vary.

Page 203

Answers will vary.

Page 204

1. lamb, lamb, lamb, lamb, snow
2. jolly, jolly, pipe, bowl, three
3. dock, mouse, down, dock
4. market, home, beef, none

Page 205

1. enemy (foe)
2. white
3. little
4. bad
5. late
6. quiet
7. old
8. small
9. high
10. soft
11. light
12. up
13. wet
14. in
15. slow

Page 206

Answers will vary.

Part 1 Answer Key *(cont.)*

Page 207

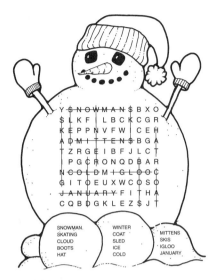

SNOWMAN.
SKATING
CLOUD
BOOTS
HAT

WINTER
COAT
SLED
ICE
COLD

MITTENS
SKIS
· IGLOO
· JANUARY

Page 208

BUTTER
CINNAMON
CITRON

COCONUT
EGGS
FLOUR

GINGER
MILK
MOLASSES

NUTMEG
PECANS
RAISINS

SALT
SUGAR
VANILLA

Page 209

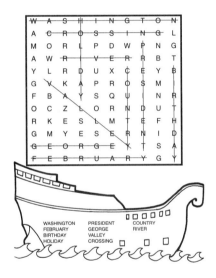

WASHINGTON
FEBRUARY
BIRTHDAY
HOLIDAY

PRESIDENT
GEORGE
VALLEY
CROSSING

COUNTRY
RIVER

Page 210

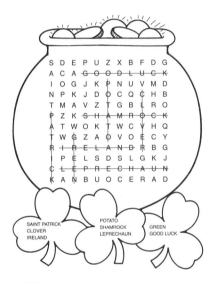

SAINT PATRICK
CLOVER
IRELAND

POTATO
SHAMROCK
LEPRECHAUN

GREEN
GOOD LUCK

Page 211

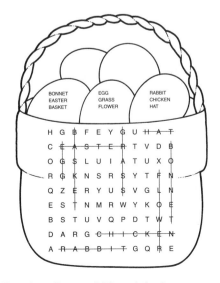

BONNET
EASTER
BASKET

EGG
GRASS
FLOWER

RABBIT
CHICKEN
HAT

Page 212

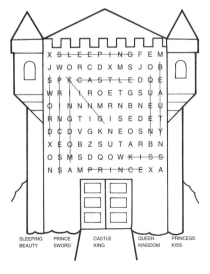

SLEEPING
BEAUTY

PRINCE
SWORD

CASTLE
KING

QUEEN
KINGDOM

PRINCESS
KISS

Part 1 Answer Key *(cont.)*

Page 213

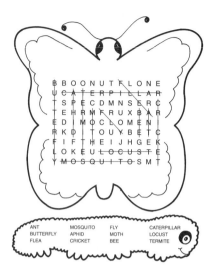

B	B	O	O	N	U	T	F	L	O	N	E
U	C	A	T	E	R	P	I	L	L	A	R
T	S	P	E	C	D	M	N	S	E	R	C
T	E	H	R	M	F	R	U	X	B	A	R
E	D	I	M	O	C	L	O	M	E	N	I
R	K	D	I	T	O	U	K	B	E	T	C
F	I	F	T	H	E	I	J	H	G	E	K
L	O	K	E	U	L	O	C	U	S	T	E
Y	M	O	S	Q	U	I	T	O	S	M	T

ANT	MOSQUITO	FLY	CATERPILLAR
BUTTERFLY	APHID	MOTH	LOCUST
FLEA	CRICKET	BEE	TERMITE

Page 214

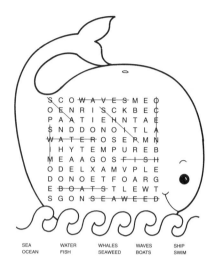

S	C	O	W	A	V	E	S	M	E	O
O	E	N	R	I	S	C	K	B	E	C
P	A	A	T	I	E	H	N	T	A	E
S	N	D	D	O	N	O	I	T	L	A
W	A	T	E	R	O	S	E	R	M	N
I	H	Y	T	E	M	P	U	R	E	B
M	E	A	A	G	O	S	F	I	S	H
O	D	E	L	X	A	M	V	P	L	E
D	O	N	O	E	T	F	O	A	R	G
E	B	O	A	T	S	T	L	E	W	T
S	G	O	N	S	E	A	W	E	E	D

SEA	WATER	WHALES	WAVES	SHIP
OCEAN	FISH	SEAWEED	BOATS	SWIM

Page 215

S	T	O	D	A	L	O	T	I	O	N
U	U	I	S	W	I	M	S	U	I	T
N	N	S	D	T	I	S	G	M	A	T
G	W	W	O	R	I	U	L	I	L	A
B	L	I	E	M	Y	R	A	J	O	N
E	A	M	L	O	T	F	S	A	N	D
A	L	O	V	H	E	I	S	H	O	T
C	R	A	C	W	A	N	E	D	W	W
H	O	A	R	K	W	G	S	N	E	S

SUN	SAND	LOTION	SWIMSUIT	SWIM
TAN	BEACH	HOT	GLASSES	SURFING

Page 216

T	S	A	F	A	R	I	F	A	S	L
P	A	J	V	I	O	T	K	N	T	E
L	L	T	L	I	W	R	H	I	F	O
A	I	S	I	Y	N	E	O	M	A	P
N	J	U	N	G	L	E	N	A	D	A
T	A	N	D	W	E	S	S	L	P	R
S	S	R	D	O	I	R	T	S	I	D
Y	R	I	V	E	R	S	E	L	O	S
R	M	O	N	K	E	Y	S	G	A	M

SAFARI	TREES	ANIMALS	LEOPARDS	PLANTS
JUNGLE	VINES	TIGER	MONKEYS	RIVERS

Page 217

L	I	G	H	T	N	I	N	G	A
P	U	D	D	L	E	R	K	T	H
C	L	O	U	D	E	Y	A	L	O
T	U	M	B	R	E	L	L	A	N
H	H	I	N	F	L	O	W	E	R
U	E	U	F	E	R	B	U	G	A
N	H	K	R	S	P	R	I	N	G
D	C	B	R	A	I	N	B	O	W
E	M	R	A	I	N	C	O	A	T
R	B	U	T	T	E	R	F	L	Y

RAINBOW	FLOWER	PUDDLE	LIGHTNING
BUTTERFLY	UMBRELLA	RAINCOAT	CLOUD
SPRING	BUG	THUNDER	

Page 218

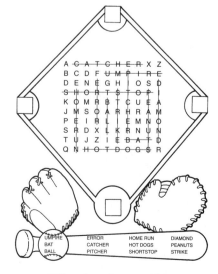

A	C	A	T	C	H	E	R	X	Z
B	C	D	F	U	M	P	I	R	E
D	E	N	E	G	H	I	O	S	D
S	H	O	R	T	S	T	O	P	
K	O	M	R	B	T	C	U	E	A
J	M	S	O	A	R	H	R	A	M
P	E	I	R	L	E	M	N	O	
S	R	D	X	L	K	R	N	U	N
T	U	J	Z	I	E	B	A	T	D
Q	N	H	O	T	D	O	G	S	R

UMPIRE	ERROR	HOME RUN	DIAMOND
BAT	CATCHER	HOT DOGS	PEANUTS
BALL	PITCHER	SHORTSTOP	STRIKE

Part 1 Answer Key *(cont.)*

Page 219

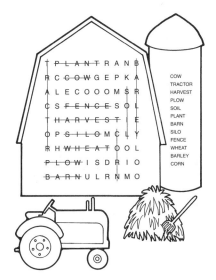

T	P L A N T R A N B								

COW
TRACTOR
HARVEST
PLOW
SOIL
PLANT
BARN
SILO
FENCE
WHEAT
BARLEY
CORN

Page 220

COW   CHICKENS   FIELDS   TRACTOR   GROW
FARMER   BARN   PIGS   CROPS   SCARECROW

Page 221

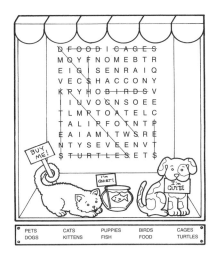

PETS   CATS   PUPPIES   BIRDS   CAGES
DOGS   KITTENS   FISH   FOOD   TURTLES

Page 222

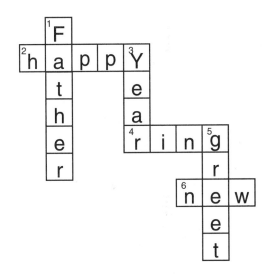

Page 223

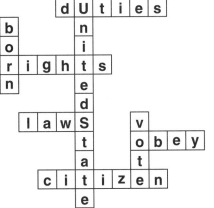

Page 224

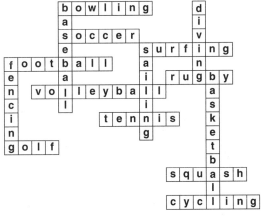

Page 225

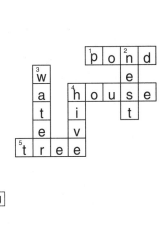

Part 1 Answer Key *(cont.)*

Page 226

Page 227

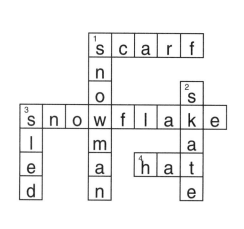

Page 228

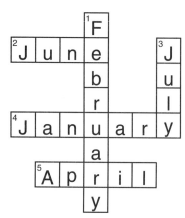

Page 229

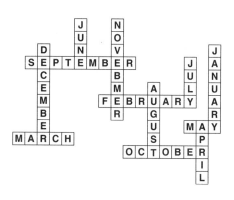

Page 230

Page 231

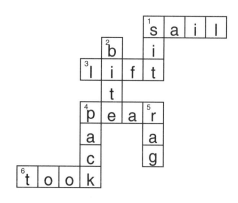

Page 232

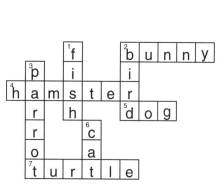

Page 233

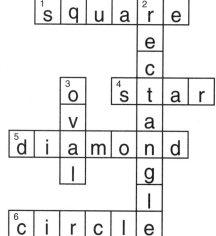

Page 234

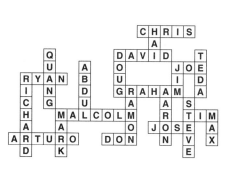

Part 1 Answer Key *(cont.)*

Page 235

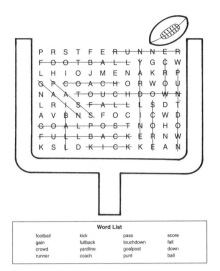

Word List

football	kick	pass	score
gain	fullback	touchdown	fall
crowd	yardline	goalpost	down
runner	coach	punt	ball

Page 236

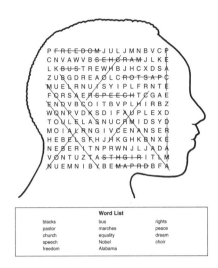

Word List

blacks	bus	rights
pastor	marches	peace
church	equality	dream
speech	Nobel	choir
freedom	Alabama	

Page 237

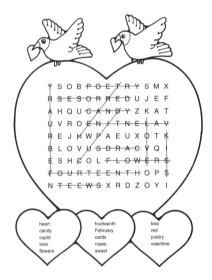

heart	fourteenth	kiss
candy	February	red
cupid	cards	poetry
love	roses	valentine
flowers	sweet	

Page 238

Page 239

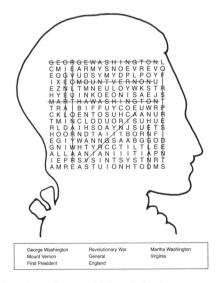

George Washington	Revolutionary War	Martha Washington
Mount Vernon	General	Virginia
First President	England	

Page 240

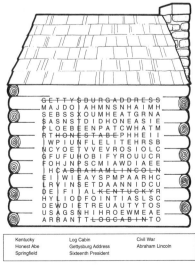

Kentucky	Log Cabin	Civil War
Honest Abe	Gettysburg Address	Abraham Lincoln
Springfield	Sixteenth President	

Part 1 Answer Key *(cont.)*

Page 241

```
H P U L N E B A T S E N O H W P B
Y R H O S M N M P C W T F V U K L
T E I U O U O X O R E K A E P S
E S F G U R I V I B G S X V Y H S
W I K H T I I K H R A U E P R D
T D Y H H L O R U G X C S C E H X
U E W A W D E B A T E S G B V L
G N I A R S D Q X K L N M Q A X E
X T R Y K Y F E C R E Y W A L Z E
K O I N T M Y V B M E N P A S I N
K E N T U C K Y L I O P N C Z F T
D E E R F B L H F I I U D C W S H
R G T Y H K C O N F E D E R A T E
T O H S I W S U Z S D F B U V N C
```

Word List			
president	sixteenth	Gettysburg	speaker
lawyer	Kentucky	North	Honest Abe
log cabin	slavery	South	debates
Civil War	freed	Union	Confederate

Page 242

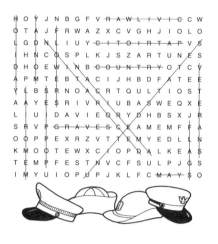

```
H O Y J N B G F V R A W L I V I C C W
O T A J F R W A Z X C V G H J I O L O
L G D N L I U Y C I T O I R T A P V S
I H N C O S P L K J S Z A R T U N E S
D H O E W J N B C O U N T R Y O T C V
A P M T E B T A C I J H B D F A T E E
Y L B S R N O A C R T Q U L T I O S T
A A Y E $ R I V R I U B A S W E Q X E
L U I D A V I E O R Y D H B S X J R
S R V P G R A V E S C E A M E M F F A
O O P P E X R Z V T T E M Y E D L L N
K M O O T E W X C I O P D A L K E A S
T E M P F E S T N V C F S U L P J G S
I M Y U I O P U P J K L F C M A Y S O
```

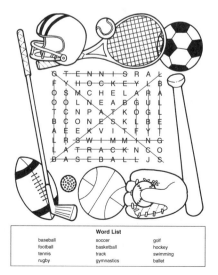

Page 243

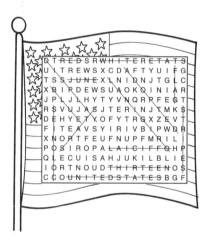

```
D T R E D S R W H I T E R E T A T S
U I T R E W S X C D A F T Y U I F G
T S S J U N E X L N I D N J T G L C
X B I R D E W S U A O K Q I N I A R
J P L J H Y T Y V N Q R F E G T
R S V U J A S J T E R I N J T M K $
D E H Y E T Y O F Y T R G X Z E V T
F I T E A V S Y I R I V B I P W D R
X N O R T F E U F N U P F M R I L
P O S I R O P A L A I C I F F Q H P
Q L E C U I S A H J U K I L B L I E
I O R T N O U D T H I R T E E N O $
C C O U N I T E D S T A T E S B G F
```

Page 244

```
U Y A D H T R I B H Y U I H F U Y T R
P Y T V G E M T F D C N G J J M J F T
H E T A R B E L E C O N R U H N J H S
I G N I N G I S K I G E N H D H G R A
L N G F C L C S T U W N F E V C S W Q
A G F R T I M A S O G T P J H B X S D
D S C P N U R G R F C E P A R A D E E
E V F C U A S K N B N R B O P W E S V
L B I Y L F S U H D U J P M Y E L A R
P P O C V G T F E F R T Y U J L G R E
H I E C U A N N I V E R S A R Y U O S
J D R T R E C H U I O L M N B V O J B
A D R T G E N B V G F T Y H U I O L O
F O U R T H N J K C O U N T R Y N G Q
```

Page 245

```
A Q T R A Y Z K L T N E E S U
V X W B C O M E T D V D M O T
V B E T U H C C I R A A S S C
S O R R P U E V E R E S H A M
U F R L I A O S A L D H C C H
Q B E C D O N N E R R E M I A
S M E V E H R E M L E R R T H
R U D O L P H L A W K I S H P
A Y V O U E O R N Y I B B E D
D A N C E R H E C E H O L I D
D O R I I N X K I R L I I R E
L W C D E I U Z L D U D T Y A
T C H D V A T D W O H Z Z U E
X Y O B U Q L P R A N C E R L
N E O T U E B E P Y P N N B S
```

Word List		
Comet	Vixen	Blitzen
Cupid	Prancer	Dancer
Donner	Rudolph	Dasher

Page 246

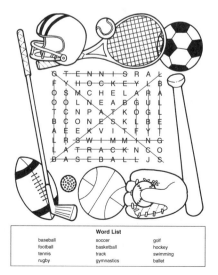

```
G T E N N I S R A L
F Y H O C K E Y L B
O $ M C H E L A R A
O L N E A B G U L
T C N P A T K O G L
B C O N E S K L B E
A E E K V I T F Y T
L R S W I M M I N G
L A T R A C K N C O
B A S E B A L L J S
```

Word List		
baseball	soccer	golf
football	basketball	hockey
tennis	track	swimming
rugby	gymnastics	ballet

Part 1 Answer Key *(cont.)*

Page 247

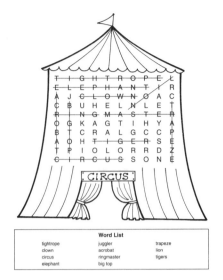

Word List

tightrope	juggler	trapeze
clown	acrobat	lion
circus	ringmaster	tigers
elephant	big top	

Page 248

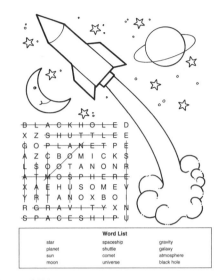

Word List

star	spaceship	gravity
planet	shuttle	galaxy
sun	comet	atmosphere
moon	universe	black hole

Page 249

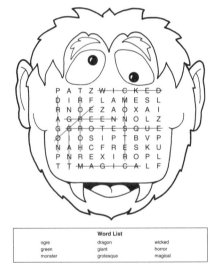

Word List

ogre	dragon	wicked
green	giant	horror
monster	grotesque	magical

Page 251

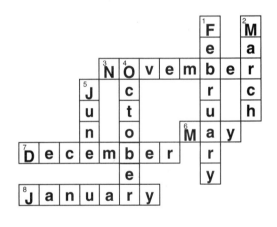

Page 252

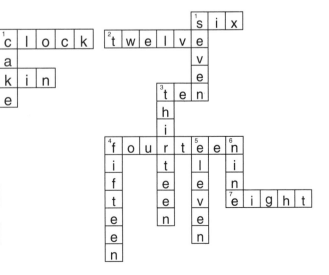

Page 253

Page 254

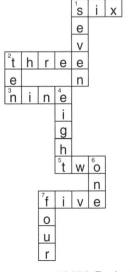

Part 1 Answer Key *(cont.)*

Page 255

Page 256

Page 257

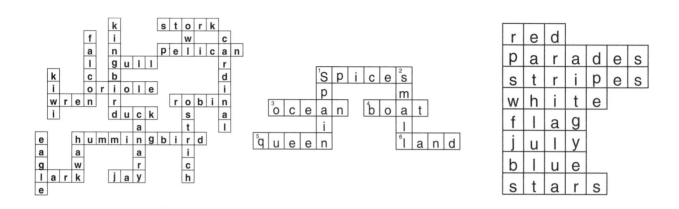

Page 258

Page 259

Page 260

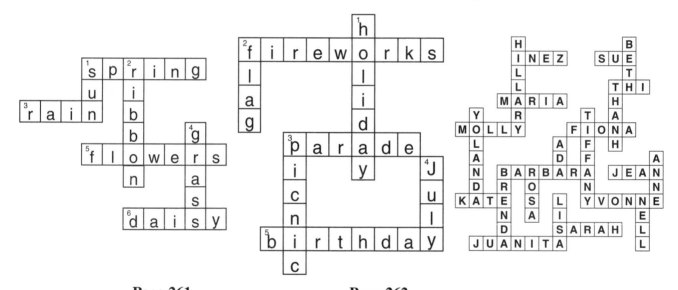

Page 261

Page 262

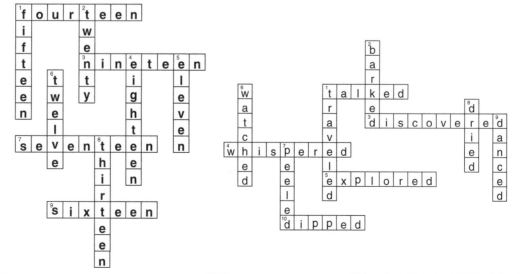

Part 1 Answer Key *(cont.)*

Page 263
1. west
2. Elvis
3. salt
4. plum
5. nest
6. Iran
7. tale
8. aunt
9. arms
10. golf

Page 264
2. doghouse
3. bedtime
4. seashore
5. blueberry
6. overcoat
7. cardboard
8. crossword

Page 265
1. will not—won't
2. should not—shouldn't
3. let us—let's
4. is not—isn't
5. it is—it's
6. how is—how's
7. they have—they've
8. who would—who'd
9. she will—she'll
10. I will—I'll

Page 266
1. parted
2. two in the bush
3. laughs best
4. saves nine
5. words
6. grow fonder
7. leap
8. healthy, wealthy, and wise
9. a pound of cure
10. should not throw stones
11. one is dead
12. never to have loved at all
13. on the other side of the fence
14. never boils
15. three's a crowd

Page 267
1. Europe
2. sight
3. road, street, highway
4. down
5. meow
6. sweet
7. shine
8. thick, fat
9. cold
10. foot
11. composer
12. son
13. egg(s)
14. Illinois
15. green

Page 268
Decoded Line: If it weren't for venetian blinds, it would be curtains for all of us!

Page 269

Elsie	Lee
leg	Elsie
hill	gobble
Lee	giggle
hi	Lee
Lee	Elsie
Elsie	gosh
egg	shell

Page 270
Steal Its Chair

Page 271
1. (35 divided by 5) x (27 divided by 3) = 63
2. (32 divided by 4) x (49 divided by 7) = 56
3. (72 divided by 9) x (24 divided by 8) = 24
4. (56 divided by 7) x (64 divided by 8) = 64
5. (36 divided by 6) x (35 divided by 7) = 30

Page 272

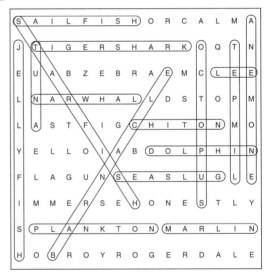

Page 273

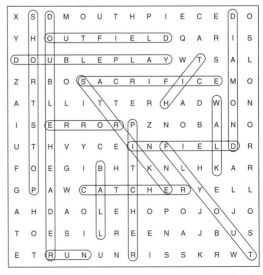

Part 1 Answer Key *(cont.)*

Page 274

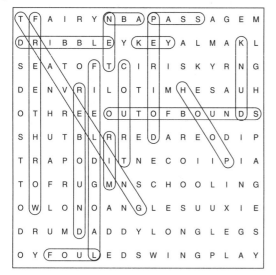

Page 277

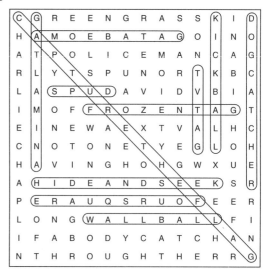

Page 275

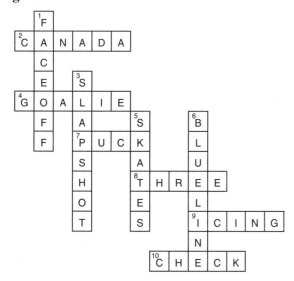

Page 278

Page 279

1. St. Louis Cardinals
2. Boston Celtics
3. Miami Dolphins
4. Anaheim Mighty Ducks
5. Cleveland Crunch

Page 280

Claudia—fencing
Maxine—biathlon
Brian—luge
Madeline—figure skating
Nicole—ski jump

Page 276

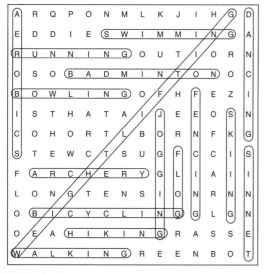

Brain Games
Part 2

Getting to Know Your Classmates

Fill each blank with the name of a classmate who fits the description. Use each person's name only once. Do not forget to include yourself!

1. _____ has ridden a horse.

2. _____ has lived on a farm.

3. _____ has green eyes.

4. _____ has been to Washington, D.C.

5. _____ has taken ballet.

6. _____ is left-handed.

7. _____ has a sibling under one year of age.

8. _____ wears glasses.

9. _____ plays ice hockey.

10. _____ has a home computer.

11. _____ collects stamps.

12. _____ likes to go fishing.

13. _____ has a pet turtle.

14. _____ was born outside the state/province.

15. _____ loves to read.

16. _____ has visited Disney World.

17. _____ rides a bike to school.

18. _____ collects baseball cards.

19. _____ had all A's on a report card once.

20. _____ has grandparents in another state.

More "Getting to Know Your Classmates"

Fill each blank with the name of a classmate who fits the description. Use each person's name only once. Do not forget to include yourself!

1. _____ lives or has lived on a farm.

2. _____ has red hair.

3. _____ has milked a cow.

4. _____ has blue eyes.

5. _____ has an unusual pet.

6. _____ is left-handed.

7. _____ was born outside the country.

8. _____ has math as a favorite subject.

9. _____ has been to a museum.

10. _____ loves to camp.

11. _____ has met a famous person.

12. _____ has seen a rainbow.

13. _____ has blue as a favorite color.

14. _____ hates to eat liver.

15. _____ has never had a cavity.

16. _____ is an Elvis fan.

17. _____ loves country music.

18. _____ loves strawberry milkshakes.

19. _____ has a middle name identical to yours.

20. _____ has 7 as a favorite number.

Still More "Getting to Know Your Classmates"

Fill each blank with the name of a classmate who fits the description. Use each person's name only once. Do not forget to include yourself.

1. _____ has been backpacking.

2. _____ loves chocolate.

3. _____ water-skis.

4. _____ collects rocks.

5. _____ has brown eyes.

6. _____ plays soccer.

7. _____ plays the piano.

8. _____ wears glasses or contact lenses.

9. _____ loves to run.

10. _____ collects football cards.

11. _____ loves to take pictures.

12. _____ has blonde hair.

13. _____ has visited Disneyland.

14. _____ plays chess.

15. _____ has red as a favorite color.

16. _____ walks to school.

17. _____ has a younger sibling.

18. _____ loves to write.

19. _____ wears braces.

20. _____ plays an instrument.

And Even More "Getting to Know Your Classmates"

Fill each blank with the name of a classmate who fits the description. Use each person's name only once. Do not forget to include yourself.

1. _____ loves classical music.

2. _____ has met a politician.

3. _____ was born at least 100 miles (kilometers) from your current location

4. _____ has a birthday in the same month as yours.

5. _____ has been on stage.

6. _____ has been snowed in.

7. _____ loves vanilla milkshakes.

8. _____ has swum in the ocean.

9. _____ has seen a tornado.

10. _____ has seen a rainbow.

11. _____ hates spinach.

12. _____ has the same first name as you.

13. _____ has had only one cavity.

14. _____ has traveled outside your country.

15. _____ has two pets.

16. _____ has hazel eyes.

17. _____ is a football fan.

18. _____ has yellow as a favorite color.

19. _____ loves pepperoni pizza.

20. _____ has seen a bear in the wild.

Complete the Phrase

Complete the following phrases with the first things that come to mind. There are no incorrect responses to this activity.

1. What I want most in the world is

_____

2. I feel sorry for

_____

3. When someone hurts me, I

_____

4. If I were 21, I

_____

5. I like to eat at

_____

6. I am really good at

_____

7. I never want to forget

_____

8. Sometimes I dream about

_____

9. When I was little

_____

10. My favorite time of day is

_____

11. I wish I could

_____

12. I would rather read than

_____

13. I do not like to

_____

14. I love it when

_____

15. I am afraid of

_____

Wacky Introductions

Fill in the form below and be prepared to share your answers with your classmates.

1. What is your full name?_____

2. What is your half name? _____

3. What would your name be, if you had named yourself?_____

4. Where do you come from? _____

5. How tall would you be if you were wearing your mom's high heels? _____

6. Do you have a pet? _____

7. How much do you weigh when you are holding your pet? _____

8. What is the color of your left eye?_____

9. What is the color of your right eye?_____

10. What color is your hair?_____

11. Has it always been this color?_____

12. If you had to wear the same color of nail polish the rest of your life, what color would it be?_____

13. What kind of nose do you have?_____

14. In your free time which would you prefer to be doing?
    ❏ screaming at the top of your lungs on a roller coaster
    ❏ playing "Candy Land"
    ❏ playing sardines at the mall
    ❏ dressing like a clown
    ❏ other_____

15. If you could take over your teacher's job, which subject would you most like to teach? _____

16. Do you like to be buried in sand up to your neck? Why or why not? _____

    _____

17. Has anyone ever called you "foofie?" _____

18. Have you ever imitated a chicken? What was the occasion? _____

19. What is your monthly income? _____

20. Are you married? _____

21. If you had a pet penguin, where would you keep it?_____

If You Were . . .

Answer each of the questions, explaining why for each one. Use a seperate piece of paper, if necessary.

1. If you were an animal, what would you be? _____

2. If you were a color, what color would you be? _____

3. If you were a musical instrument, which would you be? _____

4. If you were a fast food, what would you be?_____

5. If you were a flower, which kind would you be? _____

6. If you were able to live anywhere in the world, where would you live? _____

7. If you were an amusement park ride, what would you be? _____

8. If you were a holiday, which one would you be? _____

9. If you were an article of clothing, what would you look like? _____

10. If you were a number, which would you be? _____

11. If you were a candy, what kind would you be? _____

12. If you were a place, would you rather be a city, beach, mountain, or desert?

    _____

13. If you were to write a book, what would the title be? _____

14. If you were a movie star, what would your stage name be?_____

15. If you were a professional athlete, what sport would you play? _____

16. If you were in your first starring role, what would the title of the movie be?

    _____

17. If you were a psychiatrist, who would be your first patient? _____

18. If you were some sports equipment, what would you be? _____

19. If you were to time travel, where would you go? _____

20. If you were to step into a book and be there with the characters, which book would you choose? _____

21. If you were a grownup, what would your job be? _____

22. If you were a vegetable, what kind would you be? _____

23. If you were able to put an additional pair of eyes someplace else on your body, where would you put them?_____

24. If you were a house, what kind would you be, and how many rooms would you have? _____

25. If you were a car, what kind would you be? _____

Earliest Memories

How far back can you remember? Do you have any memories from when you were a tiny baby? How about your first day of school? Do you remember your first pair of shoes? Think for awhile about your earliest memories. Choose one or two of them and write them in the lined space below. You may also want to color the illustrations in the frame around your writing.

Map of Your House

Can you draw a map of your house? It is not as easy as you might think. Imagine that a new friend will be coming to spend a few weeks at your home. Before he or she comes, you want to draw a map of the inside of your house so that your friend will know what to expect. Show where your visitor will sleep, eat, shower, store his or her belongings, and so forth. Do not forget to add windows and doors, and be sure to show where the yards and street are in relation to the inside of your house. Use the space below to draw your map.

314

Your Bio

"Bio" is short for biography. A bio is usually a short version of a biography. People write bios to give information to others about themselves. Actors and speakers use bios, and authors often use them in the backs of their books. Magicians and clowns even write bios.

Here is your chance to write a bio about yourself! Include only the most important things. You might include your birthdate, but you will not have room to write about how it was stormy that day or how your dad locked the keys in the car at the hospital. Save these things for your biography! Instead, write about the things that make you special. If you play a musical instrument, sports, or ride horses, include that. If you have brothers and sisters, you might want to say something about them. If you want to be an astronaut or a dancer, tell your readers that, too. Make your bio one paragraph and make it fit in the space below.

My Bio

These Are a Few of My Favorite Things

Fill in the blanks with your very favorites:

1. My favorite color is _____
2. My second favorite color is _____
3. My favorite food is _____
4. My favorite story is _____
5. My favorite movie is _____
6. My favorite game is _____
7. My favorite place is _____
8. My favorite person is _____
9. My favorite animal is _____
10. My favorite number is _____
11. My favorite book is _____
12. My favorite song is _____
13. My favorite musical group is _____
14. My favorite actor is _____
15. My favorite actress is _____
16. My favorite school subject is _____
17. My favorite article of clothing is _____
18. My favorite season is _____
19. My favorite fruit is _____
20. My favorite day of the week is _____
21. My favorite amusement park is _____
22. My favorite vegetable is _____
23. My favorite holiday is _____
24. My favorite flower is _____
25. My favorite sport is _____
26. My favorite language is _____
27. My favorite ice-cream flavor is _____
28. My favorite tree is _____
29. My favorite name is _____
30. My favorite candy is _____
31. My favorite fast food is _____
32. My favorite room is _____
33. My favorite poem is _____
34. My favorite snack is _____
35. My favorite drink is _____
36. My favorite footwear is _____
37. My favorite hero is _____
38. My favorite time of the day is _____

Personal Poem

This is a good way for others to get to know you. To begin, fill in the blanks below. Then, on the poem frame on the next page, write your personal poem. Be sure to illustrate it and maybe even include a self-portrait.

First name _____

List three adjectives that describe you

Sibling (or Child/Grandchild) of _____

Lover of_____

Who feels _____

Who needs _____

Who gives_____

Who fears _____

Who would like to see _____

_____

_____

_____

_____
Last name

Here is an example to give you more ideas.

Jason

Affectionate, shy, athletic

Sibling of Michael, Chris, and Kiera

Lover of furry pets, rainy days, and cool swimming pools

Who feels affection, understanding, and generosity

Who needs friendship, comfort, and support

Who gives love, friendship, and affection

Who fears large waves, darkness, and unknown things

Who would like to see the tops of clouds, the ground from above, and the blackness of space

Buffington

Personal Poem *(cont.)*

Write your poem in the space below.

Color the Pairs

Color the two items in each row that match.

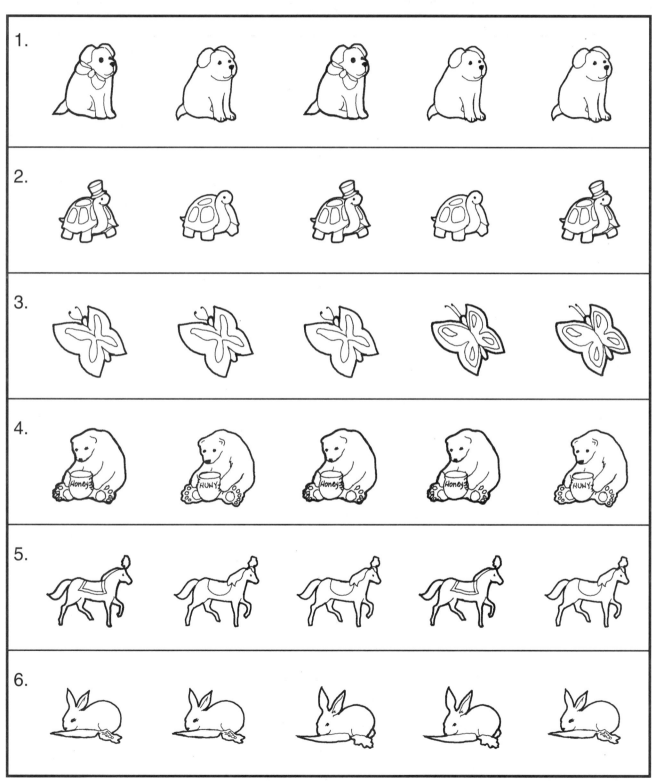

Word Pairs

Write the missing half of each word pair.

1. Hot and _____

2. Lock and _____

3. Black and _____

4. Body and _____

5. Scream and _____

6. Left and _____

7. Bacon and _____

8. Cat and _____

9. Up and _____

10. Burgers and _____

11. Peace and _____

12. Thunder and _____

13. Back and _____

14. Thick and _____

15. Tooth and _____

16. Sticks and _____

17. Aches and _____

18. Bread and _____

19. Hammer and _____

20. Hide and _____

More Word Pairs

Write the missing half of each word pair.

1. Huff and _____

2. Tar and _____

3. Law and _____

4. Peanut butter and _____

5. Nook and _____

6. Mix and _____

7. Satin and _____

8. Cats and _____

9. Cream and _____

10. Old and _____

11. Now and _____

12. Night and _____

13. Lettuce and _____

14. Prim and _____

15. Fine and _____

16. Dollars and _____

17. Peaches and _____

18. Rise and _____

19. Twist and _____

20. Duck and _____

Word Twins

Write the missing half of each word pair.

1. Lost and _____

2. Good and _____

3. Far and _____

4. Meat and _____

5. Fire and _____

6. Chips and _____

7. Bat and _____

8. Pride and _____

9. Hand and _____

10. Macaroni and _____

11. Young and _____

12. Liver and _____

13. Come and _____

14. Pins and _____

15. Touch and _____

16. Right and _____

17. Left and _____

18. Sing and _____

19. Cup and _____

20. Down and _____

21. Safe and _____

22. Nuts and _____

23. Read and _____

24. Pork and _____

25. Knife and _____

26. Yes and _____

27. Soap and _____

28. Salt and _____

29. Toss and _____

30. High and _____

Famous Pairs

Name the famous partners.

Ren and _____

Hansel and _____

Superman and _____

_____ and the Beast

_____ and Robin

_____ and Minnie

Barbie and _____

Donald Duck and _____

Popeye and _____

_____ and Miss Piggy

_____ and Judy

_____ and Mr. Hyde

Jack and _____

Lady and _____

Bert and _____

More Famous Pairs

Name the famous counterparts.

_____ and Wilma Flintstone

_____ and Wilbur Wright

_____ and the Beaver

Calvin and _____

Roy Rogers and _____

Tom and _____

_____ and Andy

_____ and Jeff

_____ and Rhett

Dick and _____

Ricky and _____

Rocky and _____

_____ and Hardy

_____ and Daisy

_____ and Jane

Even More Famous Pairs

Name the famous counterparts.

Adam and _____

Antony and _____

Ozzie and _____

Raggedy Ann and _____

Kanga and _____

Laurel and _____

Robin Hood and _____

Lewis and _____

Samson and _____

Romeo and _____

Blondie and _____

Abbott and _____

Mickey and _____

Sylvester and _____

Laverne and _____

Pick a Pair

List items that are sold in pairs.

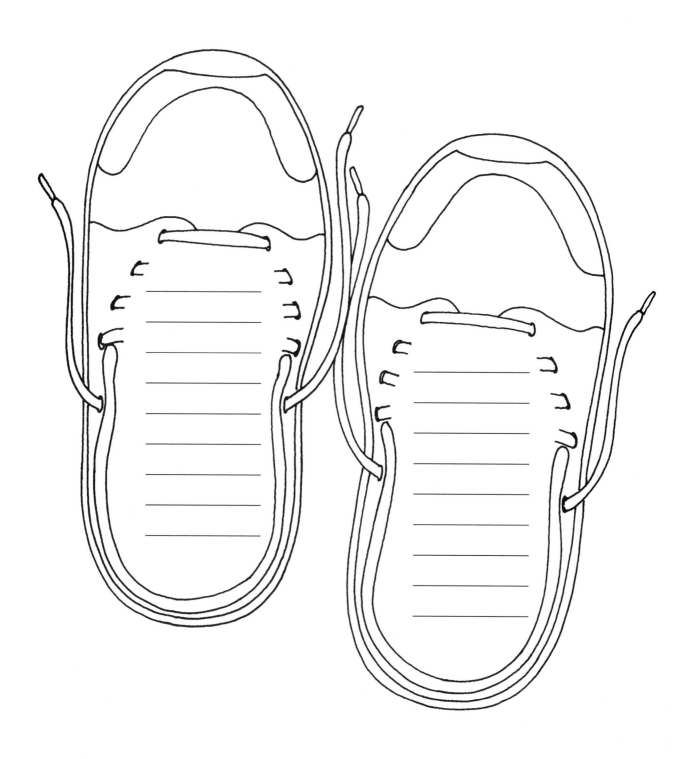

More Pick a Pair

List as many items as you can that are sold in pairs. Can you think of at least 20?

1. _____
2. _____
3. _____
4. _____
5. _____
6. _____
7. _____
8. _____
9. _____
10. _____
11. _____
12. _____
13. _____
14. _____
15. _____
16. _____
17. _____
18. _____
19. _____
20. _____

Use the other side of the paper if you can come up with more than 20.

Those famous Threes

Name each of the following threesomes.

1. The first three U.S. presidents to live in the White House

   _____   _____   _____

2. The three presidential memorials in Washington, D.C.

   _____   _____   _____

3. Dorothy's and Toto's three travelling companions to Oz

   _____   _____   _____

4. The Three Bears

   _____   _____   _____

5. The three basic primary colors

   _____   _____   _____

6. The three good fairies in the animated film, *Sleeping Beauty*

   _____   _____   _____

7. The three men in the tub

   _____   _____   _____

8. The three Wise Men

   _____   _____   _____

9. The three R's

   _____   _____   _____

10. Donald Duck's nephews

   _____   _____   _____

11. The Three Stooges

   _____   _____   _____

12. The three wise monkeys

   _____   _____   _____

Three and Four of a Kind

Complete each list.

1. Red, white, and _____

2. Stop, look, and _____

3. Sun, moon, and_____

4. Readin', writin', and_____

5. Ready, set, _____

6. Red, yellow, and _____

7. Go, fight, _____

8. Stop, drop, and _____

9. Tall, dark, and _____

10. Rain, snow, sleet, and_____

11. Larry, Moe, and _____

12. Coffee, tea, or _____

13. Animal, vegetable, or _____

14. Faith, hope, and _____

15. Eeny, meeny, miney, _____

Name Three

Name three items that belong to each category.

1. Things that are red _____

2. Things that swim _____

3. Things to do when you are ill _____

4. Months that have 30 days _____

5. Four-legged animals _____

6. Flowers _____

7. Kinds of clouds _____

8. Scary things _____

9. Reference books _____

10. Citrus fruits_____

11. Candies with nuts _____

12. American League baseball teams _____

13. Places people live _____

14. Elements (chemical) _____

15. Things that give off heat _____

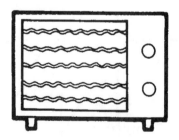

Which One Does Not Belong?

In each line below, one of the four words does not belong with the other three. Circle the one that does not fit. Explain what the others have in common. An example has been done for you.

relish, (hot dogs,) mustard, ketchup = condiments

1. Green, yellow, red, blue _____

2. April, December, November, June _____

3. cirrus, calculus, cumulus, stratus _____

4. carrots, radishes, potatoes, cabbages _____

5. fork, comb, rake, shovel _____

6. Cathy, Carol, Susan, Cheryl _____

7. carnation, peony, tomato, rose _____

8. pie, cake, brownie, candy bar _____

9. boy, lad, niece, man _____

10. North America, Australia, Asia, Canada _____

11. Dodgers, Cubs, Cowboys, Cardinals _____

12. orange, lemon, watermelon, grapefruit _____

13. laugh, giggle, chuckle, cry _____

14. duck, turkey, goose, pig _____

15. southeast, southwest, northeast, east _____

More "Which One Does Not Belong?"

One of the four words in each group below does not belong with the other three. Circle the one that does not fit. Then, explain what the others have in common. An example has been done for you.

Australia, South America, Europe, (France) : They are continents.

1. shout, whisper, scream, yell   _____

2. dark clouds, rain, sun, lightning   _____

3. knife, fork, stapler, spoon   _____

4. math, encyclopedia, thesaurus, dictionary   _____

5. mother, nephew, aunt, niece   _____

6. piglet, sow, boar, gosling   _____

7. liver, blood, heart, kidney   _____

8. Washington, Oregon, Oklahoma, California   _____

9. pig, chicken, cow, horse   _____

10. relish, hamburgers, mustard, ketchup   _____

11. Dodgers, White Sox, Bears, Orioles   _____

12. marker, eraser, chalk, pen   _____

13. bagel, muffin, bread, margarine   _____

14. dog, goldfish, parakeet, raccoon   _____

15. hat, gloves, wallet, belt   _____

Even More "Which One Does Not Belong?"

In each list below, circle the item that does not belong and explain what the other items have in common.

1. trigonometry, geometry, cirrus, calculus

   _____

2. comic book, atlas, novel, brain teasers book

   _____

3. otter, shark, dolphin, sea lion

   _____

4. kilometer, gram, acre, centimeter

   _____

5. pen, pencil, eraser, chalk

   _____

6. Golden Delicious, Bartlett, Granny Smith, Jonathan

   _____

7. angora, cocker spaniel, dachshund, schnauzer

   _____

8. iris, petunia, maple, daisy

   _____

9. pig, chicken, sheep, zebra

   _____

10. husband, father, niece, son

    _____

Specific Groups

Explain what the items in each list below have in common. Be specific. An example has been done for you.

Lemon, lime, orange, grapefruit = citrus fruits

1. hockey, soccer, football, baseball = _____

2. Yankees, Orioles, Royals, Rangers = _____

3. mermaids, unicorns, dragons = _____

4. California, Texas, New Mexico, Arizona = _____

5. Carter, Grant, Kennedy, Coolidge = _____

6. potatoes, beets, turnips, carrots = _____

7. Snickers, Almond Joy, PayDay = _____

8. Rams, Cowboys, Bears, Vikings = _____

9. jaguar, panther, tiger, lion = _____

10. Massachusetts, Virginia, Florida, Maine = _____

11. bus, bicycle, train, car = _____

12. September, June, April, November = _____

13. credit cards, pictures, license, money = _____

14. Texas, Alabama, Florida, Mississippi = _____

15. Nirvana, Beatles, Temptations, Cars = _____

334

A Visit to the Zoo

Laura, Phil, Jane, and Mike recently visited the St. Louis Zoo to see their favorite animals. One liked koalas, another liked zebras, a third liked monkeys, and a fourth liked giraffes. While at the zoo, each person ate one of the following: a corndog, a hot dog, a hamburger, or popcorn. Using the clues below, determine each person's favorite animal and what he or she had to eat. Mark an X in each correct box.

1. The girls like the koalas and giraffes while the boys like the zebras and monkeys.

2. Mike ate his food on a stick while Laura ate hers on a bun.

3. Laura's favorite animal originates in Australia.

4. The boy who loves the zebras also loves hot dogs.

	koala	zebra	monkey	giraffe	hamburger	corn dog	hot dog	popcorn
Laura								
Phil								
Jane								
Mike								

335

Birthday Parties

Eight children will all turn ten years of age this year. From the clues given, determine the month of each child's birth. Mark an X in each correct box.

1. A common holiday is celebrated on Jill's birthday.

2. Andrea's birthday is before Jeff's but after Millie's and Sarah's.

3. Sarah's birthday is exactly one month after Millie's.

4. Andrew's birthday is during the winter months.

5. Max's birthday comes after Andrea's but before Jeff's.

	Feb. 15	Mar. 24	April 1	May 1	July 10	Sept. 9	Oct. 15	Dec. 25
Andrea								
Andrew								
Sarah								
Sam								
Jill								
Jeff								
Millie								
Max								

Practice Makes Perfect

Nicole, Sean, Justin, and Janis are taking music lessons from Mrs. Reatherford. Each student is learning to play one of the following instruments: piano, flute, drums, or clarinet. Mrs. Reatherford asks that each of her students practice for at least thirty minutes per evening. Find out from the clues below what instrument is being played by which student and for how long each evening. Mark an X in each correct box.

1. Nicole practices longer than Sean but less than Janis.

2. Janis does not play the drums or flute, but Sean plays one of them.

3. Justin plays the clarinet and practices for more than 30 minutes.

4. The person who practices 45 minutes plays the piano, and the person who plays the clarinet practices less than the person who is taking flute lessons.

	Piano	Drums	Flute	Clarinet	30 min.	35 min.	40 min.	45 min.
Nicole								
Sean								
Justin								
Janis								

Sports Nuts

Matt, Brian, Jon, Neil, and Jason each love sports, but each loves to play one particular sport most of all. From the three clues given, determine which sport each boy loves to play the most. Mark an X in each correct box.

1. Matt loves baseball or hockey, Jon loves basketball or soccer, and Neil's favorite sport is not soccer or basketball.

2. Jason's favorite sport is played on the ice.

3. Brian's sport is played on a court and he hopes to become as well-known as his favorite player, Michael Jordan.

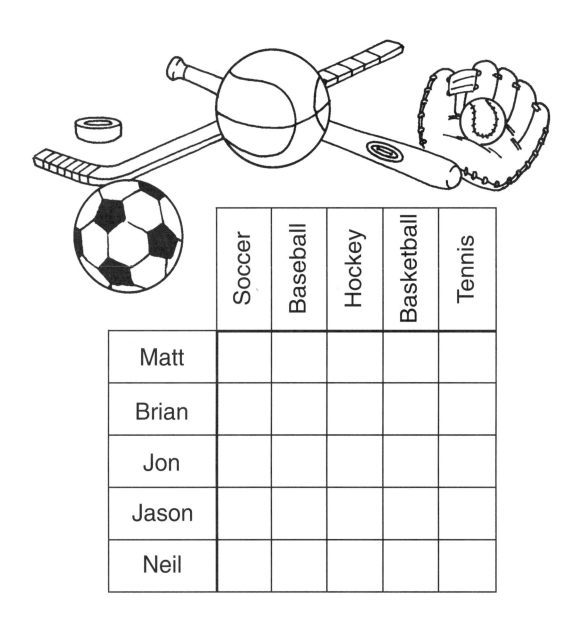

	Soccer	Baseball	Hockey	Basketball	Tennis
Matt					
Brian					
Jon					
Jason					
Neil					

Exam Time

As Mrs. Myers prepared to pass back the last math exam, five anxious students awaited their grades. Using the clues below, determine each child's grade. Mark an X in each correct box.

1. Chelsea, who did not get an A on her test, scored higher than Morgan and Linda.

2. Marcia and Linda both scored higher than Casie.

3. Morgan received a C on her test.

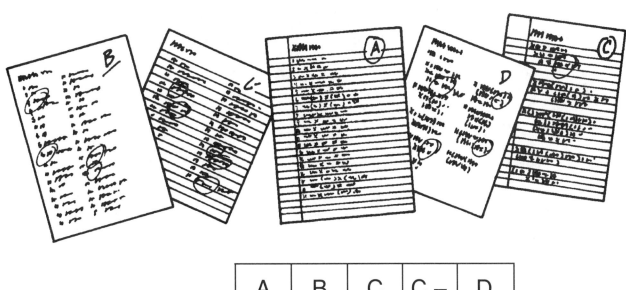

	A	B	C	C –	D
Chelsea					
Linda					
Marcia					
Morgan					
Casie					

Who's Who

Mr. Fitzpatrick has three boys in his class who go by variations of the name Andrew. From the statements below, determine each boy's full name and age. Mark an X in each correct box.

1. Jones is younger than Andrew but older than Smith.

2. Andy is not the youngest.

	Smith	Jones	Rogers	8	9	10
A. J.						
Andy						
Andrew						

Elizabeth

Mrs. Ginty has three girls in her ballet class who each go by a variation of the name Elizabeth. From the statements below, discover each girl's full name and age. Mark the correct boxes with an X.

1. Jones is younger than May but older than Smith.

2. Beth is not the youngest or the oldest.

3. Liz's last name is Smith.

	Jones	Smith	May	8	9	10
Bess						
Liz						
Beth						

Getting Fit

David, Tom, Rick, and Roger have each found a way to keep fit. One jogs, one bikes, one golfs, and one swims. They each spend different amounts of time doing these activities. Using the clues below, determine each man's activity and the time he spends doing it. Mark the correct boxes with an X.

	Jogging	Bicycling	Golf	Swimming	15	30	45	60
David								
Tom								
Rick								
Roger								

1. Roger spends more time exercising than Tom or Rick, but he does not golf or bike.

2. David jogs.

3. Rick works out for 45 minutes.

4. Tom spends less time at his activity than the person who golfs, but he spends more time than David.

A Visit to the Amusement Park

Katelyn, Kenny, Emily, and Howie recently visited their local amusement park to ride their favorite attractions—the roller coaster, the Ferris wheel, the carousel, and the bumper cars. While there, one ate a hamburger, another ate a corndog, another ate a hot dog, and the last ate bratwurst. Using the clues below, determine each person's favorite ride plus what each had to eat. Mark the correct boxes with an X.

	roller coaster	Ferris wheel	carousel	bumper cars	hamburger	corndog	hot dog	bratwurst
Katelyn								
Kenny								
Emily								
Howie								

1. The girls liked the roller coaster and bumper cars while the boys liked the Ferris wheel and the carousel.
2. Howie ate his food on a stick, while Katelyn ate hers on a hot dog bun.
3. Katelyn's favorite ride has hills.
4. The boy who loved the Ferris wheel also loves hot dogs.

Eight Birthdays

Eight children in one neighborhood will turn eleven this year. From the clues below, determine the date of each child's birthday. Mark the correct boxes with an X.

	February 3	August 25	April 12	July 13	May 12	January 1	September 2	March 30
Rita								
Jenny								
Millie								
Andrew								
Ralph								
Scott								
Andrea								
Maeve								

1. Everyone celebrates on Jenny's birthday.

2. Andrea's birthday is before Scott's but after Millie's and Rita's.

3. Rita's birthday is exactly one month after Millie's.

4. Andrew's birthday is during the winter months.

5. Ralph's birthday comes after Andrea's but before Scott's.

Favorite Foods

The favorite foods of Megan, Michael, Sergi, and Jana are pictured below. Each person has a different favorite food. Use the following clues to match the people with their favorite foods.

1. Michael likes ketchup and mustard on his favorite food.

2. Jana is allergic to cheese.

3. Sergi eats his favorite food on a bun.

4. Sometimes for something different, Michael makes his favorite food into corn dogs.

Whose favorite food?

_____

_____

_____

_____

Favorite Teams

Five boys root for five different baseball teams. Read the clues to determine which team each likes best. Mark the correct boxes with an X.

1. Will's bedroom is filled with posters and products from the A's.

2. Andrew's father is a big Cardinals fan, but Andrew is not.

3. Chad and Ryan like the Dodgers, the Reds, or the A's.

4. No boy's favorite team begins with the same letter as his name.

	Cardinals	Dodgers	A's	Reds	White Sox
Chad					
Danny					
Andrew					
Ryan					
Will					

Baseball Lineup

All nine players on the Panther baseball team are sitting on the bench in their batting order. Using the clues below, find their batting order.

1. Jeff is batting fifth, and David will bat before Carlos.

2. Jordi sits between David and Greg, and Andrew is to the right of Jeff.

3. Greg bats after Jordi but before Andrew.

4. Luis follows Andrew, but not Phil.

5. Carlos and Tom are at each end of the bench.

	1	2	3	4	5	6	7	8	9
Jeff									
David									
Carlos									
Jordi									
Greg									
Andrew									
Phil									
Tom									
Luis									

Going to the Circus

Brooke, Becky, Alexis, and Lindsey went to the circus last Saturday. Each girl saw her favorite animal and ate her favorite food. From the clues given, determine each girl's favorite animal and food.

1. Becky loves the elephants but does not like popcorn or taffy.

2. Alexis is afraid of the lions.

3. The girl who loves lions does not eat taffy or ice cream, but the girl who eats a snowcone loves the monkeys.

4. Brooke enjoys any flavor of taffy.

	Lions	Elephants	Monkeys	Horses	Taffy	Popcorn	Ice cream	Snowcone
Becky								
Alexis								
Lindsey								
Brooke								

348

Teachers' Meeting

Recently, teachers from all over the United States met together in Chicago for a national meeting. Four of the teachers decided to continue the day's discussion over dinner. From the clues below, determine the subject taught by each teacher, what state each teacher is from, and what type of food each teacher ordered.

1. Illinois is the home of the math teacher.

2. Mrs. Jackson teaches geography but doesn't live in Nevada.

3. The English teacher comes from Wisconsin and loves Italian.

4. Mrs. Jackson did not order Chinese or Italian.

5. Ms. Snow lives in Illinois but doesn't teach English and didn't order Italian.

6. Mr. Hunter loves Mexican food but isn't from Wisconsin.

	Ms. Snow	Mr. Hunter	Mr. Wong	Mrs. Jackson
Wisconsin				
Nevada				
California				
Illinois				
Geography				
Math				
English				
Science				
Italian				
Chinese				
American				
Mexican				

What's for Lunch?

Mr. Thomas is going to fix lunch for his four sons, A.J., Nick, Jim, and Tom. Each boy wants a different type of sandwich and fruit. Use the clues below to help Mr. Thomas pack the boys' lunches. Mark an X in each correct spot on the chart.

1. The boy who asked for peanut butter and jelly also asked for an orange.
2. A.J. and Nick do not care for cheese on their sandwiches, but Jim does.
3. Tom loves ham and cheese but not bananas.
4. Jim does not like apples nor to peel his fruit.
5. A.J. is allergic to bananas and apples.

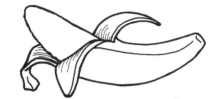

	peanut butter and jelly	ham and cheese	bologna and cheese	ham salad	banana	grapes	apple	orange
A.J.								
Nick								
Jim								
Tom								

Holiday Dinner

The Durbin family is all together for a delicious holiday dinner. Read each statement to help determine where each family member is sitting. Write their names in the correct blanks.

1. Rachel is to Dad's left.
2. Greg sits in the middle on one side of the table.
3. Dad and Mom always sit at each end of the table with Dad closest to the turkey to do the honors of carving the meat.
4. The three-year-old twins, Andrew and Andrea, sit on either side of Mom in case they need some help.
5. The daughters, including Christine, all sit on one side of the table and their brothers, including Rob, sit across from them.

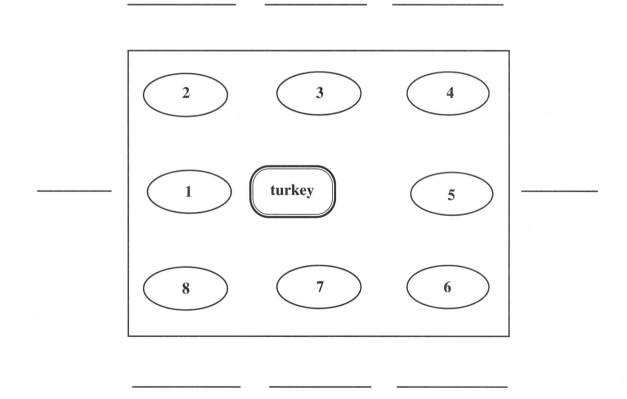

Camp Chippewa

Russ Smith, the camp counselor, and the seven boys from his cabin are sitting on blankets around the campfire, roasting marshmallows and telling ghost stories. Using the diagram and the clues below, determine where everyone is sitting. Write their names in the correct blanks.

1. Jeff is sitting on the blanket between Zac and Andrew.
2. Danny is sitting between Alan and Ryan.
3. The counselor is sitting at the top of the circle of blankets.
4. Zac is not sitting next to Russ.
5. Mark is to Russ's right.
6. Ryan is sitting across from the counselor.

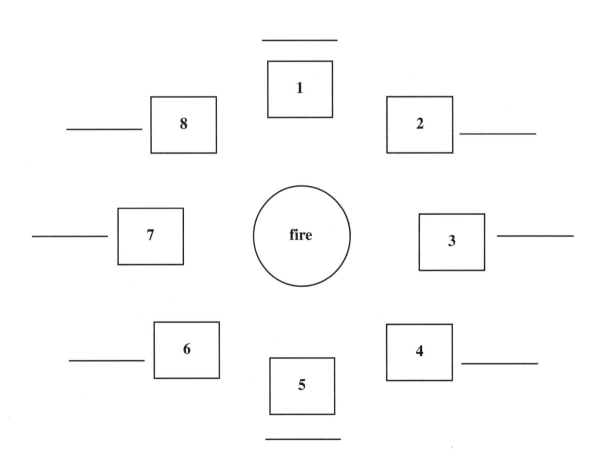

Fun at the Arcade

Jack, Ron, Charles, and Dave tried their luck playing skeeball at the local arcade. Read the clues to determine each boy's last name and his total score for the day. Mark an X in each correct spot on the chart.

1. Ron scored more points than Dave but less than Smith and Charles.
2. Dave's last name is not May and Charles' last name is not Ford.
3. Ford scored 100 points.
4. Jack got the highest total for the day and May came in second.

	Smith	May	Ford	Thompson	90 points	100 points	120 points	130 points
Jack								
Ron								
Charles								
Dave								

Play it Again

Tammy, Gina, Shannon, and Donna all play in the school band. Using the clues below, figure out each girl's last name and which instrument she plays. Mark an X in each correct spot on the chart.

1. None of the girls' first and last names begin with the same letter as their instrument.
2. Tammy strums her instrument.
3. Gina's last name is Donaldson, but Shannon's is not Thompson.
4. Donna's last name comes last alphabetically.

	drums	guitar	sax	trombone	Donaldson	Green	Simpson	Thompson
Tammy								
Gina								
Shannon								
Donna								

Antique Hunting

Four friends spent the day shopping at an antique mall. Each had a certain amount of money to spend. From the clues given below, determine how much each spent and which item she purchased.

1. The vase cost more than the lamp but less than the chair and frame.

2. Bev spent more than Janis or Mary Jo but less than the person who bought the chair.

3. Janis spent more than Mary Jo.

	chair	frame	lamp	vase	$20	$30	$40	$60
Bev								
Debbie								
Janis								
Mary Jo								

Analogies

Analogies are comparisons. Complete each analogy below. An example has been done for you.

Ear is to hearing as eye is to sight.

1. Cardinal is to St. Louis as Dodger is to _____

2. A.M. is to before noon as P.M. is to _____

3. Three is to triangle as eight is to _____

4. Tear is to tore as see is to _____

5. Springfield is to Illinois as Austin is to _____

6. Carpet is to floor as bedspread is to _____

7. Go is to green as stop is to _____

8. Purple is to grapes as red is to _____

9. Ghost is to Halloween as bunny is to _____

10. Son is to dad as daughter is to _____

11. Jelly is to toast as syrup is to _____

12. Ear is to hear as eye is to _____

13. Oink is to pig as cluck is to _____

14. Mississippi is to U.S. as Nile is to _____

15. Clock is to time as thermometer is to _____

16. V is to 5 as C is to _____

17. Up is to down as ceiling is to _____

18. Car is to driver as plane is to _____

19. Sleep is to tired as eat is to _____

20. Bird is to nest as bee is to _____

More Analogies

Analogies are comparisons. Complete each analogy below. An example has been done for you.

Nephew is to uncle as niece is to aunt.

1. _____ is to wings as fish is to fins.

2. Tennis is to _____ as baseball is to bat.

3. Jim is to James as Betsy is to _____.

4. Author is to story as poet is to _____.

5. Wide is to narrow as _____ is to short.

6. Lincoln is to _____ as Roosevelt is to Theodore.

7. _____ is to shell as pea is to pod.

8. Hard is to _____ as big is to small.

9. Dirt is to forest as _____ is to desert.

10. Frame is to picture as curtain is to _____.

11. Sing is to song as _____ is to book.

12. Braces are to _____ as contact lenses are to eyes.

13. _____ is to flake as rain is to drop.

14. Scissors are to _____ as pen is to write.

15. Hat is to head as _____ is to foot.

16. Hammer is to nail as screwdriver is to _____.

17. Scarf is to neck as _____ is to finger.

18. Fingers are to _____ as toes are to feet.

19. _____ is to pig as neigh is to horse.

20. Second is to _____ as day is to week.

Even More Analogies

Analogies are comparisons. Complete each analogy below. An example has been done for you.

Tall is to short as wide is to narrow.

1. _____ is to aunt as nephew is to uncle.

2. Eat is to _____ as sleep is to tired.

3. Zoo is to animals as _____ is to books.

4. Eye is to sight as ear is to _____.

5. November is to Thanksgiving as _____ is to Christmas.

6. Small is to _____ as little is to big.

7. _____ is to waist as bracelet is to wrist.

8. Grape is to _____ as cherry is to tree.

9. Blue is to sky as _____ is to grass.

10. Shoe is to foot as hat is to _____.

11. Cub is to lion as _____ is to cow.

12. Dusk is to _____ as night is to day.

13. _____ is to read as radio is to listen.

14. Ship is to _____ as airplane is to pilot.

15. Floor is to bottom as _____ is to top.

16. Gate is to yard as door is to _____.

17. Boy is to man as _____ is to woman.

18. Window is to _____ as floor is to rug.

19. _____ is to nest as bee is to hive.

20. Boat is to _____ as car is to road.

True or False

Before each of the following statements, circle T if the statement is true and F if the statement is false. Be prepared to explain any "false" responses.

1. T F Washington Monument is in Washington, D.C.

2. T F A telescope is used to view things that are far away.

3. T F Three is an even number.

4. T F The Pacific Ocean is on the east coast of North America.

5. T F A hexagon has fewer sides that an octagon.

6. T F There are 12 months in every Gregorian year.

7. T F The color red is a primary color.

8. T F Lincoln was the third president of the United States.

9. T F Half-past-eight is the same as 8:30.

10. T F Thanksgiving comes before Labor Day.

11. T F Pierre Trudeau is the Prime Minister of Canada.

12. T F All insects have 6 legs.

13. T F Australia is an island continent.

14. T F Happy and merry are synonyms.

15. T F In Roman numerals, IX is 11.

16. T F A triangle has four sides.

17. T F The U.S. is north of Canada.

18. T F The fourth letter of the alphabet is "D."

More "True or False"

1. T F Sir Isaac Newton discovered gravity by watching an apple fall.

2. T F The longest river in the world is the Mississippi River.

3. T F The smallest bird in the world is the hummingbird.

4. T F The moon gives off its own light.

5. T F All dinosaurs were carnivores.

6. T F The fastest land animal is the African cheetah.

7. T F Spiders have six legs.

8. T F Synonyms are words that mean the same or nearly the same.

9. T F There are over 100 planets in our solar system.

10. T F Grownups have a total of 32 permanent teeth.

11. T F The first person to walk on the moon was Neil Armstrong.

12. T F Whales can stay under water for more than an hour.

13. T F The capital of Illinois is Chicago.

14. T F Vaccinations protect you from getting diseases.

15. T F Every time you blink, you are actually crying.

16. T F A baby goat is called a kid.

17. T F Abraham Lincoln is pictured on a quarter.

18. T F An attic is below a house.

Even More "True or False"

Read each of the following statements carefully. Which of the statements are true and which are false? Be prepared to defend your answer.

1. T F   John F. Kennedy was the 35th president of the United States.

1. T F   The signal SOS means save our ship.

2. T F   Of the five Great Lakes, only Lake Superior lies entirely within the U.S.

3. T F   A dolphin is a mammal.

4. T F   Los Angeles is the capital of California.

5. T F   All prime numbers are odd numbers.

6. T F   The diamond is the hardest of all minerals.

7. T F   Numismatics is the science of numbers.

8. T F   A ladybird is a female bird.

9. T F   The Lincoln Memorial appears on the back of the American five-dollar bill.

10. T F   Arbor Day is celebrated on the same day around the world.

11. T F   The air we breathe is mostly nitrogen.

12. T F   Only four months of the year have thirty days.

13. T F   The longest river in the world is the Nile.

14. T F   In a lunar eclipse, the moon is between the earth and the sun.

15. T F   A firefly is a type of fly.

Do You Know?

1. When a car has 2 license plates (one in the front and one in the rear), which plate gets the yearly registration sticker? _____

2. How many books are in the Old Testament of the *Bible*? _____

3. Are there more red or white stripes on the U.S. flag? _____

4. From west to east, name the second president carved on Mt. Rushmore. _____

5. On the count in baseball, is the first number strikes or balls?

   _____

6. The Statue of Liberty holds her torch in which hand? _____

7. Does an insect have 6 or 8 legs? _____

8. Are there 60, 90, or 180 degrees in a right angle? _____

9. How many numbers are in a zip code? _____

10. In *A Visit from Saint Nicholas*, how many reindeer pull Santa's sleigh? _____

11. In a fraction, what is the bottom number called?

    _____

12. Which season comes after summer? _____

13. On which side of the horse do you mount and dismount?

    _____

14. Which is more, minimum or maximum? _____

Try These!

1. How many sides does a snowflake have? _____

2. Whose picture is on the American penny? _____

3. What is another name for a bison? _____

4. What two primary colors are mixed to make orange?

   _____

5. Which bird is known for its beautiful tail? _____

6. What is the commander of a ship called?_____

7. What is another name for the season of fall? _____

8. From what animal do we get wool? _____

9. Which of the seven dwarfs never speaks? _____

10. In *The Wizard of Oz*, what color is the brick road? _____

11. What is a person wearing if he has on spectacles? _____

12. What relationship is your father's brother to you?

    _____

13. What is the art of Japanese paper folding called?

    _____

14. What is a baby kangaroo called? _____

15. What color is the filling in an Oreo cookie? _____

And How About These?

1. What is another name for a moving staircase?_____

2. How often does leap year occur? _____

3. Most fairy tales begin with what four words? _____

4. What are five babies born to the same mother at the same time called?

   _____

5. What do we call a stand with three legs? _____

6. What does a philatelist collect?_____

7. What do you do with a piñata? _____

8. What color is ebony?_____

9. What is a group of lions called? _____

10. What is the left-hand side of a ship called? _____

11. What type of hat is Abraham Lincoln famous for wearing?_____

12. Who lives in Aladdin's lamp?_____

13. What do we call the water-filled ditch around a castle? _____

14. What is the hole in a sewing needle called?_____

15. What animal's foot is said to be a good luck charm? _____

Now Try These!

1. What are the five colors on the Olympic flag? _____

   _____

2. What do we call a dead body, embalmed and preserved, as in ancient

   Egypt? _____

3. Which of Disney's seven dwarfs wears glasses? _____

4. What is the "directional" name given to left-handed people? _____

5. What do we call a picture painted on a wall? _____

6. What is the hardest mineral? _____

7. What aircraft has no engine? _____

8. What is a karat used to measure? _____

9. What does a numismatist collect? _____

10. What is the name of the month of fasting in the Muslim faith?_____

    _____

11. What is a female sheep called? _____

12. What do Christians call the Friday before Easter? _____

13. If one is superstitious, over which shoulder should one throw salt?_____

14. In the film *The Sound of Music*, how many children are there? _____

15. Who is Garfield's owner? _____

How Many?

Answer each question with a number.

How many . . .

1. . . . sides in a dodecagon? _____

2. . . . books in the Bible? _____

3. . . . sheets in a quire? _____

4. . . . people aboard the *Mayflower?* _____

5. . . . rooms in the White House? _____

6. . . . items in a baker's dozen? _____

7. . . . rings on the Olympic flag? _____

8. . . . instruments in a quartet? _____

9. . . . bones in the human body? _____

10. . . . teeth in the adult mouth? _____

11. . . . keys on a piano? _____

12. . . . items in a gross? _____

13. . . . original colonies in the United States? _____

14. . . . years in a century? _____

15. . . . wheels on a unicycle? _____

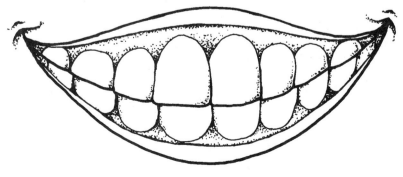

More "How Many?"

Answer each question with a number.

How many . . .

1. . . . eyes did Cyclops have? _____

2. . . . planets in our solar system have no moons? _____

3. . . . sides does a pentagon have? _____

4. . . . feet does a centipede have? _____

5. . . . degrees are in a right angle? _____

6. . . . centimeters are in a meter? _____

7. . . . faces are carved on Mt. Rushmore? _____

8. . . . musical instruments are played in an *a cappella* performance? _____

9. . . . stories are in the Sears Tower? _____

10. . . . degrees are in a circle? _____

11. . . . strings are on a guitar? _____

12. . . . events are in a decatholon? _____

13. . . . lines of verse in a sonnet? _____

14. . . . cards are in a deck? _____

15. . . . squares are on a checkerboard? _____

16. . . . years are in a millenium? _____

17. . . . days are in a leap year? _____

18. . . . sheets of paper are in a ream? _____

19. . . . hours are in a week? _____

20. . . . people are on a football team? _____

Trivia Time

1. On what side of the horse does one mount and dismount?

_____

2. Complete the following phrase: "All for one, . . ."

_____

3. Who painted the Mona Lisa?

_____

4. From what material is the lead inside a pencil made?

_____

5. A sphinx has the body of what animal?

_____

6. What vehicle is used to explore the deepest parts of the oceans?

_____

7. What does one lose when one has amnesia?

_____

8. Name the instrument that beats time for musicians.

_____

9. According to a famous saying, of what can one never have too much?

_____

10. Who sits at the center of the table in the painting *The Last Supper*?

_____

11. Which variety of oranges do not have seeds?

_____

12. What does "my true love give to me" on the first day of Christmas?

_____

13. In the painting *American Gothic*, what farm tool is the man holding?

_____

14. What does Robinson Crusoe call the only other person on the island where he is
shipwrecked?

_____

15. In "The Star-Spangled Banner," over what does the flag wave?

_____

Tallest, Largest, or Fastest

What is the . . .

1. . . . tallest mountain?_____

2. . . . tallest living thing? _____

3. . . . tallest building? _____

4. . . . largest sea animal?_____

5. . . . largest bird? _____

6. . . . largest continent? _____

7. . . . largest island?_____

8. . . . largest snake?_____

9. . . . largest land animal? _____

10. . . . fastest sea animal?_____

11. . . . fastest land animal? _____

12. . . . fastest flying animal? _____

The Largest to the Smallest

What is the . . .

1. . . . largest freshwater lake? _____

2. . . . largest reptile ever? _____

3. . . . largest country? _____

4. . . . largest ocean? _____

5. . . . largest living thing? _____

6. . . . largest sea? _____

7. . . . largest mammal? _____

8. . . . largest desert? _____

9. . . . longest mountain range? _____

10. . . . largest seashell? _____

11. . . . fastest living fish? _____

12. . . . longest river? _____

13. . . . longest venomous snake? _____

14. . . . smallest mammal? _____

15. . . . smallest reptile? _____

16. . . . smallest bird? _____

17. . . . smallest continent? _____

Which Is It?

Circle the word or number on the right that correctly corresponds to the word or words on the left.

1.	octagon	**4 sides**	**6 sides**	**8 sides**
2.	peninsula	**Cuba**	**Florida**	**Australia**
3.	state	**Oklahoma**	**Canada**	**Springfield**
4.	Thomas Jefferson	**16th president**	**3rd president**	**40th president**
5.	painter	**Picasso**	**Bach**	**Shakespeare**
6.	province	**Alaska**	**Montreal**	**Quebec**
7.	baker's dozen	**12**	**13**	**15**
8.	decagon	**10 sides**	**12 sides**	**15 sides**
9.	year	**12 months**	**50 weeks**	**360 days**
10.	percussive instrument	**trombone**	**violin**	**tambourine**
11.	cloud formation	**omnibus**	**cumulus**	**calculus**
12.	capital of California	**Sacramento**	**Los Angeles**	**Hollywood**
13.	day	**12 hours**	**24 hours**	**60 minutes**
14.	century	**10 years**	**20 years**	**100 years**
15.	chambers in the human heart	**2**	**4**	**7**
16.	Mother's Day	**February**	**May**	**June**

More "Which Is It?"

Circle the correct answer.

1.	degrees in a right angle?	**60**	**90**	**180**
2.	sides on a dodecagon?	**20**	**14**	**12**
3.	items in a gross	**64**	**103**	**144**
4.	country in South America	**Canada**	**Chile**	**Costa Rica**
5.	person who was a painter	**da Vinci**	**Bach**	**Beethoven**
6.	years in a score	**10**	**20**	**100**
7.	letter that is five hundred in Roman numerals	**X**	**L**	**D**
8.	muscles in the human body	**over 200**	**over 400**	**over 600**
9.	interjection	**Shoo!**	**neither**	**smack**
10.	type of math	**omnibus**	**calculus**	**cumulus**
11.	month with thirty days	**August**	**September**	**May**
12.	words that should be hyphenated	**attorney general**	**self conscious**	**roller skates**
13.	woodwind instrument	**tambourine**	**clarinet**	**piano**
14.	former prime minister of Canada	**Franklin**	**Trudeau**	**Jefferson**
15.	words in the Gettysburg Address	**270**	**271**	**272**
16	a musician	**Pablo Casals**	**Lou Gehrig**	**Charlie Chaplin**
17.	U.S. state called the Sooner State	**Oklahoma**	**Wyoming**	**Nebraska**
18.	primary color	**purple**	**green**	**yellow**
19.	lines in a sonnet	**12**	**14**	**16**
20.	degrees in a circle	**360**	**390**	**180**

Even More "Which Is It?"

Circle the name or number on the right that matches the words on the left.

1. state in the U.S.	**Los Angeles**	**Italy**	**Florida**
2. Abraham Lincoln	**3rd president**	**16th president**	**25th president**
3. states in the U.S.	**13**	**8**	**50**
4. rooms in the White House	**206**	**132**	**102**
5. capital of Illinois	**Springfield**	**Austin**	**Dover**
6. 16th president	**Adams**	**Carter**	**Lincoln**
7. American river	**Nile**	**Amazon**	**Mississippi**
8. people aboard the *Mayflower*	**132**	**102**	**272**
9. Great Lake that lies entirely within the U.S.	**Huron**	**Michigan**	**Superior**
10. number of amendments in the Bill of Rights	**10**	**11**	**12**
11. presidents before Eisenhower	**35**	**33**	**30**
12. face on Mt. Rushmore	**Roosevelt**	**Kennedy**	**Adams**
13. an original colony	**Illinois**	**Pennsylvania**	**Ohio**
14. pictured on a U.S. coin	**Nixon**	**Adams**	**Lincoln**
15. Republican president	**Carter**	**Ford**	**Kennedy**

American Holidays

1. Which two U.S. presidents' birthdays do we celebrate in February?

   _____

2. When is Independence Day?

   _____

3. In what month is Thanksgiving celebrated?

   _____

4. When do we observe Veterans Day?

   _____

5. What holiday is celebrated on the first Monday in September?

   _____

6. Why do we celebrate Memorial Day?

   _____

7. Which holiday is observed on the second Monday in October?

   _____

8. What famous civil rights activist is honored in January?

   _____

9. On what day is the above activist honored?

   _____

10. On what holiday is a famous parade honoring Irish ancestry held in New York City? _____

11. What holiday is celebrated on the second Sunday in September and honors the oldest family members?

    _____

12. What current holiday was originally called Constitution Day?

    _____

Social Studies Trivia

1. On which continent is Canada located? _____

2. In traveling north, what direction is to the right? _____

3. On the American flag, are there more red or white stripes? _____

4. What is the longest river in the U.S.? _____

5. What does "N" on a map normally represent? _____

6. Who invented the telephone? _____

7. What is a book of maps called? _____

8. Name the highest mountain in the world. _____

9. What do you call a piece of land surrounded with water on all sides?

   _____

10. What are the names of the three ships Columbus took on his famous journey? _____

11. On what mountain are four famous presidents' faces carved?

   _____

12. Name the five Great Lakes. _____

   _____

13. Of England, Australia, Peru, and Canada, which nation does not have English as a national language? _____

14. Name the ocean west of North America. _____

15. What is the capital of Hawaii? _____

More Social Studies Trivia

1. What is the capital of the United States' largest state? _____

2. What is a piece of land with water on three sides called? _____

3. How many white stripes are on the U.S. flag? _____

4. Who assassinated President Lincoln? _____

5. For whom is America named? _____

6. Which Great Lake lies entirely in the U.S.? _____

7. The Statue of Liberty is made of what metal? _____

8. Who wrote *Poor Richard's Almanac?* _____

9. When traveling north, what direction is to the left? _____

10. What country gave the Statue of Liberty to the U.S.? _____

11. In what city is the Liberty Bell located? _____

12. Which two states are not within the continental U.S.? _____

13. Who wrote The *Declaration of Independence*? _____

14. What American landmark stands on Liberty Island? _____

15. Who is said to have made the U.S. flag? _____

Some More
Social Studies Trivia

1. What does one call a government ruled by a king or queen?

   _____

2. Which two countries fought in the War of 1812?

   _____

3. Name the largest African desert.

   _____

4. Across which continent does the Amazon river flow?

   _____

5. Which country lies north of Germany and south of Norway?

   _____

6. Who was the captain of the *Mayflower*?

   _____

7. Of which country is Havana the capital?

   _____

8. What Spanish leader led the conquest of the ancient Aztec people?

   _____

9. To what mountain range does Mt. Everest belong?

   _____

10. Alaska was purchased by the United States from what country?

    _____

11. What type of map shows elevations and contours?

    _____

12. Along the shore of which continent lies the Great Barrier Reef?

    _____

13. During what years was World War I fought?

    _____

14. How many provinces and territories are in Canada?

    _____

15. Name the world's most populous country.

    _____

American Social Studies Trivia

1. What does *"e pluribus unum"* mean? _____

2. How long is a senator's term of office? _____

3. Which president is shown on the five-dollar bill? _____

4. Where is the Alamo? _____

5. During what years was the Civil War fought? _____

6. Who wrote "The Pledge of Allegiance"? _____

7. The president is chief of which branch of government? _____

8. Which president's former occupation was acting? _____

9. On the flag, what does red signify? _____

10. Who became president after Dwight D. Eisenhower? _____

11. Who invented the cotton gin? _____

12. Which was the last state to join the Union? _____

13. On the Statue of Liberty, is Miss Liberty carrying the torch in her left or her
    right hand? _____

14. Which English explorer sailed along the West Coast in 1579? _____
    _____

15. What is the official song of the president of the United States? _____
    _____

What Do You Know?

Fill in the answers to the clues by using the syllables in the box. The number of syllables to be used in each answer is shown in parentheses. The first answer has been done for you.

A	A	AD	AR	BRU	CAR	COLN	CON
DE	DY	FE	GIN	VER	HO	DAMS	WASH
ING	I	IA	KA	LAN	LAS	LIN	LU
LU	MAD	NO	NON	NIX	O	Y	ON
ROO	SE	SON	TED	TER	GRESS	VELT	VIR
MOUNT	TON						

1. Theodore Roosevelt's nickname (2) __Teddy__

2. The face on the quarter (3) _____

3. Franklin Roosevelt's middle name (3) _____

4. The father of the Constitution (3) _____

5. A month for celebrating presidents (4) _____

6. President whose father was also a president (2) _____

7. The capital of Hawaii (4) _____

8. A president and a peanut farmer (2) _____

9. The sixteenth president (2) _____

10. The first president to resign from office (2) _____

11. An original colony (3) _____

12. The home of George Washington (2 words) (3) _____

13. The state closest to Russia (3) _____

14. A face on Mount Rushmore (3) _____

15. The Senate and House of Representatives (2) _____

Presidents' First Names

Listed below are some last names of former presidents. Write each president's first name on the blank.

1. _____ Adams

2. _____ Eisenhower

3. _____ Reagan

4. _____ Jefferson

5. _____ Nixon

6. _____ Lincoln

7. _____ Carter

8. _____ Hoover

9. _____ Roosevelt

10. _____ Washington

11. _____ Coolidge

12. _____ Cleveland

13. _____ Grant

14. _____ Taylor

15. _____ Harrison

16. _____ Truman

17. _____ Buchanan

18. _____ Polk

19. _____ Garfield

20. _____ Johnson

Famous Women

Match these women to their major accomplishments. Put the letter of the accomplishment before the corresponding name.

_____ 1. Harriet Tubman

_____ 2. Harriet Beecher Stowe

_____ 3. Grandma Moses

_____ 4. Juliette Gordon Low

_____ 5. Shirley Chisholm

_____ 6. Pearl S. Buck

_____ 7. Mary McLeod Bethune

_____ 8. Clara Barton

_____ 9. Louisa May Alcott

_____ 10. Susan B. Anthony

_____ 11. Jane Addams

_____ 12. Amelia Earhart

_____ 13. Helen Hayes

_____ 14. Helen Keller

_____ 15. Victoria C. Woodhull

A. social worker and humanitarian

B. primitive painter

C. novelist and reformer

D. stage and screen actress

E. author of *The Good Earth*

F. aviator

G. author of *Little Women*

H. educator who worked to improve educational opportunities for blacks

I. significant "conductor" of the Underground Railroad

J. first woman to run for president of the U.S.

K. first African American woman in the U.S. Congress

L. founded the Girl Scouts of America

M. founded the American Red Cross

N. overcame physical handicaps; helped thousands of handicapped people lead fuller lives

O. reformer and leader in the American women's suffrage movement

Which President?

1. Which president was nicknamed "Honest Abe"?_____

2. Which president was called the "Father of the Constitution"?

   _____

3. Which president and his wife were the first to occupy the White House in Washington, D.C.? _____

4. Which future president was the author of the *Declaration of Independence*?

   _____

5. Which president was the only one to serve two nonconsecutive terms of office? _____

6. Which president was nicknamed "Old Rough and Ready"?

   _____

7. Which president was assassinated in Ford's Theater?_____

8. Which two presidents are buried in Arlington National Cemetery?

   _____

9. Which president served more than two terms?_____

10. Which president was in office when the White House was set on fire?

    _____

11. Which president was the grandson of another president?

    _____

12. Which president was the shortest? _____

13. Which president never married? _____

14. Which president was the first to talk to a man on the moon?

    _____

15. Which seven presidents were/are left-handed? _____

    _____

Math Trivia

1. How many minutes are in 2 hours? _____

2. How many dimes are in a dollar? _____

3. What is a 3-sided figure called? _____

4. What does a sundial do? _____

5. Two tons is equal to how many pounds? _____

6. What mark separates the hour and the minutes when one is writing down time? _____

7. How many items are in a dozen? _____

8. How many sides does a hexagon have? _____

9. What do you call the result of adding two numbers? _____

10. How many centimeters are in a meter? _____

11. How many months are in half of a year? _____

12. Which plane figure has 8 sides? _____

13. How many sides are there on a die? _____

14. How many years are in a decade? _____

15. How many hours are in a day? _____

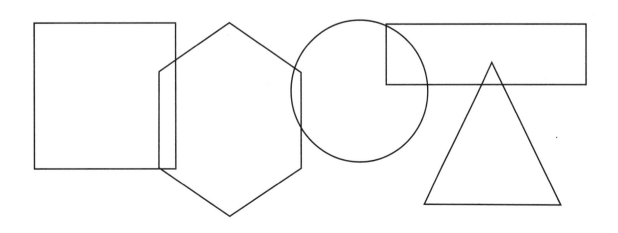

More Math Trivia

1. What do we call a chart that helps compare facts and numbers or quantities? _____

2. Does a right angle measure 60, 90, or 180 degrees? _____

3. What do we call an area where people use the same clock time?

   _____

4. What does "C" stand for in Roman numerals? _____

5. What name is given to an 8-sided figure? _____

6. How many millimeters are there in a centimeter? _____

7. How many nickels are there in 2 dollars? _____

8. How many dots are there on a die? _____

9. Will parallel lines intersect? _____

10. How much is half of 20? _____

11. How many zeros are there in the number one million? _____

12. How do we find the area of a figure? _____

13. Which number is a palindrome, 654 or 606? _____

14. The number 66 rounded to the nearest tens place is what number? _____

15. How many degrees are there in a circle? _____

Some More Math Trivia

1. Can a triangle have two right angles? _____

2. How many centimeters are there in three meters?_____

3. What does congruent mean? _____

   _____

4. Which weighs more, a pound of feathers or a pound of bricks? _____

5. What are the Roman numerals for 176?_____

6. What instrument is used to measure an angle? _____

7. In the fraction $\frac{5}{9}$, which numeral is the numerator? _____

8. How many items are in a gross? _____

9. How many sides does a decagon have? _____

10. What is $\frac{6}{8}$ reduced to its lowest terms? _____

11. How many zeros are in a billion? _____

12. Which angle is greater than 90 degrees — obtuse or acute? _____

    _____

13. Will perpendicular lines on the same plane ever touch? _____

14. What is the shortest distance between two points? _____

    _____

15. Is fifth an ordinal or a cardinal number? _____

Even More Math Trivia

1. How many grams are in one kilogram?

_____

2. In Roman numerals, what letter represents 1,000?

_____

3. What name is given to the Chinese 7-piece puzzle?

_____

4. How many feet are in a mile?

_____

5. Which is less, maximum or minimum?

_____

6. What is half of 25?

_____

7. What fraction is equivalent to 50%?

_____

8. The world is divided into how many time zones?

_____

9. What is the distance between the center and edge of a circle called?

_____

10. How many sides does a heptagon have?

_____

11. What is 3 squared?

_____

12. How does one calculate the square of any number?

_____

13. Give the place value of 7 in 0.708.

_____

14. Which angle measures less than 90 degrees, an acute or obtuse angle?

_____

15. What kind of number is divisible by only itself and 1?

_____

English Trivia

1. What are the two main parts of a sentence? _____

2. What punctuation mark is used in a contraction? _____

3. What words name a person, place, thing, or idea? _____

4. What do we call stories that are made up rather than true?

   _____

5. In the book *Charlotte's Web,* what is the rat's name?

   _____

6. In an address, what punctuation mark comes between the city and state?

   _____

7. What do we call a statement that tells what a person thinks or believes?

   _____

8. In a friendly letter, what punctuation mark is placed after the greeting?

   _____

9. Give the contraction for *will not*. _____

10. What is the mini-dictionary in the back of some textbooks called? _____

11. What is the plural of sheep? _____

12. Do antonyms mean the same as or opposite of one another?

    _____

13. In the dictionary, which comes first, maybe or maypole? _____

14. What type of story has a moral at the end? _____

15. What Japanese poetry follows a pattern of 5-7-5 syllables?

    _____

More English Trivia

1. What is a story you write about your own life called?

   _____

2. Meg, Jo, Beth, and Amy are characters in what famous book?

   _____

3. What is the name of the ancient Greek who wrote a group of fables?

   _____

4. Who wrote *The Tale of Peter Rabbit?* _____

5. What do we call a person who writes stories and books?

   _____

6. What part of speech is used to modify verbs? _____

7. What is Mark Twain's real name? _____

8. What punctuation mark is placed at the end of a declarative sentence? _____

   _____

9. What do we call words which are spelled the same forwards and
   backwards? _____

10. In *Tales of a 4th Grade Nothing,* who ate Peter's turtle?

    _____

11. Which type of nouns are capitalized? _____

12. In dialogue, what punctuation marks are put around the spoken words? ___

    _____

13. What did the Brothers Grimm write? _____

14. In a business letter, what punctuation mark is placed after the greeting? ___

    _____

15. How many syllables are there in the word *catastrophe?* _____

Some More English Trivia

1. Who wrote *Uncle Tom's Cabin?* _____

2. What reference book contains a listing of synonyms and antonyms? _____
    _____

3. In grammar, what do we call the words *and, but,* and *or?* _____

4. What do we call a sentence that gives a command or makes a request?
    _____

5. What do we call the two words at the top of each dictionary page? _____
    _____

6. What three kinds of cards or computer files will you find in a card catalog?
    _____

7. Who was Tom Sawyer's best friend? _____

8. In the novel *Bunnicula,* what is the rabbit suspected of being? _____
    _____

9. What are the six parts in a business letter? _____
    _____
    _____

10. Is "Susie saw seashells at the seashore" an example of alliteration or
    onomatopoeia? _____

11. What do we call words that sound the same but have different meanings
    and spellings? _____

12. In the book *The Cricket in Times Square,* where does Chester give his
    concerts?_____

13. What does it mean to sign your John Hancock? _____
    _____

14. In *Charlotte's Web,* what is the last word that Charlotte writes in her web?
    _____

15. What type of books are factual? _____

Even More English Trivia

1. What does one call the list of resources at the end of a research paper?

_____

2. Which is the longest poem—a sonnet, an epic, or a ballad?

_____

3. What is the name of the horse in *The Black Stallion*?

_____

4. Who devotes his life to catching the great whale in the book *Moby Dick*?

_____

5. What is the last name of Wilhelm and Jacob, the brothers who collected fairy tales?

_____

6. What is a writer's *nom de plume*?

_____

7. In one of Aesop's fables, which animal puts on a sheepskin?

_____

8. What land does Gulliver visit on his first journey?

_____

9. How many thieves help Ali Baba?

_____

10. In what grade is Margaret in *Are You There God, It's Me Margaret*?

_____

11. What is left over after Pandora lets all the evil things out of her box?

_____

12. What is the dreaded "It" in Madeline L'Engle's *A Wrinkle in Time*?

_____

13. What do we call a sentence that shows strong feeling?

_____

14. Is "The cat said 'purr'" an example of alliteration or onomatopoeia?

_____

15. What type of books are based on fact?

_____

Science Trivia

1. What instrument is used to measure temperature?

    _____

2. What are animals without backbones called? _____

3. With what does a fish breathe? _____

4. In what sea creatures are pearls found? _____

5. What instrument is used to view things that are far away?

    _____

6. Which is the sixth planet from the sun? _____

7. What animal uses its odor as a weapon? _____

8. How many legs does a spider have? _____

9. What birds can fly backwards? _____

10. What is another name for very low clouds? _____

11. What is a frog called when it still has gills? _____

12. Which mammals can fly? _____

13. What is a group of fish called? _____

14. What is another name for a mushroom? _____

15. What do we call the ends of a magnet? _____

More Science Trivia

1. What do we call an instrument that makes small things look large?

   _____

2. What is the largest planet in our solar system? _____

3. What makes a skeleton move? _____

4. What is the hardest natural substance called? _____

5. What device is used to measure air pressure?_____

6. Which is larger, the moon or Earth? _____

7. For most people, what is the normal Farenheit body temperature?

   _____

8. What is the Earth's path around the sun called? _____

9. Which planet is farthest away from the sun? _____

10. Which bones protect your lungs and heart? _____

11. What name is given to the huge group of stars that are close together?____

    _____

12. What is the colored part of the eye called?_____

13. What is the term for the remains of things found in rock? _____

14. What kind of trees lose their leaves in autumn?_____

15. What does the pulse measure? _____

Some More Science Trivia

1. What system of the body is made of the brain, the spinal cord, and the nerves? _____

2. What comet is visible every 76 years? _____

3. In what three forms can matter exist?_____

4. What instrument is used to measure air pressure? _____

5. What do we call the dirty haze that forms when air pollution combines with moisture in the air? _____

6. What part of the body is sometimes called the "funny bone"? _____

7. What substance gives plants their green color?_____

8. What do we call the energy of motion? _____

9. What happens if the earth's crust moves suddenly along a fault? _____

   _____

10. What type of animal eats only meat? _____

11. What do all living things inhale during respiration? _____

12. Which is warmer — tepid or hot water? _____

13. What tube connects the mouth and the stomach? _____

14. What do we call pieces of stone that enter the earth's atmosphere?_____

    _____

15. What is the opening at the top of a volcano called?_____

Even More Science Trivia

1. What system of the human body is made up of blood, blood vessels, and the heart?

   _____

2. Name the brightest planet.

   _____

3. Are reptiles warm- or cold-blooded?

   _____

4. What two names are given to the sun's energy?

   _____

5. What is the human bone most frequently broken?

   _____

6. If a temperature is 32 degrees Farenheit, what is the Celsius temperature?

   _____

7. What *Apollo II* assistant minded the store while Armstrong and Aldrin made

   history? _____

8. What type of climate is hot or warm all year round?

   _____

9. What liquid metal is used in thermometers?

   _____

10. Name the brightest star in the sky.

    _____

11. How many satellites travel around Mars?

    _____

12. Name the largest marsupial.

    _____

13. Which side of the human heart pumps blood to most of the body?

    _____

14. What is the opening at the top of a volcano called?

    _____

15. What type of animal eats only plants?

    _____

394

Science Names Trivia

Many of the words that we use in science come from inventors, discoverers, and researchers. For example, when you look at a container of pasteurized milk, you know that the milk went through a process called pasteurization developed by Louis Pasteur, a French bacteriologist.

Here are some more science words that come from scientists' names. Can you match the words to the scientists?

_____ 1. Watt

_____ 2. Celsius

_____ 3. Volt

_____ 4. Ohm

_____ 5. Richter scale

_____ 6. Diesel

_____ 7. Ampere

_____ 8. Fahrenheit

_____ 9. Mach number

_____ 10. Decibel

A. Charles Richter, American seismologist

B. Alessandro Volta, Italian physicist

C. Rudolf Diesel, German automotive engineer

D. Andre Ampere, French physicist

E. Georg Simon Ohm, German physicist

F. James Watt, Scottish engineer and inventor

G. Anders Celsius, Swedish astronomer and inventor

H. Alexander Bell, American inventor of the telephone

I. Gabriel Fahrenheit, German physicist

J. Ernst Mach, Austrian philosopher and physicist

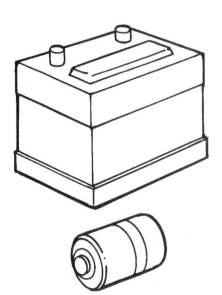

Science Clues

Using the clues, fill in the missing letters to spell the science words.

1. This is someone who travels into space.   __st__on__ut

2. This is round, and we live on it.   e__rt__

3. These are often fluffy, and they float in the sky.   __lo__ __s

4. When some animals sleep through the winter,
    they do this.   h__ber__ate

5. This creature may buzz or crawl.   in__e__t

6. Light is reflected from this at night.   m__ __n

7. When one of these comes, the wind blows
    very hard.   __urr__c__n__

8. When this happens, everything gets wet.   __ai__

9. When we eat, the food goes into this organ.   st__ __ach

10. To see very small things, scientists use this.   __icr__ __co__e

11. These are pretty, and they smell pleasant.   f__ow__ __s

12. This is very cold and white.   __no__

13. To determine your temperature, you
    need this.   t__ __rmo__et__ __

14. These animals do not lay eggs.   m__ __m __l__

15. This force keeps us on the planet Earth.   __ra__i__ __

Color this Design

Color this design so that no shapes of the same color touch one another. You may use only three colors. (**Hint:** Think about the design before you begin to color.)

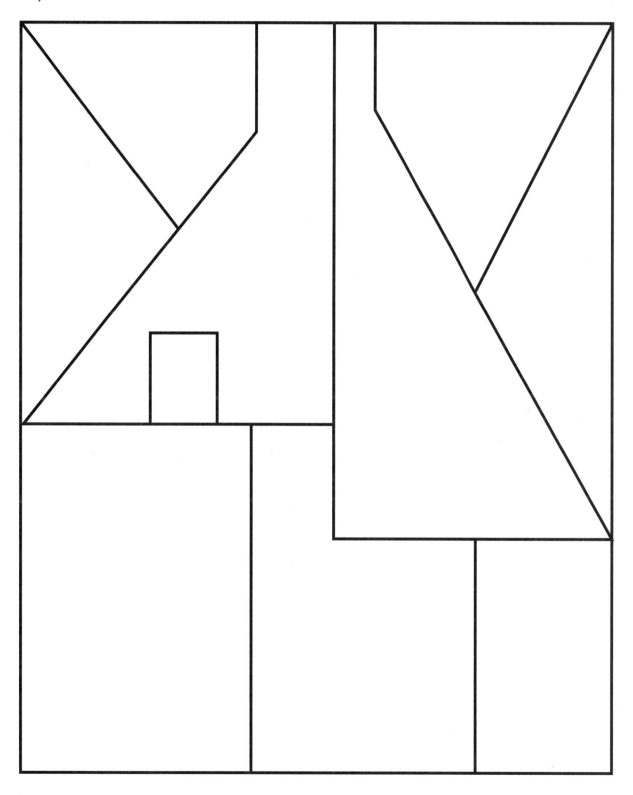

It Doesn't Fit

Circle everything in the picture that does not fit in. Color the picture.

398

Whose Baby?

Which baby goes to which parent? Find the things in common, and you will know.

A.

B.

C.

D.

Baby #_____   **Baby #_____**   **Baby #_____**   **Baby #_____**

1   **2**   **3**   **4**

Shadows

Identify each of the following objects by looking at its shadow.

1. _____

2. _____

3. _____

4. _____

5. _____

6. _____

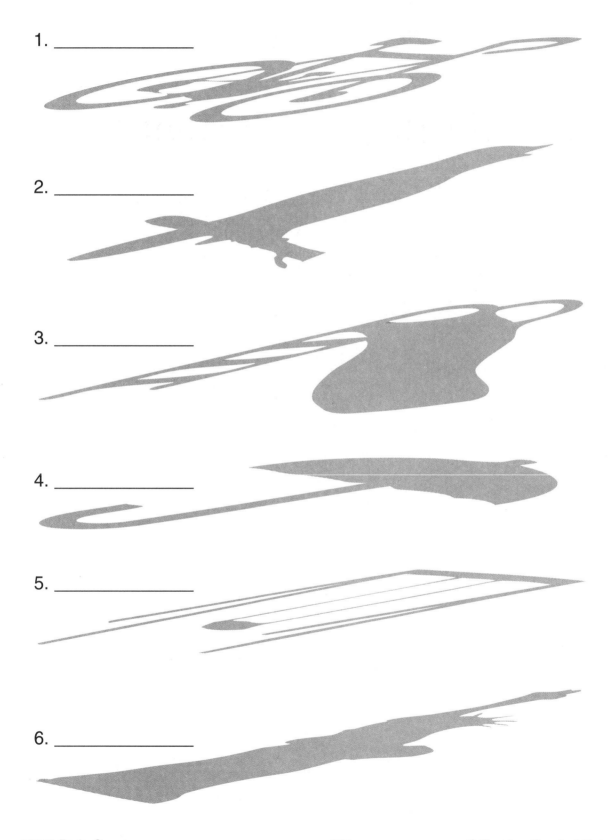

Picture Puzzle

Cut out the individual pieces to make a picture of an important event in American history.

What Is It?

Cut out the squares and put them back together to form the image of a famous Egyptian work of art.

Who Is It?

Cut out the individual pieces to form the portrait of a famous American.

If You Were a . . .

Choose three friends or family members, and ask each of them the questions below. Fill in their answers on the chart.

	Name:	Name:	Name:
What kind of ocean animal or fish would you be?			
What flavor of ice cream would you be?			
What color would you be?			
What fast food would you be?			
What kind of footwear would you be?			
What season would you be?			
Would you be the mountains, ocean, or desert?			
What kind of flower would you be?			
What kind of pet would you be?			
What kind of sport would you be?			
What kind of car would you be?			
What kind of tree would you be?			
What kind of wild animal would you be?			
What kind of building would you be?			
What kind of pajamas would you be?			

Hidden Meanings

Figure out the meaning of each box below.

Open

1._____

ARREST
YOU'RE

2. _____

D
O
DOUBLE
B
L
E

3. _____

4._____

5. _____

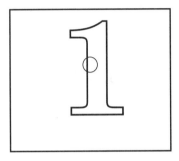

6. _____

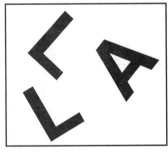

7._____

cycle
cycle
cycle

8. _____

NOON GOOD

9. _____

MAC

10._____

chair

11. _____

T
O
U
C
H

12. _____

#3670 Brain Games

More Hidden Meanings

Figure out the meaning of each box below.

Jack	Tim	**DICE DICE**
1._____	2. _____	3. _____
wear / **long**	r/e/a/d/i/n/g	 get
4._____	5. _____	6. _____
TI*JUST***ME**	**GI** / **CCCCC**	*GOING* DIET
7._____	8. _____	9. _____
SAND	T O W N	**mmoaonn**
10._____	11. _____	12. _____

Some More
Hidden Meanings

Explain the meaning of each box.

skating
thin ice

1. _____

everyrightthing

2. _____

vision

vision

3. _____

K
C
E
H
C

4. _____

r
r o a d s
o a d s
a
d
s

5. _____

$$\frac{mind}{matter}$$

6. _____

I am/myself

7. _____

s
m
o
t
t
o
b

8. _____

$$\frac{c}{deep}$$

9. _____

hahandnd

10. _____

N
W
O
T

11. _____

H IJKLMN O

12. _____

Still More
Hidden Meanings

Explain the meaning of each box.

gnivird

1. _____

HOUR

2. _____

youJUSTme

3. _____

POX

4. _____

MAN
MOON

5. _____

WORN

6. _____

LONG
due

7. _____

Loosen

8. _____

theturkeystraw

9. _____

GO
GNI
GO
GNI

10. _____

me QUIT

11. _____

SOTA

12. _____

How About Some More Hidden Meanings?

Explain the meaning of each box.

F F A A C C E E	**man** ――― **board**	LE VEL
1. _____	2. _____	3. _____
barmonkey monkey monkeyrel	d d e e r e r	s r i a t s
4. _____	5. _____	6. _____
businesspleasure	coORDERurt	the weather ――――― I'm
7. _____	8. _____	9. _____
Ban ana	0 ――― B.S. M.A. Ph.D.	MIRROR
10. _____	11. _____	12. _____

And More Hidden Meanings!

Explain the meaning of each box.

B R A I N E D	GROUND FT FT FT FT FT FT	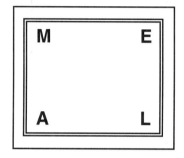
1. _____	2. _____	3. _____
knee light	League	Man Campus
4. _____	5. _____	6. _____
NEpainCK	sleeping job	rise
7. _____	8. _____	9. _____
Once ——— Lightly	your hat keep it	School
10. _____	11. _____	12. _____

A Few More
Hidden Meanings

Explain the meaning of each box.

I'm / WORLD	ECNALG	2 um / 2 um
1._____	2._____	3._____

cloud cloud cloud cloud cloud cloud she cloud cloud cloud	rain drops ————— my head	D O W N out
4._____	5._____	6._____

FAπCE	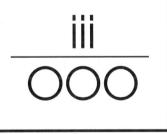	TIME A B D E
7._____	8._____	9._____

AGEBEAUTY	date date	DECI SION
10. _____	11. _____	12. _____

Finally, the Rest of the Hidden Meanings

Explain the meaning of each box.

T A H W M U S T	death life	histalkingsleep
1._____	2._____	3._____
milonelion	eggs / easy	OOO circus
4._____	5._____	6._____
GO IT IT IT IT	nowaysitways	GOOD / EVIL
7._____	8._____	9._____
one one	SLOW	STAND
10._____	11._____	12._____

Symmetry

Draw the other half of the figure, using the squares as a guide. Then, color the picture.

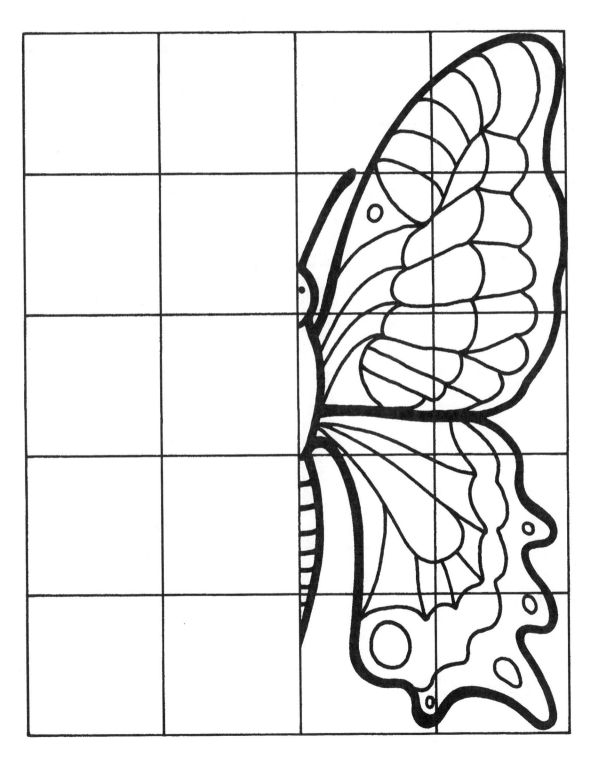

More Symmetry

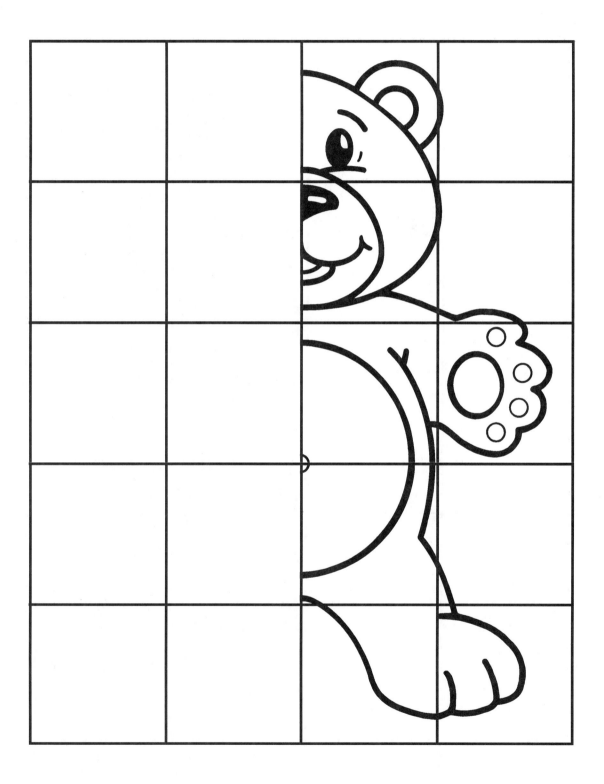

Even More Symmetry

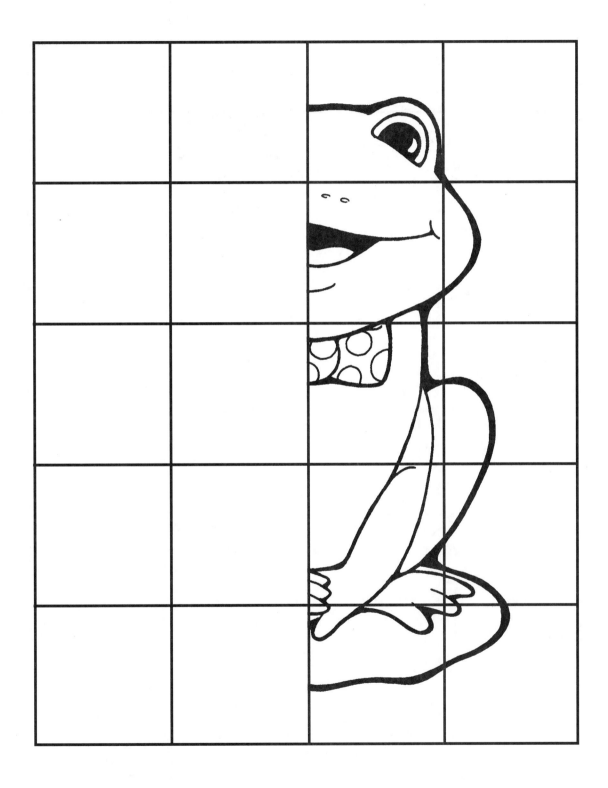

Popular Music
Rebus Writing

Decode the pictures to reveal the names of songs, groups, musicians, or places of the sixties.

More "Popular Music Rebus Writing"

Decode the pictures to reveal the names of songs or musicians of the fifties.

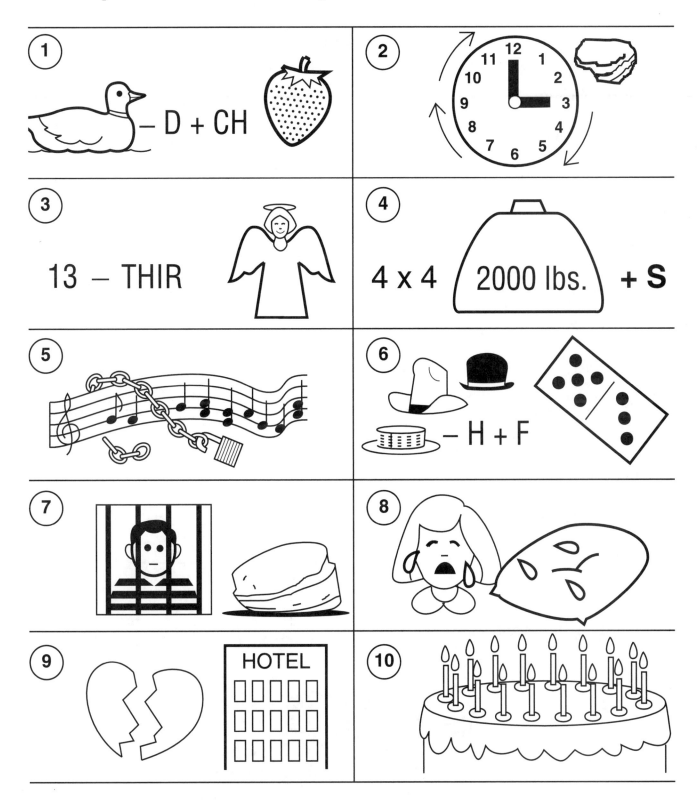

Rhyming Word Pairs

Find an adjective that rhymes with a noun so that the two words together have about the same meaning as the phrase that is given. An example has been done for you.

girl from Switzerland = Swiss miss

1. ailing William _____

2. mischievous boy _____

3. unhappy friend _____

4. bashful insect _____

5. comical rabbit _____

6. overweight referee _____

7. obese feline _____

8. unhappy father _____

9. soaked dog _____

10. watered-down red juice _____

11. large swine _____

12. flower that hates to work _____

13. tiny bug _____

14. ill hen _____

15. overweight rodent _____

More Rhyming Word Pairs

Find an adjective that rhymes with a noun so that together, the two words have about the same meaning as the phrase that is given. An example has been done for you.

soaked dog = soggy doggy

1. skinny horse _____

2. child playing hide-and-seek _____

3. smooth hen _____

4. dog with a license _____

5. burned bread _____

6. purple gorilla _____

7. downcast father _____

8. wagon full of rocks _____

9. girl from Switzerland _____

10. beetle embrace _____

11. crude man _____

12. car crash _____

13. dog kiss _____

14. Halloween evening _____

15. adorable bird _____

16. bashful man _____

17. home for a rodent _____

18. large swine _____

19. happy boy _____

20. loafing flower _____

Still More Rhyming Word Pairs

Find an adjective that rhymes with a noun so that the two words together have about the same meaning as the phrase that is given. An example has been done for you.

Soaked dog = soggy doggy

1. Friend who does not arrive on time _____

2. Carrot top _____

3. Rude fish _____

4. Nasty guy _____

5. Beetle's cup _____

6. Lengthy tune _____

7. Running Fido _____

8. Twice as much bother _____

9. Large hole _____

10. Fish you wanted to catch _____

11. Snowflake cut from paper _____

12. Hundred-watt bulb _____

13. Sugary dessert _____

14. Jewelry chest _____

15. Someone who stole your math book _____

16. Squished cap _____

17. Sunset _____

18. Without money _____

19. Irritated employer _____

20. Fake coins _____

Even More Rhyming Word Pairs

Find an adjective that rhymes with a noun so that, together, the two words have about the same meaning as the phrase that is given. An example has been done for you.

Bashful insect = shy fly

1. Scratchiness from pants _____

2. Playing checkers again _____

3. Smart-aleck girl _____

4. Sleeping twin _____

5. Comfy flower _____

6. Colorless man _____

7. Boat on fire _____

8. Blushing rodent _____

9. Skinny tailor _____

10. Great meal _____

11. Unrolled rug _____

12. Royal woman after a shower _____

13. Home of happy cows _____

14. Cage for chickens _____

15. Dejected boy _____

16. Small snack _____

17. Noisy group of people _____

18. Bloody tale _____

19. Nice bird _____

20. Clever feline _____

Synonyms, Antonyms, and Homophones

Identify each pair of words as synonyms (S), antonyms (A), or homophones (H).

1. clause; claws _____

2. problem; solution _____

3. ally; friend _____

4. following; preceding _____

5. attempt; endeavor _____

6. vast; minute _____

7. accept; except _____

8. sufficient; enough _____

9. foe; opposition _____

10. beautiful; gorgeous _____

11. manner; manor _____

12. crave; desire _____

13. individual; group _____

14. troublesome; difficult _____

15. stationery; stationary _____

16. maximum; minimum _____

17. frequently; repeatedly _____

18. join; separate _____

19. unique; different _____

20. him; hymn _____

Palindromes

Palindromes are words, phrases, sentences, or numbers that read the same forward or backward. Write a palindrome that relates to each word or phrase below. An example has been done for you.

Trick or joke = gag

1. Midday _____

2. Title for a lady _____

3. Tier_____

4. Robert's nickname _____

5. Abbreviation for #2 above _____

6. A glimpse _____

7. An organ of the body used for sight _____

8. A father's nickname _____

9. Something that fails to work _____

10. The sound of a horn _____

11. Something a baby wears _____

12. A concert engagement _____

13. A mother's nickname _____

14. Bounce in water_____

15. Hero of *Great Expectations* _____

16. Soda _____

17. Goofy person _____

18. Small dog _____

19. Brave or skillful act _____

20. Slang for "mister" _____

Art, Literature, and Music

Find an item in either the Art, Literature, or Music Box that relates to each clue below.

1. Ansel Adams _____

2. Ballet _____

3. *Moonlight Sonata* _____

4. Claude Monet _____

5. *The Adventures of Huckleberry Finn* _____

6. *Roll of Thunder, Hear My Cry* _____

7. Leonardo da Vinci _____

8. Rock and roll _____

9. *A Christmas Carol* _____

10. Opera _____

11. Grant Wood _____

12. Jazz _____

13. *Pride and Prejudice* _____

14. Michelangelo _____

15. "The Raven" _____

Art Box	**Literature Box**	**Music Box**
Mona Lisa	Charles Dickens	Beethoven
photography	Jane Austen	Duke Ellington
the Sistine Chapel	Edgar Allan Poe	*The Nutcracker*
impressionism	Mildred D. Taylor	*Aida*
American Gothic	Mark Twain	The Beatles

What's the Question?

Write an appropriate question for each of the following answers.

1. _____

    Jupiter

2. _____

    Hawaii

3. _____

    yes

4. _____

    Christopher Columbus

5. _____

    13

6. _____

    hexagon

7. _____

    no

8. _____

    red, yellow, and blue

9. _____

    50

10. _____

    apple pie

More "What's the Question?"

Write a question for each of the following answers.

1. _____

    Genesis

2. _____

    1848

3. _____

    Amerigo Vespucci

4. _____

    206

5. _____

    Ludwig van Beethoven

6. _____

    an octogon

7. _____

    Alaska

8. _____

    88

9. _____

    yes

10. _____

    Pluto

11. _____

    a stethoscope

12. _____

    The Statue of Liberty

What's the Question Now?

Write a question for each of the following answers.

1. _____

   the ocean

2. _____

   cherry pie

3. _____

   the zoo

4. _____

   64

5. _____

   Johann Bach

6. _____

   100° Celsius

7. _____

   a tornado

8. _____

   100

9. _____

   the Indianapolis 500

10. _____

    Dr. Seuss

What Is the Question?

Write a question for each of the following answers.

1. _____

    across the street

2. _____

    6,000

3. _____

    in the year 2000

4. _____

    Peter Pan

5. _____

    Susan B. Anthony

6. _____

    Claude Monet

7. _____

    Not now, but later.

8. _____

    27

9. _____

    the Eiffel Tower

10. _____

    shortbread

11. _____

    No one knows for sure.

12. _____

    Mercury

13. _____

    Barcelona

14. _____

    Bugs Bunny

15. _____

    Albert Einstein

Try These Brain Twisters

Can you answer each of these brain twisters?

Men and Women at Work and Play

1. If it takes six men one hour to dig six holes, how long does it take one man to dig half a hole?

2. Two men play five complete games of checkers. Each man wins the same number of games. There are no ties. How?

3. A man builds a rectangular house, and all the sides have a southern exposure. A bear walks by; what color is the bear? Why?

4. A farmer has seventeen sheep. All but nine of them die. How many sheep does he have left?

5. How many animals of each species did Moses take in his ark?

6. A clerk in a butcher shop is 5' 10" tall. What does he weigh?

7. A woman applied for a job advertised in the newspaper. The boss who interviewed her offered her two pay rates: a straight ten dollars a day or one cent the first day, two cents the second day, four cents the third day, eight cents the fourth day, and so on, the pay doubling each day. The girl chose the second pay rate. The boss hired her. Why?

8. An archaeologist reports that he has discovered two gold coins dated 435 B.C. in the desert near Jerusalem. His fellow scientists refuse to take him seriously. Why?

9. Three men on a business trip go into a hotel, and each pays ten dollars for a room they are sharing. After they get back to the room the hotel manager realizes he overcharged for the room; it should have been $25. He gives the bellhop five one-dollar bills and sends him to refund the money to the men. As he walks toward the room, the bellhop puts two dollars into his pocket. When the bellhop gets to the room, he gives each man one dollar. Here is the problem. Each man has paid nine dollars (ten at the counter minus the dollar the bellhop returned equals nine dollars) for the room. The amount the three men paid for the room equals twenty-seven dollars. When you add the two dollars the bellhop has in his pocket, the total is twenty-nine dollars. Where did the last dollar go?

10. Last weekend, Derek and Joey were camping, and around midnight, while they were having s'mores, Joey bet Derek that in exactly one week it would not be sunny. Joey knows that he will win this bet. How does he know?

The Passing of Time

1. Do they have a fourth of July in England?

2. A famous Italian composer born in February 1792, wrote the opera *The Barber of Seville.* He died shortly after his eighteenth birthday at the age of seventy-six! How could that be?

3. The doctor gives you three pills and tells you to take one every half hour. How long before you run out of pills?

4. Some months have 31 days; how many have 28?

5. How many birthdays does the average man have?

Try Some More Brain Twisters

Can you answer each of these brain twisters?

Mathematical Mayhem

1. I have two U.S. coins that when added together total fifty-five cents, but one is not a nickel. What two coins do I have?

2. If there are 3 apples and you take 2 away, how many do you have?

3. You have four nines (9,9,9,9). Using only these four nines, arrange them to total 100. You can use any mathematical function you want, but each nine can only be used once.

4. How many thirty-two cent stamps are there in a dozen?

5. Divide 30 by half and add 10. What is the answer?

6. If the earth weighs six trillion tons and you built a stone and mortar wall around the equator weighing one-trillion tons, what would be the weight of the earth with the wall?

7. Jackie took a piece of paper and wrote all the numbers from 300 to 400 on it. How many times did she write the digit 3?

If You're Not Groaning Already, These Will Do the Trick

1. Why can't a man living in the U.S.A. be buried in Canada?

2. How far can a dog run into the woods?

3. If you have only one match and you walk into a room where there is a kerosene lamp, a wood burning stove, and an oil burner, which one would you light first?

4. You have a bottle with a dime in it and the bottle is closed with a cork. You need to get the dime out without taking the cork out or damaging the bottle. How would you do it?

5. If an international airplane crashes exactly on the border of the United States and Mexico, where do they bury the survivors?

6. A woman gave a beggar 50 cents. The woman is the beggar's sister, but the beggar is not the woman's brother. Why not?

7. Can you figure out how this one can be true? In the bedroom, the nearest lamp to the bed is 12 feet away. Alone in the room, and without using any special devices such as cords, pulleys, remotes, or "The Clapper," a person can turn off the lamp and make it to the bed before the room is dark. How?

Names and Numbers

1. Name the five senses.

    _____

2. Name the Three Bears.

    _____

3. Name the seven colors of the rainbow.

    _____

4. Name the three R's.

    _____

5. Name Santa's nine reindeer.

    _____

6. Name the five Great Lakes.

    _____

7. Name the four months that have exactly thirty days.

    _____

8. Name the three basic primary colors.

    _____

9. Name the two colors of the Canadian flag.

    _____

10. Name the seven dwarfs in Disney's *Snow White and the Seven Dwarfs*.

    _____

    _____

More Names and Numbers

1. Name the two planets with no moons.

   _____

2. Name the three cities where the U.S. capital has been located.

   _____

3. Name the three Wise Men.

   _____

4. Name the four figures carved into Mt. Rushmore.

   _____

5. Name the nine planets of our solar system.

   _____

6. Name the six questions a reporter asks.

   _____

7. Name the seven Wonders of the Ancient World.

   _____

   _____

8. Name the seven continents.

   _____

9. Name the 12 provinces and territories of Canada.

   _____

   _____

10. Name the original 13 colonies of the United States.

   _____

   _____

Change for Fifty Cents

There are over 75 ways to make change for 50 cents. Work with a friend to list as many ways as you can. List the coins in order on each line, from largest to smallest. (Hint: Working from large to small coins will also help you find more ways to make change.) The list has been started for you. If you need more space, continue your list on the back of this paper.

Use the following abbreviations:

hd (half dollar)   **q** (quarter)   **d** (dime)   **n** (nickel)   **p** (penny)

1. 1 hd

2. 2 q

3. _____

4. _____

5. _____

6. _____

7. _____

8. _____

9. _____

10. _____

11. _____

12. _____

13. _____

14. _____

15. _____

Calculator Fun

Answer each math problem with a calculator. When you have the answer, turn the calculator upside-down to find an answer for each of the clues in parentheses. The first one is done for you.

1. (Too big) 21,000 + 14,001 = <u>35,001</u> (loose)

2. (A sphere) 21,553 + 16,523 = _____

3. (Make honey) 10,000 - 4662 = _____

4. (Petroleum) 142 x 5 = _____

5. (Tool for watering the garden) 7008 ÷ 2 = _____

6. (Not feeling well) 348 + 424 - 1 = _____

7. (To cry) 0.02004 + 0.02004 = _____

8. (Boy's name) 9376 - 1658 = _____

9. (City in Idaho) 27413 + 7695 = _____

10. (Antonym for "tiny") 206 + 206 + 206 = _____

More Calculator Fun

Do each math problem on your calculator. Then, turn the calculator upside-down to find an answer for each of the following clues.

	Number	Word

1. 1,000 − 229 = not feeling well

2. 5,285 + 1251 + 1199 = the opposite of buy

3. 70,000 − 34,999 = not secured

4. 314 + 215 + 181 = petroleum

5. 0.5731 + 0.2003 = hola

6. 0.09 − 0.07 = a place for animals

7. 188,308 + 188,308 = to laugh in a silly way

8. 2,000 + 95 + 700 + 250 = foot apparel

9. 1080 − 272 = Robert's nickname

10. 0.20202 + 0.20202 = Santa's laughter

11. 926 x 2 x 2 = an empty space

12. 3544 + 3011 + 550 = synonym for dirt

13. 801 − 163 = to ask earnestly

14. 101 x 5 = a call for help

15. .3 x .3 = the opposite of stop

Scrambled Math

Can you unscramble the following words to find the math terms?   Write the correct word on the line after each scrambled word.

1. dad _____

2. mus _____

3. roze _____

4. lahf _____

5. slup _____

6. sinum _____

7. nitodida _____

8. geanevit _____

9. gidit _____

10. citsaamthem _____

11. trasucbt _____

12. simet _____

13. viddie _____

14. tracifon _____

15. bumner _____

Addition and Subtraction

Place + and – signs between the digits so that both sides of each equation are equal.

1. 6   4   1   2   6   2   =   15

2. 9   1   3   1   4   1   =   5

3. 9   3   4   1   2   3   =   14

4. 5   1   1   3   4   6   =   18

5. 9   8   6   3   5   3   =   8

6. 2   1   8   9   3   5   =   20

7. 5   3   2   4   1   5   =   12

8. 4   9   3   7   3   1   =   11

9. 7   6   2   8   7   1   =   3

10. 9   9   9   2   2   8   =   1

More Addition and Subtraction

Place + and - signs between the digits so that both sides of each equation are equal.

1.   9   8   6   3   5   1   =   6

2.   5   3   4   4   2   9   =   17

3.   5   3   2   4   1   5   =   2

4.   3   2   1   4   1   3   =   6

5.   5   1   1   3   4   8   =   18

6.   4   9   3   7   3   1   =   19

7.   2   1   8   9   3   5   =   20

8.   8   7   1   4   4   6   =   14

9.   7   6   2   9   9   3   =   0

10.   3   5   3   9   6   5   =   15

All Things Being Equal

What is equal to one dime, one hour, or one foot? See how many of these you know by completing the equations.

1 cup = _____ ounces

1 inch = _____ centimeters

1 nickel = _____ cents

1 minute = _____ seconds

1 pound = _____ ounces

1 penny = _____ cent

1 month = _____ weeks

1 foot = _____ inches

1 pint = _____ cups

1 quarter = _____ cents

1 meter = _____ feet

1 hour = _____ minutes

1 yard = _____ feet

1 yard = _____ inches

1 dollar = _____ cents

1 day = _____ hours

1 quart = _____ pints

1 year = _____ months

1 ton = _____ pounds

1 gallon = _____ quarts

What's the Message?

Use the "phone code" (letters on the phone that correspond to numbers) to spell out words related to these famous people.

1. Amelia Earhart   284-2867   _____

2. Moses   776-7438   _____

3. Beverly Cleary, Judy Blume   288-4677   _____

4. Ted Kennedy   736-2867   _____

5. George W. Carver   732-6887   _____

6. Wright Brothers   354-4487   _____

7. Milton Hershey   226-3437   _____

8. Liberace   742-6478   _____

9. Tommy Lasorda   363-4377   _____

10. Franklin Roosevelt   639-3325   _____

11. Helen Keller   272-4553   _____

12. George Washington   765-3437   _____

13. Norman Rockwell   724-6837   _____

14. Kristi Yamaguchi   752-8464   _____

15. Colin Powell   436-3725   _____

What's the Message Again?

Use the phone code (letters on the phone that correspond to numbers) to spell out words related to these famous people and places.

1. Jonas Salk   822-2463 _____

2. Jack the Ripper   845-5246 _____

3. Fred Astaire   326-2464 _____

4. Marie Curie   243-6478 _____

5. Harvard   265-5343 _____

6. Mary Lou Retton   496-6278 _____

7. Dian Fossey   467-4552 _____

8. Bill Gates   946-3697 _____

9. Anne Sullivan   832-2437 _____

10. Albert Einstein   749-7427 _____

11. Disneyland   868-7478 _____

12. Michelangelo   234-5464 _____

13. Dr. M. L. King, Jr. and Sitting Bull 532-3377 _____

14. Brothers Grimm   786-7437 _____

15. Benjamin Franklin   256-2622 _____

The Value of Words

In the value box, each letter of the alphabet has been given a dollar value. To find the value of a word, add the values of all the letters. For example, the word "school" would be worth $72 (19 + 3 + 8 + 15 + 15 + 12 = 72). Write words with appropriate values in each of the boxes below.

$10–$20 Words	$21–$50 Words

$51–$75 Words	$76–$100 Words

$101–$150 Words	$151–$200 Words

VALUE BOX

A = $1
B = $2
C = $3
D = $4
E = $5
F = $6
G = $7
H = $8
I = $9
J = $10
K = $11
L = $12
M = $13
N = $14
O = $15
P = $16
Q = $17
R = $18
S = $19
T = $20
U = $21
V = $22
W = $23
X = $24
Y = $25
Z = $26

Change, Please

List the coins you would give each person below to make change for his or her dollar.

1. Dolly wants one coin for her $1. _____

2. Zac wants six coins for his $1. _____

3. Holly wants seven coins for her $1. _____

4. Andrew wants 10 coins for his $1. _____

5. Casie wants 15 coins for her $1. _____

6. Thomas wants 16 coins for his $1. _____

7. Chelsea wants 17 coins for her $1. _____

8. Austin wants 19 coins for his $1. _____

9. Marc wants 25 coins for his $1. _____

10. Roberto wants 28 coins for his $1. _____

Change for a Dollar

There are over 200 ways to make change for a dollar. Work with a friend to list as many ways as you can. List the coins in order on each line, from largest to smallest. (**Hint:** Working from large to small coins will help you find more ways to make change, too.) The list has been started for you. If you need more space, continue your list on the back of this paper.

Use the following abbreviations:

hd *(half dollar)*   **q** *(quarter)*   **d** *(dime)*   **n** *(nickel)*   **p** *(penny)*

1. 2hd
2. 1hd and 2q
3. 1hd and 5d
4. 1hd and 10n
5. _____
6. _____
7. _____
8. _____
9. _____
10. _____
11. _____
12. _____
13. _____
14. _____
15. _____
16. _____
17. _____
18. _____
19. _____
20. _____
21. _____
22. _____
23. _____
24. _____
25. _____

26. _____
27. _____
28. _____
29. _____
30. _____
31. _____
32. _____
33. _____
34. _____
35. _____
36. _____
37. _____
38. _____
39. _____
40. _____
41. _____
42. _____
43. _____
44. _____
45. _____
46. _____
47. _____
48. _____
49. _____
50. _____

Numbers, Numbers, Numbers

Answer each question with a number. How many . . .

1. starting players on a soccer team? _____

2. rings on the Olympic flag? _____

3. squares on a checkerboard? _____

4. lines of verse in a limerick? _____

5. queen bees in a hive? _____

6. U.S. senators? _____

7. starting players on a basketball team? _____

8. zeros in one million? _____

9. sides on a decagon? _____

10. years in a score? _____

11. starting players on a baseball team? _____

12. cards in a deck? _____

13. games in a major league baseball season? _____

14. millimeters in a meter? _____

15. feet in a mile? _____

16. milliliters in a liter? _____

17. parts of speech? _____

18. events in a pentatholon? _____

19. notes in an octave? _____

20. atoms in a water molecule? _____

Strike It Rich!

Whose picture is on the $100,000 bill?

To discover the answer, find the difference in each problem below. Decode the name by matching the answer to its letter. Write the letter in the box below the difference.

9371	3313	4530	6000	6230	3917	6792
−4528	−1834	−3051	−3781	−1357	−2438	−1949

7927	7203	5361	4079	7455	5386
−3084	−3427	−2805	−2834	−5976	−2174

1479 O	3776 I	4843 W	2219 D
4873 R	2556 L	3212 N	1245 S

The $100,000 bill is the highest-value bill ever printed by the United States. It was used only by government banks. The bill is no longer issued. The $100 bill is the highest value U.S. bill in circulation today.

446

Money Maze

Find your way through the money maze. Mark the path of correct money amounts. You may go ↑ ←→ ↗ or ↘ .

$ End	7 pennies + 7 dimes = 70 cents	Start $	4 nickels + 3 dimes = 60 cents
3 pennies + 2 dimes +2 quarters = 73 cents	4 nickels + 2 dimes + 3 quarters = $1.25	5 nickels + 1 dime + 1 quarter = 55 cents	6 pennies + 6 dimes + 1 quarter = 91 cents
8 pennies + 5 dimes = 58 cents	2 pennies + 3 quarters = 76 cents	8 nickels + 3 quarters = $1.15	11 pennies + 7 dimes = 78 cents
4 quarters + 2 dimes = $1.25	2 pennies + 6 nickels + 7 dimes = $1.02	1 penny + 1 dime + 2 quarters = 61 cents	2 nickels + 3 dimes = 45 cents
8 dimes = 40 cents	17 nickels = 85 cents	7 pennies + 5 nickels = 33 cents	10 quarters = $2.50
2 pennies + 5 nickels + 3 quarters = 87 cents	11 pennies + 4 nickels = 41 cents	7 nickels + 7 dimes = $1.05	3 nickels + 1 dime + 1 quarter = 45 cents
3 pennies + 3 dimes = 35 cents	4 pennies + 7 nickels = 39 cents	3 nickels + 3 dimes + 3 quarters = $1.20	4 pennies + 3 nickels = 19 cents

Drawing-To-Scale Activity

1. Use graph paper with ¼" (.64 cm) squares. Make a few measurements before you decide on an appropriate scale to use. You can tape sheets of graph paper together if necessary.

2. Pick out a large building or feature on your school's campus to measure and use as a guide for estimating the size of the other buildings or rooms. (Get an idea of size by "pacing off" the length or width of something. Measure your stride and then count the number of steps you take. This is not exact, but it will help.)

3. Make a rough sketch in the space below. Then make some more exact measurements before you try to draw a final plan on the graph paper.

Cookie Math

The following word problems are based on some interesting statistics about chocolate chip cookies.

> **Fact A:** *Seven billion chocolate chip cookies are consumed annually in the United States.*

Exercises

1. Write seven billion in numerals. _____

2. In order to find out how many cookies are consumed on average by every person in the United States, what other information would you need to know in order to solve the problem? _____

3. Where could you find that information? _____

4. How would you solve the problem? _____

> **Fact B:** *Ninety million bags of chocolate morsels are sold each year, enough to make 150 million pounds (67.5 kg) of cookies.*

Exercises

1. Write a ratio to show the number of bags of chocolate morsels to the number of pounds of cookies. _____

   Reduce it to its lowest terms. _____

2. How many pounds of cookies can be made from 30 million bags of chocolate morsels? How could this problem be solved? _____

> **Fact C:** *The 150 million pounds (67.5 million kg) of cookies in fact number 2 above is enough to circle the globe 10 times.*

Exercises

1. How many cookies does it take to circle the globe once? _____

2. How many cookies would it take to circle the globe 15 times? _____

> **Fact D:** *Although the original Toll House burned to the ground in 1984, it was still baking cookies in an annex until the new one was rebuilt. Some thirty-three thousand cookies a day were baked there.*

Exercises

1. If 33,000 cookies were baked there each day, how many cookies will be baked in a week? _____

2. If baking goes on 24 hours a day, how many cookies, on the average, are baked each hour? _____

Energy Facts

Directions: Learn some interesting facts about energy as you solve the problems below. Then write the letters from the box on the sentence blanks, matching the letters with the corresponding answers below the blanks.

A	C	D	E	G	H
37 x 12 = ____	659 + 13 = ____	720 ÷ 16 = ____	316 − 105 = ____	67 + 39 = ____	374 ÷ 22 = ____
I	**K**	**L**	**M**	**N**	**O**
823 − 78 = ____	16 X 15 = ____	361 + 19 = ____	957 ÷ 33 = ____	500 − 135 = ____	17 X 9 = ____
R	**S**	**T**	**U**	**W**	**Y**
369 + 72 = ____	216 ÷ 8 = ____	999 −955 = ____	62 X 4 = ____	416 + 41 = ____	488 ÷ 4 = ____

Energy Facts

1. Anything that moves has energy of ____ ____ ____ ____ ____ ____.
   29   153   44   745   153   365

2. Energy of motion is called ____ ____ ____ ____ ____ ____ ____ energy.
   240   745   365   211   44   745   672

3. ____ ____ ____ ____ and waterfalls have kinetic energy.
   457   745   365   45

4. All light is ____ ____ ____ ____ ____ ____.
   211   365   211   441   106   122

5. ____ ____ ____ ____ is energy.
   17   211   444   44

6. ____ ____ ____ ____ ____ is energy.
   27   153   248   365   45

7. ____ ____ ____ ____ ____ ____ ____ ____ ____ ____ ____ is energy.
   211   380   211   672   44   441   745   672   745   44   122

8. One kind of energy can be ____ ____ ____ ____ ____ ____ ____ to another kind of energy.
   672   17   444   365   106   211   45

450

Children's Tales

Fill in the missing words from the fairy tale titles.

1. The Three Little _____

2. Goldilocks and the Three _____

3. The Three _____ Goats Gruff

4. _____ White and the _____ Dwarfs

5. The _____ Mermaid

6. Beauty and the _____

7. Aladdin and the Magic _____

8. _____ and the Beanstalk

9. The _____ That Laid the Golden _____

10. The Bremen _____ Musicians

11. _____ Beauty

12. The _____ Princess

13. The Steadfast _____ Soldier

14. The Tale of Peter _____

Word Jumbles

Unscramble the letters to find the things used in a house.

1. dbe _____

2. mlpa _____

3. voen _____

4. lvsnteeiio _____

5. batle _____

6. nkis _____

7. salgs _____

8. hraic _____

9. lewto _____

10. lptea _____

11. ubt _____

12. rkfo _____

13. oniwdw _____

14. chuco _____

15. toiap _____

16. escoobka _____

17. resdres _____

18. ringyf nap _____

19. noops _____

20. antpingi _____

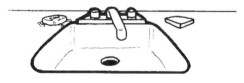

It's the Cat's Meow

Each word or phrase below is a clue for a word that contains the letters CAT.

1. Baseball position _____

2. Condiment _____

3. To make more of _____

4. Prescription drug _____

5. Scram! _____

6. Underground burial sites _____

7. Time off _____

8. Religion _____

9. Career _____

10. Mimic _____

11. 10-event contest _____

12. Faithful _____

13. Cows _____

14. To teach _____

15. Disaster _____

Re"CON"struct These Words

Each phrase below is a clue for a word that contains the letters CON.

1. U.S. state whose capital is Hartford _____

2. Woman's name _____

3. The end _____

4. Seasonings for food _____

5. To hide _____

6. To go on _____

7. To extend good wishes _____

8. Mixed up _____

9. To make up _____

10. A musical entertainment _____

11. Letters other than vowels _____

12. The seven main land masses on Earth _____

13. To become friends again _____

14. Strong building material _____

15. Bits of colored paper thrown at celebrations _____

Car Word Parts

Each word or phrase below is a clue for a word that contains the letters CAR.

1. Saturday morning television shows _____

2. Kind of candy _____

3. Major league baseball team _____

4. Box _____

5. Traveling show _____

6. Flower _____

7. Floor covering _____

8. Animals that feed chiefly on meat _____

9. Unit of weight for precious stones _____

10. A merry-go-round _____

11. Part of the engine of a car _____

12. To get rid of _____

13. Type of sweater Mr. Rogers wears _____

14. A picture that exaggerates a person's features _____

15. To imprison _____

No! No! A Thousand Times No!

Each phrase below is a clue for a word that contains the letters NO.

1. No person _____

2. City in Tennessee _____

3. Rap on the door _____

4. Wanderer _____

5. Range of information a person has _____

6. Lengthy story _____

7. Sound _____

8. The Biblical man who built an ark _____

9. The two times each year when day and night are of equal length

   _____

10. A pig's nose, mouth, and jaws _____

11. Small, elf-like, imaginary being _____

12. A loop with a slip knot that tightens as the rope is pulled _____

13. Foolishness _____

14. Body part used for smelling _____

15. A macaroni-like food made in flat strips _____

Bar None

Each phrase below is a clue for a word that contains the word BAR.

1. Backyard cookout _____

2. Building for lodging soldiers _____

3. Weight-lifting equipment _____

4. Uncivilized person _____

5. Farm building _____

6. Type of shrub _____

7. Founder of the American Red Cross _____

8. Sale-priced item _____

9. Deep voice _____

10. Baron's wife _____

11. Popular doll _____

12. River vessel _____

13. Predatory fish _____

14. Riding without a saddle _____

15. City in Spain _____

Cold as Ice

Each phrase below is a clue for a word or phrase that contains the word ICE.

1. 200th birthday _____

2. The cost of _____

3. Sliver or piece _____

4. Rodents _____

5. Large mass of ice floating in the sea _____

6. Black or red candy _____

7. Flavoring or seasoning _____

8. Island country in the North Atlantic _____

9. Grain _____

10. Dinosaur _____

11. Second in commmand_____

12. Lewis Carroll book_____

13. Suggestion about what should be done _____

14. Room in which to conduct business _____

15. Liquid part of fruits_____

16. Large muscles in the upper arms _____

17. Gadget _____

18. Attract or tempt _____

19. Persons whose duty is keeping order _____

20. Cut into small cubes _____

21. Of fine quality _____

22. Observe _____

23. Three times _____

24. Small, wingless, parasitic insect _____

25. Long-running television game show _____

The Midas Touch

Each phrase below is a clue for a word or phrase that contains the word GOLD.

1. James Bond movie _____

2. Small orange-colored fish _____

3. To avoid work _____

4. Ghana _____

5. Young girl in *The Three Bears* _____

6. Person who extracts money or gifts by coaxing or flattery _____

7. Gold in very small bits or powder _____

8. Bright yellow _____

9. Wild duck _____

10. Principle to live by _____

11. Site where gold is obtained _____

12. Event of 1848 _____

13. 50 years after a wedding _____

14. Gold held by the central bank _____

15. Fall plant with tall stalks _____

16. Person who makes articles of gold _____

17. Small yellow songbird _____

All Thumbs

Each phrase below is a clue for a word or phrase that contains the word THUMB.

1. Gardener's gift _____

2. Barnum and Bailey attraction _____

3. Go-ahead sign _____

4. Tiny fairy tale character _____

5. Impression made by underside of the thumb _____

6. Hitchhike _____

7. Signal of disapproval _____

8. To search the pages of a book _____

9. Push pin _____

10. Guideline _____

11. Clumsy in handling something _____

12. Completely dominated by someone _____

13. Treat or regard with disdain _____

Go Team Go

Each phrase below is a clue for a word or phrase that contains the word GO.

1. Animal _____

2. Sport _____

3. Water taxi _____

4. Valuable mineral _____

5. Past participle of go_____

6. Guiding principle _____

7. Type of dog _____

8. End or aim _____

9. Another name for a peanut _____

10. Intermediary_____

11. To eat hurriedly _____

12. Mischievous or scary elf _____

13. Beautiful _____

14. Ape _____

15. Stew _____

16. To annoy or irritate _____

17. Drinking glass with a stem _____

18. Spectacles used to protect the eyes _____

19. Movie and book title about the old South _____

20. Giant in the Bible _____

21. Loose, flowing garment _____

22. Fruit _____

23. Dance _____

24. Fruit of a trailing or climbing plant _____

25. Type of bird _____

Putting the
Pieces Together

Choose one syllable each from columns A, B, and C to form three-syllable words. Write the new words in column D. Use each syllable only once. One has been done for you.

Column A	Column B	Column C	Column D
as	ta	cine	1. _aspirin_
guar	di	tion	2. _____
med	pi	tone	3. _____
set	por	er	4. _____
im	fer	sine	5. _____
con	ou	tant	6. _____
o	an	mal	7. _____
ear	di	est	8. _____
lim	for	um	9. _____
dif	li	mins	10. _____
brav	tle	ent	11. _____
ra	on	tee	12. _____
pris	i	ment	13. _____
in	ver	y	14. _____
vi	er	rin	15. _____

Hidden Animals

Hidden in each sentence is the name of an animal. Each can be found either in the middle of a word or by combining the end of one word with the beginning of the next. Circle or underline the animal name in each sentence.

1. Eric owns his own computer store.

2. Is Mr. Roy Sterwin our new teacher?

3. Try some of these green grapes.

4. Sarah entered the building from the back door.

5. Sheryl, I only have 25 cents in my pocket.

6. The teacher made Ernie stay after school to get his work made up.

7. We will leave for the picnic at 11:45.

8. Please allow me to introduce you.

9. She cannot stand to be around people who smoke.

10. I can go at 7:30.

More Hidden Animals

Hidden in each sentence is the name of an animal. Each can be found either in the middle of a word or by combining the end of one word with the beginning of the next. Underline the animal name in each sentence. An example has been done for you.

Mar**c ow**ns a sporting goods store. **(cow)**

1. Cuba won the gold medal, and America took the silver. _____

2. To and fro goes the pendulum. _____

3. Eating oatmeal was Charles' favorite thing to do. _____

4. "Ski down the beginner's slope," said the instructor. _____

5. They do good work. _____

6. The politician said, "We, as elected officials, are employees of the public.".

   _____

7. Susan came late to the party. _____

8. If your answers differ, retry the problem. _____

9. Sara made Eric apologize for being mean. _____

10. Magnus ate a whole bowl of popcorn while watching the movie.

    _____

11. Noah entered the ark with his family. _____

12. Chris' new-found prestige really has gone to his head. _____

13. Steffi should be pleased with the results. _____

14. Jesse allowed only four goals the entire season. _____

15. John scraped his elbow on the pavement. _____

Corn-fed Words

Each phrase below is a clue for a word or phrase that contains the letters CORN.

1. A horn of plenty _____

2. Something of fundamental importance _____

3. Where two streets meet _____

4. A type of sandwich meat_____

5. The center part of an ear of corn _____

6. A building for storing corn _____

7. A position in football _____

8. A product used in cooking and salads _____

9. An instrument that looks like a trumpet_____

10. The kind of joke that makes people groan _____

11. The outer covering of the eyeball _____

12. A way to save money, time, or effort (two words)_____

13. A thickening agent in gravy_____

14. An ornamental molding along the top of a wall_____

15. A breakfast cereal _____

Far Out

Each phrase below is a clue for a word or phrase that contains the letters FAR.

1. The price of a bus ride _____

2. A minor league club _____

3. A paid worker on a farm _____

4. A litter of pigs _____

5. At a greater distance _____

6. One who raises crops _____

7. Remote _____

8. Good-by _____

9. A former British coin of little value _____

10. Not ordinarily believable _____

11. A region of Asia _____

12. Up to this point all is well _____

13. Humor based on ridiculous happenings _____

14. To overstep reasonable limits _____

15. Having widespread influence _____

Pet Peeves

Each phrase below is a clue for a word or phrase that contains the letters PET.

1. A man's name _____

2. Turned to stone _____

3. Part of a flower _____

4. A floor covering _____

5. Occurring again and again _____

6. A figure controlled by the movement of strings or hands _____

7. Small, tiny _____

8. A flower _____

9. An underskirt _____

10. Liquid used to make gasoline _____

11. A naval officer _____

12. Small amounts of money for incidental expenses _____

13. A formal request, often signed by a large number of people _____

14. A shallow glass container used to prepare cultures in science labs_____

    _____

15. A small cake with fancy frosting _____

This "Ore" That

Each phrase below is a clue for a word or phrase that contains the letters ORE.

1. Land next to a body of water _____

2. An ancestor _____

3. In a plentiful amount _____

4. A state in the U.S. _____

5. Took an oath _____

6. The finger next to the thumb _____

7. A routine task _____

8. To breathe loudly during sleep _____

9. A seasoning used in cooking _____

10. To love or worship _____

11. To predict the weather _____

12. Woods _____

13. Opposite of less _____

14. Animals that eat only meat _____

15. To choose not to pay attention _____

"The" Words

Each phrase below is a clue for a word or phrase that contains the letters THE.

1. Used to keep liquids warm or cold _____

2. Near that place or time _____

3. The study of numbers _____

4. Instrument used to measure temperature_____

5. Melody used to identify a certain show_____

6. To bring together _____

7. The act of stealing_____

8. A dictionary of synonyms and antonyms _____

9. An essay submitted by a candidate for a university degree_____

10. To wash; to immerse in liquid _____

11. An explanation; an opinion _____

12. At that time _____

13. A black leopard _____

14. The atmospheric conditions of a place _____

15. A place where movies are shown _____

Man Hunt

Each phrase below is a clue for a word or phrase that contains the letters MAN.

1. A large insect _____

2. A tropical fruit _____

3. A shelf above a fireplace _____

4. A feeding trough for cattle _____

5. A province in Canada _____

6. To make by hand or by machine _____

7. Numerous _____

8. A small orange _____

9. A stringed musical instrument _____

10. Treatment for fingernails _____

11. An opening to a sewer _____

12. Person in charge _____

13. A large house _____

14. To treat roughly _____

15. A model for displaying clothes _____

Weather Words

Hidden in each sentence is a word that a meteorologist might use in a weather report. Each "weather word" can be found either in the middle of a word or by combining the end of one word with the beginning of the next. Underline the weather word in each sentence and then write it in the answer blank provided. An example has been done for you.

Do you like sp<u>icy</u> foods? icy

1. Alexis is now working at the mall. _____

2. Be sure the sign is clearly visible from the road. _____

3. We found mildew around the tub in the bathroom. _____

4. My dad drives a Thunderbird. _____

5. Heather is my best friend. _____

6. Robert is unlikely to win the race. _____

7. Andres sprained his ankle while riding his skateboard. _____

8. Who could have torn a door from its hinges? _____

9. According to Cedric, loud is the only way to sing! _____

10. Wouldn't it be fun to sail the seas on a yacht? _____

11. War might break out soon between the two nations. _____

12. Dad had to scold Chris for disobeying. _____

13. Ha! Illness will never stop me! _____

14. We'll have the show indoors this year because of rain. _____

15. Greg went hunting and shot his first deer. _____

Compound Words

Write a word in the blank between each set of words. The trick is that the new word must complete a compound word both to the left and to the right of it. The first one has been done for you.

1. dug   **out**   side

2. foot   _____ ladder

3. arrow   _____ line

4. country _____ walk

5. tea   _____ belly

6. camp   _____ place

7. basket _____ room

8. touch   _____ stairs

9. drug   _____ keeper

10. girl   _____ ship

11. flash   _____ house

12. hill   _____ walk

13. look   _____ doors

14. quarter _____ bone

15. some   _____ ever

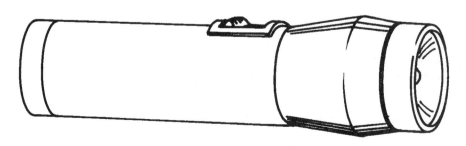

More Compound Words

Choose a word from column A or B and combine it with a word from column C or D to make a compound word. Some words will go together in more than one combination, but there is only one combination that will use all words.

A	B	C	D
any-	south-	-road	-ball
school-	back-	-ever	-board
sea-	snow-	-shore	-east
grand-	who-	-day	-paper
home-	head-	-made	-where
under-	cow-	-doors	-boy
every-	news-	-one	-bone
black-	bed-	-room	-stand
rail-	after-	-father	-time
else-	out-	-noon	-line

_____   _____

_____   _____

_____   _____

_____   _____

_____   _____

_____   _____

_____   _____

_____   _____

Still More Compound Words

Choose a word from column A or B and combine it with a word from column C or D to make a compound word. Some words will go together in more than one combination, but there is only one combination that uses all of the words.

A	B	C	D
any-	hand-	-pole	-side
base-	down-	-come	-ball
under-	paint-	-where	-port
in-	flag-	-box	-father
camp-	light-	-brush	-town
rail-	eye-	-ground	-line
grand-	mail-	-road	-house
north-	over-	-shake	-lid
quarter-	text-	-back	-book
sea-	junk-	-east	-yard

_____   _____

_____   _____

_____   _____

_____   _____

_____   _____

Clipped Words

The following words are written in their shortened forms. Write the long form of each word in the blank to its right.

1. phone _____

2. champ _____

3. gas _____

4. vet _____

5. pop _____

6. bike _____

7. plane _____

8. tux _____

9. math _____

10. ref _____

11. auto _____

12. fridge _____

13. sub _____

14. prom _____

15. gym _____

16. taxi _____

17. burger _____

18. specs _____

19. limo _____

20. exam _____

Which Word Shall I Use?

Circle the correct word on the right that matches the word or phrase on the left.

1. Story   **tale/tail**

2. Rabbit   **hare/hair**

3. Bus token   **fair/fare**

4. Odor   **sent/scent**

5. Make a purchase   **buy/by/bye**

6. One   **lone/loan**

7. Also   **to/two/too**

8. Assistant   **aid/aide**

9. Land by an ocean   **beach/beech**

10. Two   **pare/pair**

11. Large   **great/grate**

12. Change   **alter/altar**

13. Atmosphere   **air/heir**

14. Grief   **mourning/morning**

15. Land   **aisle/isle**

Which Word?

Words that sound alike or look alike often have meanings that are not alike. Decide which word is the correct one for each clue below and circle it.

1. Dry land   **dessert/desert**

2. Complete   **through/thorough**

3. Belonging to both of them   **there/their/they're**

4. Completely prepared   **all ready/already**

5. To go forward   **proceed/precede**

6. Writing paper   **stationary/stationery**

7. Second in a series of two   **latter/later**

8. A basic law   **principle/principal**

9. Hush   **quite/quiet**

10. Contraction for it is   **its/it's**

11. To recline   **lie/lay**

12. The result of a cause   **affect/effect**

13. A part of speech   **preposition/proposition**

14. In any case   **any way/anyway**

15. To rest the body on something   **sit/set**

Which Word Now?

Words that sound alike or look alike often have meanings that are not alike. Decide which word is the correct one and circle it.

1. To leave out   **accept/except**

2. A building   **capital/capitol**

3. To give advice   **consul/counsel**

4. To hint at or suggest   **imply/infer**

5. Second of two things   **later/latter**

6. A fear of   **mania/phobia**

7. The first of two   **former/latter**

8. Immovable   **stationary/stationery**

9. The beginning of life   **birth/berth**

10. State of the atmosphere   **whether/weather**

11. Occurring yearly   **annual/perennial**

12. Temperament   **disposition/deposition**

13. Lesson   **morale/moral**

14. Belonging to you   **your/you're/yore**

Around Your House

Complete each expression with items found around your house. A word may be used more than once.

1. The mouse ran up the _____.

2. My _____ runneth over.

3. The _____ was bare.

4. The _____ ran away with the spoon.

5. Out of the _____ and into the fire

6. The butcher, the baker, the _____ maker

7. Rub-a-dub-dub, three men in a _____

8. _____, mirror on the wall

9. Life is just a _____ of cherries.

10. Home on the _____

11. Blue-_____ special

12. Strike while the _____ is hot

13. Skeleton in the _____

One Word Plus Another

Add one word to another word to make a third word. The first one has been done for you.

1. A water barrier plus a writing utensil equals a verb that means "to make slightly wet."

   dam + pen = dampen

2. A large body of water plus a male child make a period of time.

   _____ + _____ = _____

3. A lightweight bed of canvas plus 2,000 pounds make a type of fabric.

   _____ + _____ = _____

4. A vegetable plus an edible kernel make a seed that ripens underground and is usually roasted before being eaten.

   _____ + _____ = _____

5. The nearest star plus the antonym of *wet* make an adjective meaning "various" or "several."

   _____ + _____ = _____

6. A male offspring plus something used to catch fish make a form of poetry.

   _____ + _____ = _____

7. The antonym of *on* plus frozen water make a place for business.

   _____ + _____ = _____

8. A rodent plus a shade of brown make a plant used to make furniture.

   _____ + _____ = _____

9. Male adults plus the highest playing card make a threat.

   _____ + _____ = _____

10. A man's name plus a male child make the name of a former U.S. president.

    _____ + _____ = _____

Another Word Plus Another

Add the first word to the second word to make a third word.

1. A standard score for a hole of golf _____
   plus to get possession of _____
   make a word meaning to participate. _____

2. A flower that is not fully open _____
   plus "to obtain" _____
   make a plan for income and expenses. _____

3. A kind of tree _____
   plus a rock from which metal can be extracted
   _____
   make a word meaning "on land." _____

4. To decay _____
   and the past tense of eat _____
   make a word meaning "to revolve." _____

5. A lower limb of the human body _____
   plus the antonym for begin _____
   make a story handed down from the past.
   _____

6. An auto _____
   plus an animal that is treated with affection
   _____
   make a type of floor covering. _____

7. "To put on" _____
   and something used to unlock _____
   make a member of the horse family. _____

8. To succeed in competition _____
   and "to make an attempt" _____
   make a word meaning "cold." _____

Colorful Words

Answer each clue with a word or phrase that has the name of a color in it. There may be more than one answer.

1. A bridge in California _____

2. A chocolate cookie-like cake _____

3. A flower _____

4. A bird _____

5. A person without training or experience _____

6. A fruit _____

7. A contagious disease _____

8. A wasp _____

9. A bus line _____

10. A piece of slate on which to write with chalk _____

11. An automobile tire _____

12. Beef, lamb, and veal _____

13. A medal _____

14. A famous pirate _____

A Maze of Letters

Follow the letters to spell out the sentence the children say as they leave for school.

Complete the Phrase

1. Blood, sweat, and _____

2. Eat, drink, and _____

3. Knife, fork, and _____

4. Morning, noon, and _____

5. Snap, crackle, and_____

6. Up, up, and _____

7. The butcher, the baker, and _____

8. A hop, a skip, and _____

9. Hook, line, and _____

10. Wynken, Blynken, and _____

11. Bacon, lettuce, and _____

12. Truth, justice, and _____

13. Men, women, and _____

14. Healthy, wealthy, and_____

15. Papa Bear, Mama Bear, and_____

16. Yes, no, or _____

17. Huffed and puffed and _____

18. Person, place, or _____

Abbreviations

Write the meaning of each abbreviation.

1. N _____

2. St. _____

3. RR _____

4. B.A. _____

5. M.C. _____

6. C.O.D. _____

7. Wed. _____

8. A.M. _____

9. chap. _____

10. doz. _____

11. qt. _____

12. pkg. _____

13. P.S.T. _____

14. Ave. _____

15. Sept. _____

16. yr. _____

17. bldg. _____

18. no. _____

19. temp. _____

20. P.O. _____

More Abbreviations

Write the meaning of each abbreviation.

1. Pres. _____

2. ASAP _____

3. Adj. _____

4. Lbs. _____

5. Max. _____

6. Etc. _____

7. Dec. _____

8. M.A. _____

9. I.O.U. _____

10. B.C. _____

11. P.M. _____

12. R.S.V.P. _____

13. S.A.S.E. _____

14. S.A. _____

15. Bldg. _____

16. RR _____

17. Prep. _____

18. Hdqrs. _____

19. D.A. _____

20. D.S.T. _____

Anagrams

Reorder the letters of each word below to make a new word.

1. ocean _____

2. snap _____

3. Brian _____

4. owl _____

5. melon _____

6. pots _____

7. flea _____

8. ring _____

9. art _____

10. gum _____

11. heart _____

12. bat _____

13. paws _____

14. ape _____

15. tone _____

16. tap _____

17. stop _____

18. not _____

19. pore _____

20. wee _____

Proverbs

Proverbs are old, familiar sayings that often give advice for daily living. Complete each of the following proverbs and explain what they mean.

1. Early to bed and early to rise, _____

   _____

2. Don't count your chickens _____

   _____

3. Birds of a feather _____

   _____

4. A penny saved _____

   _____

5. Two wrongs _____

   _____

6. When the cat's away, _____

   _____

7. Look before _____

   _____

8. Never look a gift horse _____

   _____

9. Never put off until tomorrow _____

   _____

10. All work and no play _____

    _____

More Proverbs

Proverbs are old, familiar sayings that often give advice for daily living.
Complete each of the following proverbs.

1. Never put off until tomorrow . . .

   _____

2. A friend in need . . .

   _____

3. Don't cry over . .

   _____

4. A stitch in time, . . .

   _____

5. Two heads . . .

   _____

6. Absence makes the heart . . .

   _____

7. All that glitters . . .

   _____

8. The grass is always greener . . .

   _____

9. The early bird . . .

   _____

10. Haste makes . . .

    _____

489   #3670 Brain Games

A Puzzling Proverb

Fill in the answers to the following clues. Then, transfer the letters to the corresponding numbered blanks to reveal a famous proverb.

1. If the capital of Hawaii is Honolulu, circle P. If not, circle O.

2. If there are five rings on the Olympic flag, circle O. If there are six, circle A.

3. If an insect has eight legs, circle T. If not, circle W.

4. If the result of two numbers added together is called the sum, circle C. If not, circle N.

5. If 131 is a numerical palindrome, circle F. If not, circle H.

6. If there are 14 in a baker's dozen, circle T. If not, circle D.

7. If antonyms mean the opposite, circle Y. If not, circle N.

8. If a comma is used in a contraction, circle N. If not, circle T.

9. If a name for low clouds is fog, circle R. If it is not, circle A.

10. If an eight-sided figure is called an octagon, circle A. If not, circle M.

11. If a baby kangaroo is a kid, circle Y. If it is a joey, circle M.

12. If Washington is one of the four presidents carved on Mt. Rushmore, circle U. If not, circle H.

13. If your mother's sister is your grandmother, circle H. If not, circle N.

14. If 2,000 pounds equals one ton, circle H. If not, circle F.

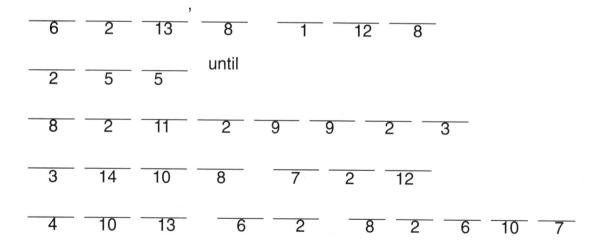

$$\overline{}_{6} \quad \overline{}_{2} \quad \overline{}_{13} \; {}^{,} \quad \overline{}_{8} \qquad \overline{}_{1} \quad \overline{}_{12} \quad \overline{}_{8}$$

$$\overline{}_{2} \quad \overline{}_{5} \quad \overline{}_{5} \qquad \text{until}$$

$$\overline{}_{8} \quad \overline{}_{2} \quad \overline{}_{11} \quad \overline{}_{2} \quad \overline{}_{9} \quad \overline{}_{9} \quad \overline{}_{2} \quad \overline{}_{3}$$

$$\overline{}_{3} \quad \overline{}_{14} \quad \overline{}_{10} \quad \overline{}_{8} \qquad \overline{}_{7} \quad \overline{}_{2} \quad \overline{}_{12}$$

$$\overline{}_{4} \quad \overline{}_{10} \quad \overline{}_{13} \quad \overline{}_{6} \quad \overline{}_{2} \quad \overline{}_{8} \quad \overline{}_{2} \quad \overline{}_{6} \quad \overline{}_{10} \quad \overline{}_{7}$$

Another Puzzling Proverb

Fill in the answers to the following clues. Then, transfer the letters to the corresponding numbered blanks to reveal a famous proverb. (**Note:** Not all of the letters will be used.)

1. Food prepared scrambled or fried

   $\overline{}$ $\overline{}$ $\overline{}$ $\overline{}$
   31 20 4   8

2. To keep out of sight

   $\overline{}$ $\overline{}$ $\overline{}$ $\overline{}$
   2   38 39 23

3. Plural of *this*

   $\overline{}$ $\overline{}$ $\overline{}$ $\overline{}$ $\overline{}$
   29 34 22 7   40

4. Solitary

   $\overline{}$ $\overline{}$ $\overline{}$ $\overline{}$
   10 17 28 25

5. Feeling regret

   $\overline{}$ $\overline{}$ $\overline{}$ $\overline{}$ $\overline{}$
   19 32 36 5   13

6. Australian tree-climbing animal

   $\overline{}$ $\overline{}$ $\overline{}$ $\overline{}$ $\overline{}$
   18 27 6   15 12

7. By preference

   $\overline{}$ $\overline{}$ $\overline{}$ $\overline{}$ $\overline{}$ $\overline{}$
   21 9   1   30 35 26

8. Not old

   $\overline{}$ $\overline{}$ $\overline{}$
   24 3   11

9. To throw without force

   $\overline{}$ $\overline{}$ $\overline{}$ $\overline{}$
   33 16 14 37

$\overline{}$ $\overline{}$ $\overline{}$ $\overline{}$ $\overline{}$ $\overline{}$ $\overline{}$ $\overline{}$
1   2   3   4   5   6   7   8

$\overline{}$ $\overline{}$ $\overline{}$ $\overline{}$ $\overline{}$ $\overline{}$ $\overline{}$ $\overline{}$
38 19   9   10 11 12 13 14

$\overline{}$ $\overline{}$ $\overline{}$ $\overline{}$ $\overline{}$ $\overline{}$ $\overline{}$ $\overline{}$ $\overline{}$
20 21 22 23 24 25 26   27 28

$\overline{}$ $\overline{}$ $\overline{}$ $\overline{}$ $\overline{}$ $\overline{}$ $\overline{}$ $\overline{}$ $\overline{}$ $\overline{}$ $\overline{}$ $\overline{}$
29 30 31   32 33 34 35 36   37 38 39 40

School Days

Acrostics are word puzzles or poems in which the first or last letter of each line forms a word or words. In the example below, the first letters of each line form the words "school days." Complete the acrostic by writing a phrase or sentence on each line that begins with the letter given and relates to the subject "school days."

S _____

C _____

H _____

O _____

O _____

L _____

D _____

A _____

Y _____

S _____

Acrostics

Acrostics are word puzzles or poems in which the first or last letter of each line forms a word or words. The first letters of each line below form the words *recess* and *friends.* Complete the acrostics by writing a phrase or sentence on each line that begins with the letter given and relates to the subjects "recess" or "friends."

R _____

E _____

C _____

E _____

S _____

S _____

F _____

R _____

I _____

E _____

N _____

D _____

S _____

Letter Answers

Use one or two letters of the alphabet to respond to each of the clues. The first one has been done for you.

1. Not difficult   **EZ** _____

2. Cold   _____

3. Goodbye   _____

4. Vegetable   _____

5. Body of water   _____

6. Girl's name   _____

7. Exclamation   _____

8. Organ used for sight _____

9. Pronoun   _____

10. Tent home   _____

11. Plant or vine   _____

12. Question   _____

13. Something to drink   _____

14. Insect   _____

15. Radio announcer   _____

More Letter Answers

Use one, two, or three letters of the alphabet to "spell" a word corresponding to each of the following clues. The first one has been done for you.

1. Used in a pool game   Q

2. Happiness   _____

3. A foe   _____

4. Jealousy   _____

5. A woman's name   _____

6. In debt   _____

7. A written composition   _____

8. What makes a movie exciting   _____

9. A boy's name   _____

10. To say good-bye   _____

11. The number after 79   _____

12. A drink, hot or iced   _____

13. An exclamation   _____

14. To be good at something   _____

15. To rot   _____

Word Winders

Use the clues to help you fill in the blanks and circles. Only the circled letters change from one word to the next.

1. Antonym for hot

2. Pony

3. Stroke of lightning

4. Courageous

5. Without hair

6. Object used in a soccer game

7. Device that rings

8. Item worn around the waist

9. To soften by using heat

10. To shed skin

11. Fine, furry growth of fungi

12. Small, burrowing animal

13. Empty space

14. To hang on to something

15. Yellow metallic element

16. To bend and crease

17. What you eat

18. One who lacks good sense

19. Object used to do work

20. Place to swim

More Word Winders

Use the clues to help you fill in the blanks and circles. Only the circled letters change from one word to the next. The first two have been done for you. (**Note:** When a word has fewer spaces than the word above it, simply drop the letter above the empty space.)

1. Pointed — s h a r (p)

2. A fish that can be dangerous — s h a r (k)

3. To use together — __ __ __ __ ( )

4. To be concerned — __ __ __ ( )

5. A navigator's map — __ __ __ __ ( )

6. To delight — __ __ __ __ ( )

7. Not soft — __ __ __ ( )

8. Synonym for rabbit — __ __ __ ( )

9. Money paid to ride a bus — ( ) __ __ __

10. Land used to raise crops — __ __ __ ( )

11. A signal used to give warning — __ ( ) __ __ __

12. A small songbird — __ __ __ ( )

13. The sound a dog makes — ( ) __ __ __

14. Without light — ( ) __ __ __

15. To have sufficient courage — __ __ ( )

16. A fruit — __ __ ( ) __

17. After the usual time — ( ) __ __ __

18. A bowling alley — __ __ ( ) __

19. A walking stick — ( ) __ __ __

20. A wafer for holding ice cream — __ ( ) __ __

Double Anyone

Use the following clues to find words that contain consecutive double letters, like b**oo**th or sho**pp**ing.

1. An animal _____

2. One of the four seasons _____

3. Sport played in the fall_____

4. High level of understanding_____

5. To draw aimlessly _____

6. Pirate _____

7. Winged insect _____

8. Animal with a long neck _____

9. Person who asks for handouts _____

10. Earth's natural satellite _____

11. Seasoning _____

12. Flock of geese _____

13. Move from side to side _____

14. To take for a period of time _____

15. Grief, sadness _____

16. Poem of fourteen lines _____

17. Paper used in secret voting_____

18. Great work of literature _____

Word Chain

Use the last two letters of the previous words in the word chain to begin the next word. Continue throughout the chain. The first two have been done for you.

1. To bite repeatedly   ch<u>ew</u>

2. A female sheep   <u>ew</u>e

3. An undesirable in the garden _____

4. Wholesome to eat _____

5. A character in the alphabet _____

6. To rub out _____

7. A division of the year _____

8. One time _____

9. To observe some special occasion _____

10. A message transmitted by telegraph _____

11. A word for love _____

12. One of the planets _____

13. Ordinary _____

14. To permit _____

15. An animal that hoots _____

Who Can This Be?

Fill in the blanks to complete the five letter words. When read from top to bottom, the word made by the center letters will spell the name of a famous U.S. personality. The first one has been done for you.

1.
```
C  H  A  N  T
F  A  D  E  S
C  L  A  M  P
G  A  M  E  S
W  I  S  E  R
```

2.
```
F  I  __  T  Y
B  L  __  W  S
C  U  __  L  Y
W  I  __  E  R
```

3.
```
B  O  __  B  S
C  R  __  M  P
B  A  __  L  Y
W  H  __  L  E
L  O  __  E  R
C  R  __  S  S
W  I  __  K  S
```

4.
```
P  A  __  E  S
C  R  __  F  Y
P  A  __  T  Y
F  I  __  T  Y
D  R  __  N  K
F  L  __  S  H
B  U  __  L  H
W  I  __  E  N
```

5.
```
M  A  __  O  R
C  H  __  W  S
J  I  __  F  Y
R  A  __  T  S
S  H  __  L  S
B  A  __  K  L
B  A  __  K  S
C  H  __  R  E
C  A  __  D  Y
```

6.
```
C  L  __  A  N
C  L  __  M  B
D  U  __  T  Y
G  U  __  A  Y
G  O  __  E  R
A  S  __  E  R
S  T  __  N  S
T  O  __  E  R
C  H  __  A  T
D  I  __  T  Y
```

7.
```
C  L  __  M  P
B  I  __  T  H
C  O  __  B  S
M  U  __  T  S
G  U  __  S  Y
F  O  __  C  Y
C  H  __  K  E
F  I  __  A  L
A  N  __  E  R
```

8.
```
S  E  __  E  N
D  R  __  A  D
T  A  __  T  E
P  A  __  E  R
B  R  __  S  H
P  I  __  K  S
K  I  __  K  S
B  L  __  M  P
```

9.
```
P  L  __  A  D
M  A  __  A  M
S  H  __  R  T
P  A  __  T  E
C  L  __  C  K
D  A  __  C  E
```

10.
```
D  R  __  S  S
P  L  __  N  T
P  A  __  T  Y
O  T  __  E  R
G  L  __  S  R
T  H  __  E  S
W  I  __  C  H
```

Competitive Word Chain

To play, two or more players start at the same time. The object is to fill in all the blanks with a three-, four-, or five-letter word, depending on the number of blanks given. Each word must begin with the last letter of the preceding word. The first word may start with any letter. (Words may not be repeated.) The first player to complete all the words wins.

1. ____ ____ ____

2. ____ ____ ____ ____

3. ____ ____ ____ ____ ____

4. ____ ____ ____ ____ ____

5. ____ ____ ____

6. ____ ____ ____ ____

7. ____ ____ ____ ____ ____

8. ____ ____ ____ ____

9. ____ ____ ____

10. ____ ____ ____ ____ ____

11. ____ ____ ____ ____

12. ____ ____ ____ ____

13. ____ ____ ____

14. ____ ____ ____ ____

15. ____ ____ ____ ____ ____

16. ____ ____ ____ ____

17. ____ ____ ____ ____

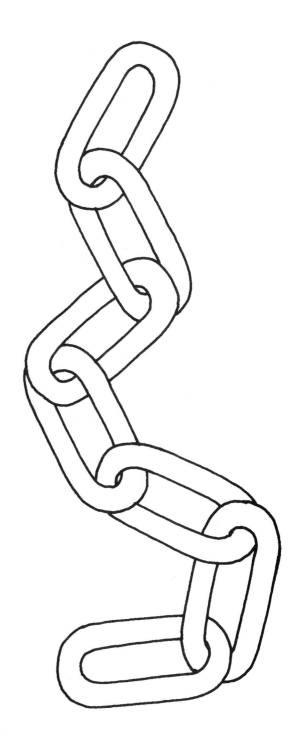

#3670 Brain Games

Another Competitive Word Chain

Two or more players begin at the same time to fill in all the blanks with a three-, four-, five-, or six-letter word, depending on the number of blanks given. Each word must begin with the last letter of the preceding word. The first word may start with any letter. (Words may not be repeated.) The first player to complete all the words wins.

1. _____ _____ _____
2. _____ _____ _____ _____
3. _____ _____ _____ _____
4. _____ _____ _____ _____ _____
5. _____ _____ _____
6. _____ _____ _____ _____
7. _____ _____ _____ _____
8. _____ _____ _____ _____ _____
9. _____ _____ _____ _____
10. _____ _____ _____
11. _____ _____ _____ _____
12. _____ _____ _____ _____
13. _____ _____ _____
14. _____ _____ _____ _____
15. _____ _____ _____ _____ _____
16. _____ _____ _____ _____
17. _____ _____ _____
18. _____ _____ _____ _____
19. _____ _____ _____ _____ _____
20. _____ _____ _____ _____
21. _____ _____ _____

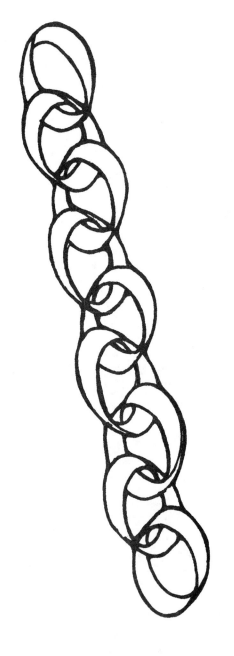

Get the Message

The telegraph was one of the greatest inventions of the mid-nineteenth century. It was invented in 1838 by Samuel F.B. Morse. He devised a code using a series of "dots" and "dashes" that represented the letters of the alphabet. Messages were tapped out on a telegraph key that made clicking sounds. A dot would be a short click and a dash would be a longer click. Messages would be carried electrically to another key where a second operator would translate the message back into English and write it down on paper.

Directions: Use the following code to change the words below into Morse Code. (You may find slight variations from other codes.) You may also wish to use the Morse Code to send messages back and forth to friends.

A	• —	J	• — — —	S	• • •	2	• • — — —
B	— • • •	K	— • —	T	—	3	• • • — —
C	— • — •	L	• — • •	U	• • —	4	• • • • —
D	— • •	M	— —	V	• • • —	5	• • • • •
E	•	N	— •	W	• — —	6	— • • • •
F	• • — •	O	— — —	X	— • • —	7	— — • • •
G	— — •	P	• — — •	Y	— • — —	8	— — — • •
H	• • • •	Q	— — • —	Z	— — • •	9	— — — — •
I	• •	R	• — •	1	• — — — —	0	— — — — —

S _____

A _____

M _____

U _____

E _____

L _____

F. _____

B. _____

M _____

O _____

R _____

S _____

E _____

T _____

H _____

O _____

M _____

A _____

S _____

A _____

L _____

V _____

A _____

E _____

D _____

I _____

S _____

O _____

N _____

E _____

L _____

E _____

C _____

T _____

R _____

I _____

C _____

I _____

T _____

Y _____

T _____

E _____

L _____

E _____

G _____

R _____

A _____

P _____

H _____

Unfinished Sayings

Use the code in the box below to complete each of the following sayings.

A	B	C	D	E	F	G	H	I	J	K	L	M
22	5	14	18	7	20	3	19	16	24	1	10	17

N	O	P	Q	R	S	T	U	V	W	X	Y	Z
4	26	12	23	2	21	8	11	15	6	25	9	13

1. Don't throw stones at your neighbors' house, if your own
   __ __ __ __ __ __ __ are glass.
   6 16 4 18 26 6 21

2. Make __ __ __ __ __ slowly.
   19 22 21 8 7

3. Beware of little __ __ __ __ __ __ __ __ , a small leak will sink a great
   ship. 7 25 12 7 4 21 7 21

4. Fish and __ __ __ __ __ __ __ __ stink in three days.
   15 16 21 16 8 26 2 21

5. A good __ __ __ __ __ __ __ is the best sermon.
   7 25 22 17 12 10 7

6. Men and __ __ __ __ __ __ are hard to know.
   17 7 10 26 4 21

7. Lend money to an __ __ __ __ __ , and thou'lt gain him, to a
   7 4 7 17 9

   __ __ __ __ __ __ and thou'lt lose him.
   20 2 16 7 4 18

8. Three may keep a __ __ __ __ __ __ if two of them are dead.
   21 7 14 2 7 8

9. Tart words make no friends; a spoonful of honey will catch more flies than a gallon of
   __ __ __ __ __ __ __ .
   15 16 4 7 3 22 2

The words and terms used by printers today would probably confuse and amaze Johann Gutenberg. See if you can figure out the terms described in each sentence below by using the code in the box. Write your answers on the lines at the beginning of each sentence.

A	B	C	D	E	F	G	H	I	J	K	L	M
3	6	9	12	15	18	21	24	27	30	33	36	39

N	O	P	Q	R	S	T	U	V	W	X	Y	Z
38	37	35	34	32	31	29	28	26	25	23	22	20

1. A ___ ___ ___ ___ ___ ___ is a large dot used at the beginning of a sentence or
     6   28   36   36   15   29
group of words to help set it off from the rest of the text.

2. Letters that slant to the right are called ___ ___ ___ ___ ___ ___ ___ .
     27   29   3   36   27   9   31

3. ___ ___ ___ ___ ___ refers to the type of paper used.
  31 29 37 9 33

4. A short line of type is called a ___ ___ ___ ___ ___ .
     25 27 12 37 25

5. The ___ ___ ___ ___ consists of the written words that will be set into type.
    9 37 35 22

6. Printers sometimes use ___ ___ ___ ___ ___ ___ ___ ___ or typographic
     12 27 38 21 6 3 29 31
decorations to dress up the pages and make text more appealing to the eye.

7. Small rough sketches are known as ___ ___ ___ ___ ___ ___ ___ ___ ___ .
           29 24 28 39 6 38 3 27 36 31

8. A ___ ___ ___ ___ ___ is the arrangement of the layout of a page.
    12 28 39 39 22

9. The ___ ___ ___ ___ ___ is the page number.
    18 37 36 27 37

10. Individual letters and numerals are called
___ ___ ___ ___ ___ ___ ___ ___ ___ ___ .
 9 24 3 32 3 9 29 15 32 31

         #3670 Brain Games

All Alike

Read the words on each line. Explain how they are alike. An example has been done for you.

Duck, chicken, goose = poultry

1. East, west, south _____

2. Niece, daughter, grandma _____

3. One, nine, fifteen _____

4. Gorgeous, glamorous, beautiful _____

5. North America, South America, Australia _____

6. April, November, June _____

7. California, Illinois, Georgia _____

8. Armstrong, Aldrin, Loveall _____

9. Phil, Paul, Peter _____

10. Saturn, Jupiter, Earth _____

11. Rose, carnation, peony _____

12. Triangle, tripod, tricycle _____

13. Sneezy, Doc, Grumpy _____

14. Red, yellow, blue _____

15. Almanac, thesaurus, dictionary _____

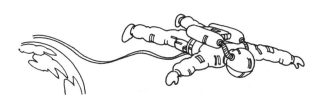

More All Alike

Read the words on each line. Explain how they are alike. An example has been done for you.

North, South, East = cardinal directions

1. Ash, pine, sycamore _____

2. Football, baseball, hockey _____

3. London, Paris, Madrid _____

4. Cougar, lion, panther _____

5. Cake, ice cream, pie _____

6. Saw, hammer, screwdriver _____

7. Angry, sad, happy _____

8. Dragons, unicorns, mermaids _____

9. Hamburger, milk, butter _____

10. Alone, single, solo _____

11. Orange, basketball, marble _____

12. Bicycle, train, car _____

13. Corn, asparagus, squash _____

14. Baby Ruth, Almond Joy, Snickers _____

15. Carol, Cathy, Casie _____

Things With Holes

Brainstorm a list of things with holes. Can you think of at least twenty?

_____   _____

_____   _____

_____   _____

_____   _____

_____   _____

_____   _____

_____   _____

_____   _____

_____   _____

_____   _____

Use the other side of the paper if you can come up with more than 20.

Things With Stripes

Brainstorm a list of things with stripes. Can you think of least 20?

1. _____

2. _____

3. _____

4. _____

5. _____

6. _____

7. _____

8. _____

9. _____

10. _____

11. _____

12. _____

13. _____

14. _____

15. _____

16. _____

17. _____

18. _____

19. _____

20. _____

Use the other side of the paper if you can come up with more than 20.

Things With Spots

Brainstorm a list of things with spots. Can you think of at least twenty?

1. _____
2. _____
3. _____
4. _____
5. _____
6. _____
7. _____
8. _____
9. _____
10. _____
11. _____
12. _____
13. _____
14. _____
15. _____
16. _____
17. _____
18. _____
19. _____
20. _____

Use the other side of the paper if you can come up with more than 20.

Things To Do With a Brick

Brainstorm a list of things you could do with a brick. Can you think of at least twenty?

1. _____
2. _____
3. _____
4. _____
5. _____
6. _____
7. _____
8. _____
9. _____
10. _____
11. _____
12. _____
13. _____
14. _____
15. _____
16. _____
17. _____
18. _____
19. _____
20. _____

Use the other side of the paper if you can come up with more than 20.

Summertime

List words related to summertime that begin with each letter of the alphabet.

A _____

B _____

C _____

D _____

E _____

F _____

G _____

H _____

I _____

J _____

K _____

L _____

M _____

N _____

O _____

P _____

Q _____

R _____

S _____

T _____

U _____

V _____

W _____

X _____

Y _____

Z _____

Name Three of Each

Write three words that belong in each category named below.

1. Things on your face _____

2. Things that come in pairs _____

3. Things found in your mom's purse _____

4. Palindromes _____

5. Things that float _____

6. Fairy tale characters _____

7. Sports _____

8. Vegetables _____

9. Things with stripes _____

10. Authors _____

11. Toys _____

12. Things to keep you warm _____

13. Colors _____

14. Kinds of dogs _____

15. Places people live _____

16. Bodies of water _____

17. Snack foods _____

18. Farm animals _____

More "Three of Each"

Name three items that belong to each category.

1. Places animals live _____

2. Things that are green _____

3. Things with stripes _____

4. Book characters _____

5. Kinds of candy _____

6. Mammals that live in the water _____

7. Things in dozens _____

8. Things you drink _____

9. Things on your body _____

10. Authors' names _____

11. Things that float _____

12. Shades of colors _____

13. Things that give off light _____

14. Kinds of houses in which people live _____

15. Provinces in Canada _____

Even More "Three of Each"

Name three items that belong to each category.

1. Works of Shakespeare_____

2. Kinds of dances _____

3. Things to collect_____

4. Authors of science fiction_____

5. Parts of a book_____

6. Metamorphic rocks_____

7. Things that are black _____

8. Ingredients for cookies_____

9. Things with holes _____

10. Professional women in sports _____

11. Kinds of hats _____

12. Inventors _____

13. Things to celebrate _____

14. Phobias _____

15. Things to read _____

16. Sports equipment_____

17. Pieces of furniture _____

18. Things that are small _____

19. Countries in Africa _____

20. Cities in Canada _____

515   *#3670 Brain Games*

Grandparent's Day

There are at least 50 words (of 3 letters or more) hidden in the words "Grandparent's Day." Can you find them? If you run out of room, use the back side of this page.

1. _____
2. _____
3. _____
4. _____
5. _____
6. _____
7. _____
8. _____
9. _____
10. _____
11. _____
12. _____
13. _____
14. _____
15. _____
16. _____
17. _____
18. _____
19. _____
20. _____
21. _____
22. _____
23. _____
24. _____
25. _____
26. _____
27. _____
28. _____
29. _____
30. _____
31. _____
32. _____
33. _____
34. _____
35. _____
36. _____
37. _____
38. _____
39. _____
40. _____
41. _____
42. _____
43. _____
44. _____
45. _____
46. _____
47. _____
48. _____
49. _____
50. _____

Four-Letter Words

Below are listed the middle letters of some four-letter words. Fill in the blanks to make four-letter words.

____ a n __   ____ i d __

____ e a __   ____ o v __

____ a r __   ____ a i __

____ e l __   ____ a m

____ o a __   ____ f a __

____ i k __   ____ a v __

____ o l __   ____ o r __

____ a r __   ____ v e __

____ o u __   ____ y p __

____ o o __   ____ a s __

Here are the initial and final letters of some four-letter words. Fill in the blanks to make four-letter words.

c ____ ____ t   b ____ ____ d

s ____ ____ t   m ____ ____ t

d ____ ____ e   t ____ ____ e

r ____ ____ n   p ____ ____ t

l ____ ____ d   b ____ ____ t

f ____ ____ d   h ____ ____ e

s ____ ____ d   d ____ ____ r

s ____ ____ r   e ____ ____ n

a ____ ____ e   g ____ ____ e

h ____ ____ t   m ____ ____ t

Double Letters

Each word or phrase below is a clue for a word that contains consecutive double letters.

1. Someone who tosses trash in public areas _____

2. Greeting _____

3. Joyful _____

4. To eat hurriedly _____

5. Not easy _____

6. Small pool of water _____

7. Awful _____

8. Duck _____

9. Farewell _____

10. Large monkey _____

11. Cushion for the head _____

12. To talk a lot and quickly _____

13. Opposite of defense _____

14. Elk _____

15. Designation where an envelope should be sent _____

More Double Letters

Use the following clues to find words that contain consecutive double letters.

1. A favorable set of circumstances _____

2. To see or view _____

3. A storm with wind and snow _____

4. Mental ability _____

5. Not guilty _____

6. To move with short, quick movements; squirm _____

7. A space with nothing in it, not even air _____

8. One who expects bad things to happen _____

9. To use or acquire temporarily _____

10. A sport in which touchdowns are scored _____

11. Part of a word pronounced as a unit _____

12. A sale of goods to raise funds, especially for charity _____

13. To make something seem larger or better than it is _____

14. A long, tapering flag _____

15. Time after midday _____

Begin and End

Each phrase below is a clue for an answer that begins and ends with the same letter.

1. Child's sidewalk game_____

2. A continent _____

3. Songs sung alone _____

4. A majestic bird_____

5. A type of drum_____

6. Rudolph _____

7. One of the sense organs_____

8. A common man's name _____

9. To quiet down _____

10. Blue-green color _____

11. A young bird's noise _____

12. Midday_____

13. Old-fashioned type of margarine_____

14. The hardest mineral _____

15. The day before today _____

Beginning and End

Each of the following clues has an answer in which the first letter is the same as the last letter.

1. Loss of memory _____

2. The fireplace floor _____

3. A type of bird _____

4. A type of boat _____

5. A province in Canada _____

6. Opposite of minimum _____

7. One who is vacationing _____

8. The act or words of welcoming someone _____

9. To regain health after an illness _____

10. The most abundant gas in the atmosphere _____

11. To roll about _____

12. Having made twice as much _____

13. To rub out _____

14. A gas used in lighted signs _____

Begin and End Once More

Each phrase below is a clue for an answer that begins and ends with the same letter.

1. A continent at the south pole _____

2. Payment to stockholders_____

3. A word used by magicians _____

4. Physical exertion done for fitness _____

5. One television show in a series _____

6. One who reviews and gives judgements _____

7. A brief advertisement _____

8. A place for performers_____

9. An amount over and above what is needed _____

10. A great work of art or literature _____

11. A ray of moonlight_____

12. An edible seed of a bean plant _____

13. Accepting of others _____

14. Handwriting skill _____

15. Anxiety_____

16. An official list of names _____

17. One thousand years _____

Animals, Animals, Everywhere

Using the letters of the alphabet, A through Z, brainstorm a list of animals. Then, try to start a second list.

A _____

B _____

C _____

D _____

E _____

F _____

G _____

H _____

I _____

J _____

K _____

L _____

M _____

N _____

O _____

P _____

Q _____

R _____

S _____

T _____

U _____

V _____

W _____

X _____

Y _____

Z _____

ABCDEFG

How many words can you spell using only the first seven letters of the alphabet?
The letters may be used more than one time within a word.

_____   _____

_____   _____

_____   _____

_____   _____

_____   _____

_____   _____

_____   _____

_____   _____

_____   _____

_____   _____

_____   _____

Back to School

List words related to school that begin with each letter of the alphabet. Then try to start a second list.

A _____

B _____

C _____

D _____

E _____

F _____

G _____

H _____

I _____

J _____

K _____

L _____

M _____

N _____

O _____

P _____

Q _____

R _____

S _____

T _____

U _____

V _____

W _____

X _____

Y _____

Z _____

Two of a Kind

Make a list of words that contain two of one letter of the alphabet. Examples include *aardvark, baby, cartoon,* and *dawdle.*

_____   _____

_____   _____

_____   _____

_____   _____

_____   _____

_____   _____

_____   _____

_____   _____

_____   _____

_____   _____

_____   _____

_____   _____

_____   _____

_____   _____

_____   _____

_____   _____

_____   _____

More Two of a Kind

Make a list of words that contain two of each letter. For example, for "A" you might write *Asia* or *anteater*.

A _____

B _____

C _____

D _____

E _____

F _____

G _____

H _____

I _____

J _____

K _____

L _____

M _____

N _____

O _____

P _____

Q _____

R _____

S _____

T _____

U _____

V _____

W _____

X _____

Y _____

Z _____

Education

List all the words you can make from the letters in the word "education". (**Note:** All the words in your list must have at least three letters, and each letter can be used only once in each word.)

_____   _____

_____   _____

_____   _____

_____   _____

_____   _____

_____   _____

_____   _____

_____   _____

_____   _____

_____   _____

_____   _____

_____   _____

_____   _____

_____   _____

_____   _____

_____   _____

_____   _____

Encyclopedia

List all the words you can make from the letters in the word "encyclopedia." All the words in your list must have at least three letters, and each letter in the word can be used only once in each word.

_____   _____

_____   _____

_____   _____

_____   _____

_____   _____

_____   _____

_____   _____

_____   _____

_____   _____

_____   _____

_____   _____

_____   _____

_____   _____

_____   _____

_____   _____

_____   _____

_____   _____

I Am Terrific

List all the words you can make from the letters in the phrase "I am terrific." All the words in your list must have at least three letters, and each letter can be used only once in each word for each time it appears in the original phrase.

_____   _____   _____

_____   _____   _____

_____   _____   _____

_____   _____   _____

_____   _____   _____

_____   _____   _____

_____   _____   _____

_____   _____   _____

_____   _____   _____

_____   _____   _____

_____   _____   _____

_____   _____   _____

_____   _____   _____

_____   _____   _____

_____   _____   _____

All Five Vowels

Make a list of words that contain these vowel combinations within them. (**Note:** The vowels can appear in any order within the word.)

Example: AE <u>seat</u>

AE

_____
_____
_____
_____
_____
_____

EU

_____
_____
_____
_____
_____
_____

AEI

_____
_____
_____
_____
_____
_____

AIO

_____
_____
_____
_____
_____
_____

EIO

_____
_____
_____
_____
_____
_____

IOU

_____
_____
_____
_____
_____
_____

EOU

_____
_____
_____
_____
_____
_____

AEOU

_____
_____
_____
_____
_____
_____

EIOU

_____
_____
_____
_____
_____
_____

Challenge: Try finding three words that each contain all five vowels.

_____   _____   _____

Complete a Word

Use the twenty-six letters of the alphabet to complete the words below. Use each letter only one time. (Cross off the letters as you use them.)

A B C D E F G H I J K L M N O P Q R S T U V W X Y Z

1. ___ A ___ Z

2. ___ U I E ___

3. ___ U ___ C A

4. E ___ T R ___

5. ___ I O ___ ___ N

6. ___ A ___ ___ F U L

7. ___ R O ___ ___

8. ___ E ___ ___ A T

9. ___ ___ A L A

10. ___ O L A ___

11. ___ O R C ___ P I N E

Complete a Word II

Use the twenty-six letters of the alphabet to complete the words below. Use each letter only one time. (Cross off the letters as you use them.)

A B C D E F G H I J K L M N O P Q R S T U V W X Y Z

1. __ O __ E L

2. __ A __ K __ A R D

3. __ N C __ E

4. __ __ U I __ T

5. R E __ U __ N

6. __ O __ __ E R

7. __ A C __ __ L

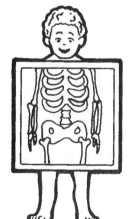

8. __ R A __

9. __ __ I C E

10. R E L __ __ __

11. __ O O M

Animal, Vegetable, or Mineral

Without using a dictionary, how many words can you list to complete the chart below? Each word must begin with the letter of the alphabet given. There are many different answers for some, but not all spaces have an answer.

	Animals	Vegetables	Minerals
A			
B			
C			
D			
E			
F			
G			
H			
I			
J			
K			
L			
M			
N			
O			
P			
Q			
R			
S			
T			
U			
V			
W			
X			
Y			
Z			

Another A to Z

How many words can you spell by using the letters given and filling in the other blanks?

a	—	—	—	—
—	b	—	—	—
—	—	c	—	—
—	—	—	d	—
—	—	—	—	e
—	—	—	f	—
—	—	g	—	—
—	h	—	—	—
i	—	—	—	—
—	j	—	—	—
—	—	k	—	—
—	—	—	l	—
—	—	—	—	m
—	—	—	n	—
—	—	o	—	—
—	p	—	—	—
q	—	—	—	—
—	r	—	—	—
—	—	s	—	—
—	—	—	t	—
—	—	—	—	u
—	—	—	v	—
—	—	w	—	—
—	x	—	—	—
y	—	—	—	—
—	z	—	—	—

—	—	—	—	a
—	—	—	b	—
—	—	c	—	—
—	d	—	—	—
e	—	—	—	—
—	f	—	—	—
—	—	g	—	—
—	—	—	h	—
—	—	—	—	i
—	—	—	j	—
—	—	k	—	—
—	l	—	—	—
m	—	—	—	—
—	n	—	—	—
—	—	o	—	—
—	—	—	p	—
—	—	—	—	q
—	—	—	r	—
—	—	s	—	—
—	t	—	—	—
u	—	—	—	—
—	v	—	—	—
—	—	w	—	—
—	—	—	x	—
—	—	—	—	y
—	—	—	z	—

What Is It?

Check the correct box for each location on the chart.

	City	State/Province	Country	Continent
1. Mexico				
2. Montreal				
3. Lima				
4. Africa				
5. Reno				
6. North America				
7. Alberta				
8. Germany				
9. Toronto				
10. Oklahoma				
11. Europe				
12. Los Angeles				
13. Switzerland				
14. Illinois				
15. Australia				
16. Canada				
17. Asia				
18. Budapest				
19. Maine				
20. Italy				

Where In the United States?

Use the letters in the words "United States" to write the answers to the following clues.

1. To make fun of in a playful or unkind way _____

2. To rise to one's feet _____

3. A female relative _____

4. To be in want of _____

5. To be present at _____

6. Five plus five _____

7. An exam _____

8. Earth's source of energy _____

9. Past tense of eat _____

10. To sample a food _____

11. Tiny grains on the beach _____

12. A body of water _____

13. To join together _____

14. A lodging for campers _____

15. The home of a lion _____

16. A large sea fish _____

17. When the sun goes down _____

18. A place to sit _____

19. A melody _____

20. To finish _____

Country and City Match

Match the cities to their countries.

1. Chicago _____

2. Paris _____

3. Tokyo _____

4. Buenos Aires _____

5. Lima _____

6. Johannesburg_____

7. Marrakech _____

8. Rome _____

9. Quebec _____

10. Lagos _____

11. Hanoi _____

12. Sydney _____

13. Christchurch _____

14. Moscow _____

15. Peking_____

16. London _____

17. Stockholm _____

18. Berlin _____

19. New Delhi _____

20. Guadalajara _____

Country Box
Argentina
Australia
Canada
China
England
France
Germany
India
Italy
Japan
Mexico
Morocco
New Zealand
Nigeria
Peru
Russia
South Africa
Sweden
United States
Vietnam

Continent Match

List the countries from the Country Box under the correct continent.

North America

South America

Europe

Asia

Africa

Country Box

Argentina
Austria
Bahamas
Belgium
Bolivia
Brazil
Canada
Chile
China
Columbia
Congo
Costa Rica
Cuba
Denmark
Ecuador
Egypt
France
Germany
Ghana
Greece
Guatemala
India
Israel
Italy
Ivory Coast
Jamaica
Japan
Lebanon
Liberia
Mexico
Morocco
Nepal
Nicaragua
Nigeria
Norway
Pakistan
Panama
Paraguay
Peru
Philippines
Portugal
Somalia
Swaziland
Sweden
Thailand
Turkey
United States
Uruguay
Venezuela
Zambia

Name the Countries

Name the countries in which you would find the following cities and geographical features.

1. Lake Vänern, Stockholm, Dal River _____

2. Buenos Aires, Parana River, Pampas _____

3. Toronto, Victoria Island, Rocky Mountains _____

4. Cape Town, Drakensberg Mountains, Johannesburg _____

5. Vienna, Danube River, Alps _____

6. Madrid, Barcelona, Iberian Mountains _____

7. Amazon River, the rain forest, Rio de Janeiro _____

8. Wicklow Mountains, Limerick, Dublin _____

9. Yangtze River, Beijing, Kunlun Mountains _____

10. Thames River, Edinburgh, London _____

11. Ganges River, Deccan Plateau, New Delhi _____

12. St. Petersburg, Ural Mountains, Moscow _____

13. Baja California, Rio Grande, Acapulco _____

14. Osaka, Hiroshima, Mount Fuji _____

15. Hamburg, Black Forest, Danube River _____

16. Rome, Mount Vesuvius, Naples _____

17. Rabat, Atlas Mountains, Casablanca _____

18. Sydney, Melbourne, Great Victoria Desert _____

19. Alps, Paris, Marseille _____

20. Nile River, Suez Canal, Cairo _____

This Map Is Making Me Hungry!

Many foods are named for the place where they were first made. Other foods share their names with places in the world. Read the following clues to help find the location of these yummy place names.

1. It is a kind of mustard and a city of Europe.

   Where do you go to find Dijon? _____

2. It is a kind of sandwich and a city of Europe.

   Where do you go to find Hamburg? _____

3. It is a pepper sauce and a state in North America.

   Where do you go to find Tabasco? _____

4. It is a red wine and a city in Western Europe.

   Where do you go to find Bordeaux? _____

5. It is a cold cut and a city in Europe.

   Where do you go to find Bologna? _____

6. They are two kinds of cheese and two cities in Europe.

   Where do you go to find Gouda and Edam? _____

7. It is a kind of orange and cities in Europe and the U.S.A. are named for it.

   Where do you go to find Valencia? _____

8. An American might call it a hot dog, and it is a city in Europe.

   Where do you go to find Frankfurt? _____

9. It is a brand of chocolate and a city in the U.S.A.

   Where do you go to find Hershey? _____

10. It is a cheese and a village in Europe.

    Where do you go to find Cheddar? _____

11. It is a hot southwestern dish and a country.

    Where do you go to find Chile? _____

12. It is two slices of bread with ham, cheese, etc., in the middle and a borough in Europe.

    Where do you go to find Sandwich? _____

13. It is a citrus fruit and a city in Western Europe.

    Where do you go to find Orange? _____

14. It is usually part of the Thanksgiving feast and also a country.

    Where do you go to find Turkey? _____

15. It is a kind of steak and a plain in Europe.

    Where do you go to find Salisbury? _____

North America In ABC Order

Picture yourself on the continent of North America. Look around. What do you see? Think of at least one sight you might see for each letter of the alphabet and list your ideas below. (**Hint:** Think of the different land areas, man-made structures, animals and people.)

A _____

B _____

C _____

D _____

E _____

F _____

G _____

H _____

I _____

J _____

K _____

L _____

M _____

N _____

O _____

P _____

Q _____

R _____

S _____

T _____

U _____

V _____

W _____

X _____

Y _____

Z _____

Europe In ABC Order

Picture yourself on the continent of Europe. Look around. What do you see? Think of at least one sight you might see for each letter of the alphabet and list your ideas below. (**Hint:** Think of the different land areas, man-made structures, animals and people.)

A _____

B _____

C _____

D _____

E _____

F _____

G _____

H _____

I _____

J _____

K _____

L _____

M _____

N _____

O _____

P _____

Q _____

R _____

S _____

T _____

U _____

V _____

W _____

X _____

Y _____

Z _____

The World In ABC Order

In the first column, list a country of the world for each letter of the alphabet. In the second column, write the name of the continent in which the country is located.

Country	Continent
A _____	_____
B _____	_____
C _____	_____
D _____	_____
E _____	_____
F _____	_____
G _____	_____
H _____	_____
I _____	_____
J _____	_____
K _____	_____
L _____	_____
M _____	_____
N _____	_____
O _____	_____
P _____	_____
Q _____	_____
R _____	_____
S _____	_____
T _____	_____
U _____	_____
V _____	_____
W _____	_____
X _____	_____
Y _____	_____
Z _____	_____

Web Sites of the U.S.A.

If each state of the U.S.A. had a Web site on the Internet, what might its address be? Some states might want to use the name of a national park located within its boundaries as an address. Read the following addresses and think of the state that might list it as an address. (**Note:** These are not actual sites!)

1. www.grandcanyon.geo _____

2. www.grandteton.geo _____

3. www.bigbend.geo _____

4. www.rockymountain.geo _____

5. www.mammothcave.geo _____

6. www.craterlake.geo _____

7. www.everglades.geo _____

8. www.glacierbay.geo _____

9. www.yosemite.geo _____

10. www.hotsprings.geo _____

11. www.haleakala.geo _____

12. www.mountrainier.geo _____

13. www.windcave.geo _____

14. www.shenandoah.geo _____

15. www.carlsbadcaverns.geo _____

Write your own Web site addresses for a state in the U.S.A.:

_____   _____

Web Site of North America

The three largest countries in North America are Canada, the United States and Mexico. Each of these countries has several states. A Web site has been created for each state, using its capital city as the address. Decode the following addresses to find the state and country. (**Note:** These are not actual sites!)

	State/Province	Country
1. www.winnipeg.geo		
2. www.carsoncity.geo		
3. www.albany.geo		
4. www.batonrouge.geo		
5. www.helena.geo		
6. www.raleigh.geo		
7. www.edmonton.geo		
8. www.juneau.geo		
9. www.austin.geo		
10. www.hermosillo.geo		
11. www.salem.geo		
12. www.toronto.geo		
13. www.santafe.geo		
14. www.durango.geo		
15. www.augusta.geo		
16. www.monterrey.geo		
17. www.victoria.geo		
18. www.sacramento.geo		
19. www.concord.geo		
20. www.ciudadvictoria.geo		

Write your own North American Web site addresses:

_____   _____

Web Sites of Australiasia

Australia, New Guinea, New Zealand, and other nearby islands make up the area known as Australasia. If each of the states, countries, and territories of Australasia had a Web site on the Internet, what would the addresses be? Read each address and find out what state or territory might list itself in this way. (**Note:** These are not actual sites!)

1. www.adelaide.geo _____

2. www.portmoresby.geo _____

3. www.brisbane.geo _____

4. www.canberra.geo _____

5. www.wellington.geo _____

6. www.perth.geo _____

7. www.jakarta.geo _____

8. www.hobart.geo _____

9. www.darwin.geo _____

10. www.kualalumpur.geo _____

11. www.sydney.geo _____

12. www.melbourne.geo _____

Write your own Australasian Web site addresses:

_____   _____

Web Sites of Africa

If each country of Africa had a Web site on the Internet, what might its address be? Read each address and find the country that might list itself in this way. (**Note:** These are not actual sites!)

1. www.cairo.geo _____

2. www.kinshasa.geo _____

3. www.bamako.geo _____

4. www.capetown.geo _____

5. www.yamoussoukro.geo _____

6. www.ndjamena.geo _____

7. www.luanda.geo _____

8. www.addisababa.geo _____

9. www.tripoli.geo _____

10. www.lusaka.geo _____

11. www.freetown.geo _____

12. www.rabat.geo _____

13. www.antananarivo.geo _____

14. www.kampala.geo _____

15. www.lome.geo _____

Write your own African Web site addresses:

_____   _____

Web Sites of South America

If each country of South America had its own Web site, what would it be? Match the name of the country, island, or dependency of South America that goes with each of the following Web site addresses. (**Note:** These are not actual sites!)

1. www.quito.geo _____

2. www.brasília.geo _____

3. www.georgetown.geo _____

4. www.buenosaires.geo _____

5. www.cayenne.geo _____

6. www.santiago.geo _____

7. www.bogota.geo _____

8. www.asuncion.geo _____

9. www.lima.geo _____

10. www.montevideo.geo _____

11. www.paramaribo.geo _____

12. www.caracas.geo _____

13. www.portofspain.geo _____

14. www.lapaz.geo _____

15. www.stanley.geo _____

Write your own South American web site addresses:

_____   _____

Web Sites of Asia

If each country in Asia had a Web site on the Internet, what might its address be? Read each address and find out what country might list itself in this way. (**Note:** These are not actual sites!)

1. www.bangkok.geo _____

2. www.ulanbator.geo _____

3. www.riyadh.geo _____

4. www.islamabad.geo _____

5. www.dhaka.geo _____

6. www.beijing.geo _____

7. www.seoul.geo _____

8. www.tehran.geo _____

9. www.jerusalem.geo _____

10. www.hanoi.geo _____

11. www.newdelhi.geo _____

12. www.tokyo.geo _____

13. www.amman.geo _____

14. www.ankara.geo _____

15. www.damascus.geo _____

Write your own Asian Web site addresses:

_____   _____

Web Sites of Europe

If each major city in Europe had a Web site on the Internet, what might its address be? Read each address and find the country that might list its famous sites in this way. (**Note:** These are not actual sites!)

1. www.eiffel.geo _____

2. www.bigben.geo _____

3. www.bullfight.geo _____

4. www.parthenon.geo _____

5. www.redsquare.geo _____

6. www.dutch.geo _____

7. www.pizza.geo _____

8. www.alps.geo _____

9. www.blarneystone.geo _____

10. www.mozart.geo _____

11. www.fjord.geo _____

12. www.kilt.geo _____

13. www.grimms.geo _____

14. www.midnightsun.geo _____

15. www.nato.geo _____

Write your own European Web site addresses:

_____   _____

Geography Scramblers

Unscramble these letters to write geography words.

1. crifaA _____

2. thaweer _____

3. virre _____

4. urterapmeet _____

5. catantAric _____

6. heheripsem _____

7. wodame _____

8. totganeevi _____

9. yerGman _____

10. noonsom _____

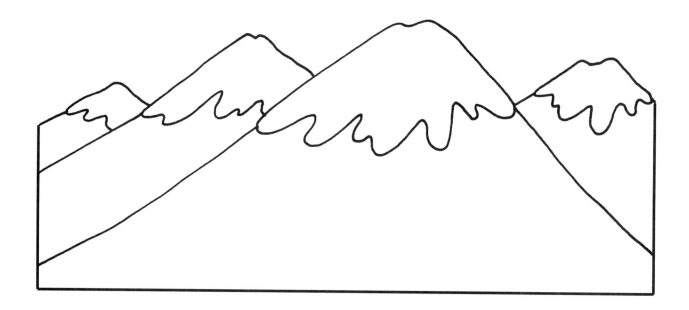

Geography Clues

Using the clues, fill in the spaces to write geography words.

1. This is a mountain that "blows its top."

   v__ __c__n__

2. It is very cold in this place.

   S __ __ th __ o l __

3. When the earth starts shaking, it could be this.

   __ a __ t __ q__ a __ e

4. This country is known for its cheeses.

   __r __ __ c __

5. A large body of water might be this.

   __ a __ __

6. This U.S. state is far away from the other 49 states.

   __ a w a i __

7. You might find a koala bear here.

   __ u s __ r __ l __ __

8. To find your way around, you will need this.

   __ a __

9. These are at a high altitude.

   __ o u __ t __ i n __

10. A place with thick vegetation and lots of animals and reptiles might be this.

    __ u n __ l __

Monuments and Statues

1. What do we call the statue on top of the Capitol Building?

   _____

2. What famous statue is located in New York City's harbor?

   _____

3. What famous memorial in Washington, D.C., is surrounded by hundreds of Japanese cherry trees? _____

4. Three monuments in Washington, D.C., were erected in honor of what men?

   _____

5. In what city would we find the Gateway Arch?

   _____

6. Where is the Tomb of the Unknown Soldier? _____

   _____

7. What does the sword in the right hand of the Statue of Freedom represent?

   _____

8. What is the tallest structure in Washington, D.C.?

   _____

9. Where is the Iwo Jima memorial statue located?

   _____

10. What does the Iwo Jima statue memorialize?

    _____

11. What monument was erected in Washington, D.C., in honor of the people who died during the war in Vietnam? _____

12. In what city would you find the Liberty Bell? _____

    _____

Which One Does Not Belong?

Listed below are four geographic areas of the world. In each set, three of them have something in common with each other, while the fourth does not. Circle the area that does not fit and then tell why.

1. Libya, Egypt, Zaire, Turkey

    Why? _____

2. Madagascar, Cuba, India, Japan

    Why? _____

3. Alaska, Canada, U.S.A., Mexico

    Why? _____

4. Pacific, Arctic, Mediterranean, Atlantic

    Why? _____

5. Algeria, Chad, Turkey, Spain

    Why? _____

6. Hawaiian, Canary, Marshall, Caroline

    Why? _____

7. South America, Africa, Australia, Antarctica

    Why? _____

8. Tasmania, New Zealand, Queensland, New South Wales

    Why? _____

9. Brazil, Zaire, South Africa, Ecuador

    Why? _____

10. Somalia, Angola, India, Australia

    Why? _____

Write your own "Which one does not belong?"

_____   _____   _____   _____

Which one does not belong? _____

Why? _____

What's the Population?

Can you guess how many people live in each of these places? This will not be easy, so go ahead and make guesses. When you finish, check the answers to see how well you guessed. Use the population choices below to answer the questions.

1. How many people live in Bombay, India? _____

2. How many people live in Buenos Aires, Argentina? _____

3. How many people live in Calcutta, India? _____

4. How many people live in Mexico City, Mexico?   _____

5. How many people live in New York City, New York, U.S.A? _____

6. How many people live in Osaka-Kobe-Kyoto, Japan? _____

7. How many people live in Sao Paulo, Brazil?_____

8. How many people live in Seoul, Korea?   _____

9. How many people live in Tokyo-Yokohama, Japan? _____

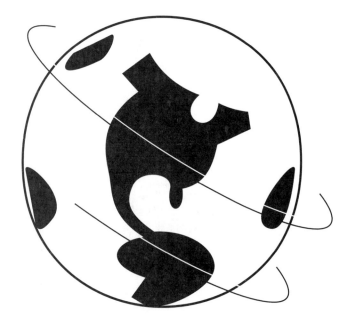

Population Choices:

26,952,000
20,207,000
18,052,000
16,268,000
14,622,000
13,826,000
11,777,000
11,663,000
11,518,000

Money, Money, Everywhere!

Each country of the world has its own basic unit of money. Match the countries listed below with the word used there for the basic unit of money.

Country

1. Mexico _____

2. U.S.A. _____

3. South Africa _____

4. Great Britain _____

5. France _____

6. Germany _____

7. Greece _____

8. India _____

9. Japan _____

10. Italy _____

11. Spain _____

12. Israel _____

13. Austria _____

14. South Korea _____

15. Panama _____

16. Venezuela _____

17. Netherlands _____

18. Russia _____

19. Finland _____

20. Sweden _____

Units of Money

balboa

bolivar

dollar

drachma

franc

guilder

krona

lira

mark

markka

peseta

peso

pound

rand

ruble

rupee

schilling

shekel

won

yen

U.S.A. Geography Sandwiches

Sandwiches are made with two pieces of bread and a filling in the middle. In these geography sandwiches, you are given the "bread" but not the "filling." Study a map of the United States to make a proper sandwich.

1. Mississippi _____ Georgia

2. North Dakota _____ Nebraska

3. Wisconsin _____ Michigan

4. New York _____ Rhode Island

5. Oklahoma _____ Texas

6. California _____ Utah

7. Texas _____ Mexico

8. Illinois _____ Ohio

9. Arizona _____ Texas

10. Missouri _____ Illinois

11. Canada _____ Mexico

12. Vermont _____ Maine

13. Minnesota _____ Missouri

14. Pacific Ocean _____ Nevada

15. Washington _____ California

Make your own sandwich:

_____   _____   _____

Europe Geography Sandwiches

Sandwiches are made with two pieces of bread and a filling in the middle. In these geography sandwiches, you are given the "bread" but not the "filling." Study a globe or a map of the world to make a proper sandwich.

1. Germany	_____	Belarus
2. France	_____	Spain
3. Switzerland	_____	Austria
4. England	_____	France
5. Europe	_____	Africa
6. Iceland	_____	Norway
7. Corsica	_____	Sardinia
8. Italy	_____	Croatia
9. Europe	_____	Asia
10. Sweden	_____	Poland
11. Greece	_____	Crete
12. England	_____	Denmark
13. Estonia	_____	Lithuania
14. Romania	_____	Bulgaria
15. Netherlands	_____	France

Make your own sandwich:

_____   _____   _____

World Geography Sandwiches

Sandwiches are made with two pieces of bread and a filling in the middle. In these geography sandwiches, you are given the "bread" but not the "filling." Study a globe or a map of the world to make a proper sandwich.

1. North America _____ Europe

2. Northern Hemisphere _____ Southern Hemisphere

3. Australia _____ New Zealand

4. Arizona _____ Texas

5. Africa _____ Australia

6. North America _____ South America

7. Eastern Hemisphere _____ Western Hemisphere

8. Australia _____ Antarctica

9. Europe _____ Africa

10. Australia _____ South America

11. South America _____ Africa

12. Tropic of Cancer _____ Tropic of Capricorn

13. Africa _____ Asia

14. South America _____ Antarctica

15. Asia _____ North America

Make your own sandwich:

_____   _____   _____

How Is Your Memory?

Study the picture for three minutes. Then, put it out of sight. On another sheet of paper, list as many items from the picture as you can remember.

Another Memory Challenge

Look at the items on this page for two minutes. Then turn the page over, and on another piece of paper, list or draw all the items you can remember. When you finish, look at this page again. How did you do?

And Another Memory Challenge

Look at the items on this page for two minutes. Then turn the page over, and on another piece of paper, list or draw all the items you can remember. When you finish, look at this page again. How did you do?

Try This Memory Challenge

Look at the items on this page for two minutes. Then turn the page over, and on another piece of paper, list or draw all the items you can remember. When you finish, look at this page again. How did you do?

Another Kind of Memory Challenge

While you are looking at the items on this page, make up a story using each of the items. When two minutes have passed, turn to the next page and write and illustrate your story, but do not look at this page while you are writing. When you finish writing your story, check back here to see how well you did.

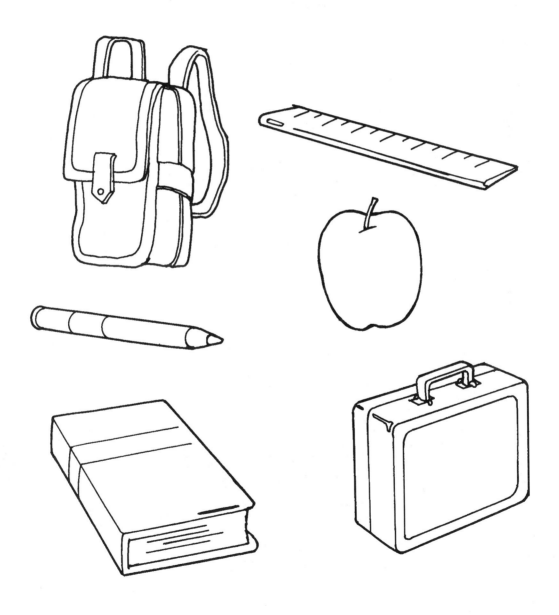

Another Kind of Memory
Challenge *(cont.)*

Write and illustrate your story here.

Try Another Memory Challenge

While you are looking at the items on this page, make up a story using each of the items. When two minutes have passed, turn to the next page and write and illustrate your story, but do not look at this page while you are writing. When you finish writing your story, check back here to see how well you did.

Try Another Memory Challenge *(cont.)*

Write and illustrate your story here.

Memory Game

Glue this page and the next onto a piece of colored construction paper. Cut out the cards on both pages. Turn them facedown, mix them up, and arrange them into rows. Turn over one card and then another. If they are a match, take them. If they are not a match, turn them back over and try two more cards. Repeat until you have matched all the cards.

Memory Game *(cont.)*

Another Memory Game

Glue this page and the next onto a piece of colored construction paper. Cut out the cards on both pages. Turn them facedown, mix them up, and arrange them into rows. Turn over one card and then another. If they are a match, take them. If they are not a match, turn them back over and try two more cards. Repeat until you have matched all the cards. (**Note:** This game will be more challenging than the last because unusual shapes are more difficult to remember than objects.)

Another Memory Game *(cont.)*

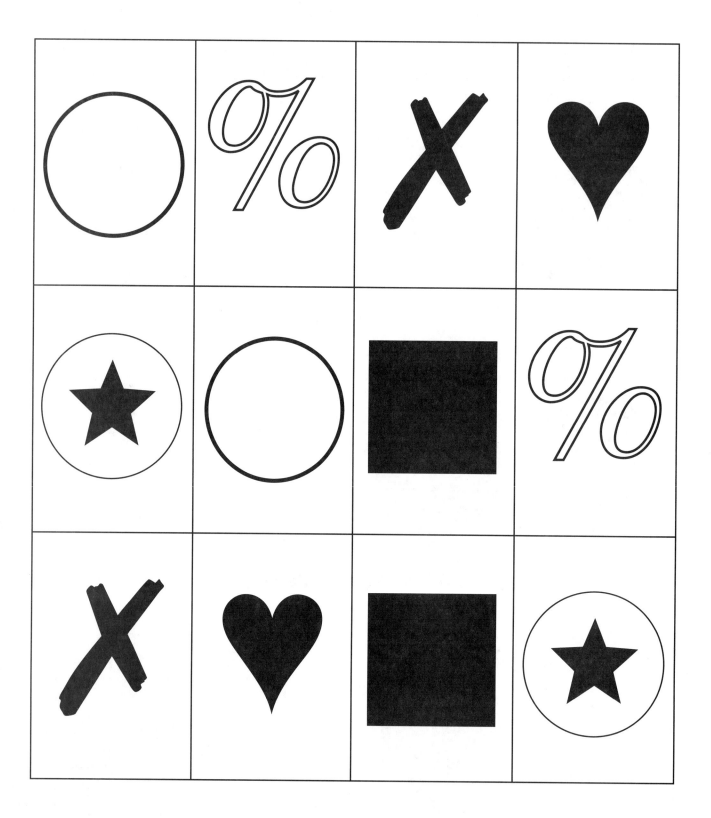

Money Memory

Every day you see and handle coins: dimes, pennies, nickels, and quarters. But do you remember what they look like? Do you remember enough to draw them? Try filling in the coins below. You may choose to enlarge the drawings or make them the same size as the coins. You can try drawing both sides or make two attempts to draw one side of the coin. On the next page, you will find what they really look like. Remember, do not take out any coins. Just see how well you can remember them.

Life size

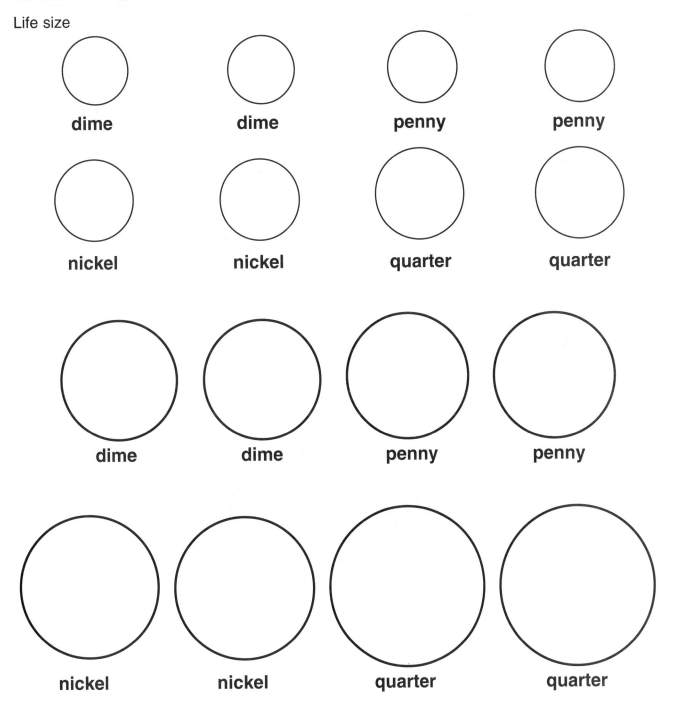

Money Memory *(cont.)*

Compare these coin drawings to yours. How well did you do? Do not feel bad; most people of all ages would have a hard time remembering what the coins look like. Of course, you will probably look more closely at coins — and everything else — from now on!

penny

dime

nickel

quarter

Simonide's Trick

Simonide was a Greek orator with a terrific memory. In ancient Greece, speakers did not have teleprompters or note cards to remind them of their speaking topics. Instead, they had to rely on memory. Simonide had a special way of remembering. He would look at his audience and where they were seated, and then he would assign each of the points or topics to a face somewhere in his audience. He would go to them one after another. Maybe the man sitting over by the passageway represented the opening remarks, and the really tall woman near the back represented the exciting story he wanted to share as background. Simonide was so good at this that he once helped to solve a murder mystery by remembering where each person in the room had been sitting.

You can use Simonide's trick, too. Look at this picture of a room. Below the picture there is a list of ten objects. Imagine places where you could put each of these objects in the picture. You will remember better if you can make some sense of where you put each item in your mind. Give yourself two minutes to imagine where to place each object and then turn the page.

Using only your mind, "place" these objects in various places in the room:

camera	jacket	pair of shoes	soccer ball	backpack
poster	pizza	boa constrictor	bucket of fish	wading pool

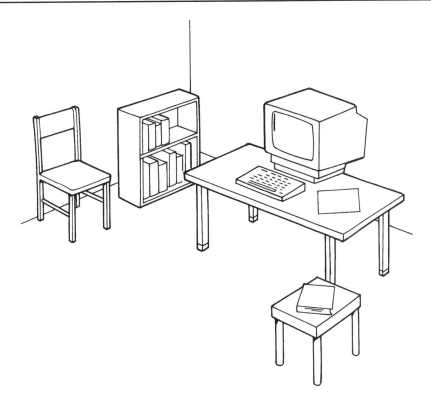

Simonide's Trick *(cont.)*

Here is the room again. Write the names of the ten objects, or if you prefer, draw each of the objects in the places where you imagined placing them. When you finish placing the objects and cannot remember any more, turn back to the list of objects. Did you remember them all? If you did, congratulations!

Now, think of ways you can use Simonide's Trick to help you in your schoolwork. If you missed some, do not worry. Like anything else, it takes practice. The next time you have a list to remember, try to find a place to put each item in the room.

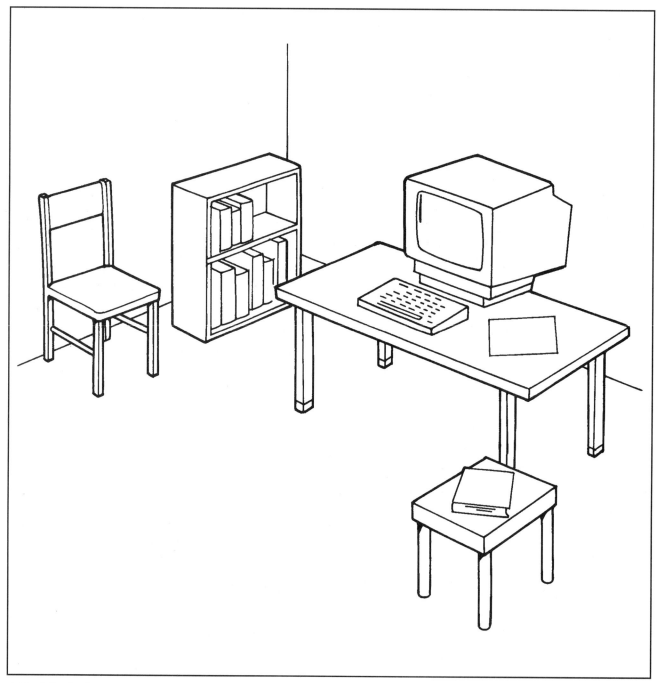

Mnemosene's Trick

Mnemosene is the Greek goddess of memory. Indeed, remembering how to spell her name would be challenge enough! From her name we get mnemonics, which is a method or trick for remembering. Here is an example of a mnemonic:

Every Good Boy Does Fine.

This sentence represents EGBDF, or the notes of the treble clef from bottom to top.

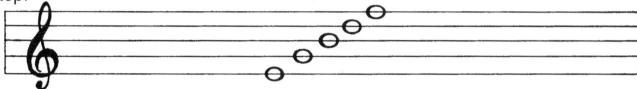

Here is another example for you:

General Eisenhower's Oldest Girl Rode A Pony Home Yesterday.

Do you see how the first letter of each word spells geography?

Here is one more example, and then you should have it:

HOMES

The letters stand for Huron, Ontario, Michigan, Erie, and Superior (the Great Lakes of North America). You probably will not be able to forget them now!

Mnemosene's Trick *(cont.)*

See if you can come up with a mnemonic to help you remember the four oceans of the world. They are the Indian, Arctic, Atlantic, and Pacific. Use the space below to write your mnemonic.

How about a mnemonic to remember how to spell "arithmetic"? Be creative and write it in the space provided.

Here's a challenge for you. Write a mnemonic to help you to remember the planets in order (Mercury, Venus, Earth, Mars, Jupiter, Saturn, Uranus, Neptune, Pluto).

Think of other things you would like to be able to remember more easily, such as your locker combination, your school schedule, a list of chores, the names of all your relatives, insects, reptiles, the states, or provinces. In the space below, brainstorm your ideas for a mnemonic for the topic of your choice. When you come up with a good one, write it in the box at the bottom of the page.

Memory Doodles

You have two minutes to memorize these drawings. Then turn to the next page.

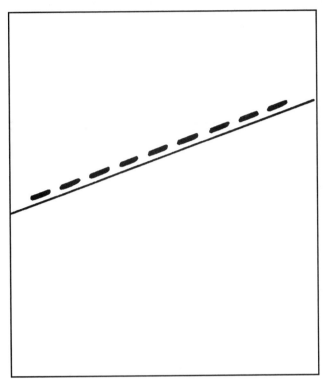

Hime

Pell

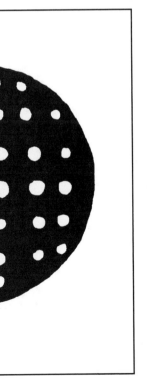

Shair

Neff

Memory Doodles *(cont.)*

Draw the doodles in the boxes. When you finish, turn back the page to see if you got them right. Then read what is written at the bottom of this page.

Hime

Pell

Shair

Neff

How well did you do? Do not be discouraged if you did not do as well as you thought you would. You have another try on the next page!

Memory Doodles *(cont.)*

Look at this page for two minutes and memorize the doodles. After two minutes, turn to the next page.

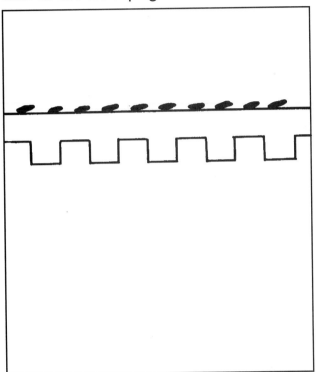

ants crawling along a ledge

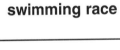

swimming race

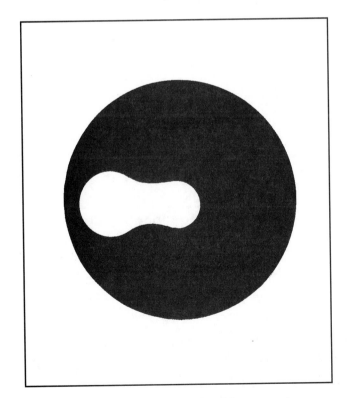

view of the world from inside a soda can

spaghetti boiling over

581

Memory Doodles *(cont.)*

Draw the doodles in the boxes. When you finish, turn back the page to see how well you did. When you have looked, read what is written at the bottom of this page.

spaghetti boiling over

swimming race

view of the world from inside a soda can

ants crawling along a ledge

Did you do better this time than on the previous activity? Why do you think that is? Write what you think in the space._____

_____

Here is why you did better this time: the doodles made sense this time, and they matched what was said about them.   Before, you only had a nonsense word to try to match with the doodle. This time you had a doodle with words to explain what it was. Didn't that make it easier for you to remember?

Plastic Memory Game

Look carefully at the picture below. It shows 12 different objects. Each object is made completely out of plastic or plastic parts. Looked long enough? On the back of this page, write a list of as many items as you can remember.

In My School Room

Study the picture and the words below. Then cover the pictures and words. In the box draw a picture of a school room with the correct items in it.

  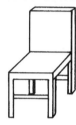  

1 chalkboard   1 picture   4 books   3 chairs   3 tables

Part 2 Answer Key

Page 319
1. the first and third puppies
2. the second and fourth turtles
3. the fourth and fifth butterflies
4. the second and fifth bears
5. the first and fourth horses
6. the third and fourth rabbits

Page 320
Accept all reasonable answers. These are most likely:
1. cold
2. key
3. white (or blue)
4. soul
5. holler (or shout)
6. right
7. eggs
8. mouse
9. down
10. fries
11. quiet
12. lightning
13. forth
14. thin
15. nail
16. stones
17. pains
18. butter
19. nails
20. seek

Page 321
1. puff
2. feather
3. order
4. jelly
5. cranny
6. match
7. lace
8. dogs
9. sugar
10. grey (or new)
11. then (or later)
12. day
13. tomato
14. proper
15. dandy
16. cents
17. cream
18. shine (or fall)
19. shout
20. cover

Page 322
1. found
2. bad
3. wide (or near)
4. potatoes
5. ice
6. dip (or salsa)
7. ball
8. joy (prejudice)
9. foot
10. cheese
11. old
12. onions
13. go
14. needles
15. go
16. left
17. right
18. dance
19. saucer
20. out
21. sound
22. bolts
23. write
24. beans
25. fork
26. no
27. water
28. pepper
29. turn
30. low (dry)

Page 323
1. Stimpy
2. Gretel
3. Lois Lane
4. Beauty
5. Batman
6. Mickey
7. Ken
8. Daisy
9. Olive Oyl
10. Kermit
11. Punch
12. Dr. Jeckyll
13. Jill
14. the Tramp
15. Ernie

Page 324
1. Fred
2. Orville
3. Wally
4. Hobbes
5. Dale Evans
6. Jerry
7. Amos
8. Mutt
9. Scarlett
10. Jane
11. Lucy
12. Bullwinkle
13. Laurel
14. Donald Duck
15. Tarzan

Page 325
1. Eve
2. Cleopatra
3. Harriet
4. Raggedy Andy
5. Roo
6. Hardy
7. Maid Marian
8. Clark
9. Delilah
10. Juliet
11. Dagwood
12. Costello
13. Minnie
14. Tweety
15. Shirley

Part 2 Answer Key (cont.)

Page 326

Answers will vary. Here are some examples:
mittens
gloves
socks
sandals
slippers
ice skates
roller skates
skis
boots
shoelaces
jeans
shorts
pajamas
earrings
glasses
pliers
binoculars
scissors
dice

Page 327

Answers will vary. See page 24 answers for examples.

Page 328

1. Adams, Jefferson, Madison
2. Lincoln, Jefferson, Washington
3. Cowardly Lion, Tin Man, Scarecrow
4. Papa Bear, Mama Bear, Baby Bear
5. red, yellow, blue
6. Flora, Fauna, Merriwether
7. butcher, baker, candlestick maker
8. Casper, Melchior, and Balthasar
9. reading, 'riting, 'rithmetic
10. Huey, Dewey, Louie
11. Curly, Moe, Larry
12. Mizaru, Mikazaur, Mazaru

Page 329

1. blue
2. listen
3. stars
4. 'rithmetic (arithmetic)
5. go
6. blue
7. win
8. roll
9. handsome
10. hail
11. Curly
12. milk
13. mineral
14. charity
15. moe

Page 330

Answers will vary.

Page 331

1. green; primary colors
2. December; months with thirty days
3. calculus; types of clouds
4. cabbage; underground vegetables
5. shovel; have prongs
6. Susan; girls' names beginning with C
7. tomato; flowers
8. candy bar; baked goods
9. niece; males

10. Canada; continents
11. Cowboys; baseball teams or Dodgers; teams beginning with C
12. watermelon; citrus fruits
13. cry; about happiness
14. pig; poultry
15. east; intermediate directions

Page 332

1. whisper; noisy expressions
2. sun; signs of bad weather
3. stapler; eating utensils
4. math; reference books
5. nephew; female relatives
6. gosling; hog family
7. blood; organs of the body
8. Oklahoma; states bordering the Pacific Ocean
9. chicken; animals with four legs
10. hamburgers; condiments
11. Bears; baseball teams
12. eraser; writing tools
13. margarine; grain products
14. raccoon; common household pets
15. wallet; things that one wears

Page 333

1. cirrus; mathematics
2. atlas; leisure books
3. shark; marine mammals
4. acre; metric measurements
5. chalk; desk tools
6. Bartlett; varieties of apple
7. angora, breeds of dog
8. maple; flowers
9. zebra; animals found on farms
10. niece; male relatives

Page 334

1. sports teams (team sports)
2. baseball teams (American League baseball teams)
3. mythical creatures
4. southwestern states (states bordering Mexico)
5. U.S. presidents
6. vegetables (vegetables grown underground)
7. candy bars (candy bars with nuts)
8. football teams (NFC football teams)
9. members of the cat family
10. eastern states (states bordering the Atlantic Ocean)
11. transportation (ground transportation)
12. months (months with thirty days)
13. things found in a wallet
14. southern states (states bordering the Gulf of Mexico)
15. musical groups

Page 335

Laura: koala and hamburger
Phil: zebra and hot dog
Jane: giraffe and popcorn
Mike: monkey and corn dog

Page 336

Andrea: July 10
Andrew: February 15
Sarah: May 1
Sam: March 24
Jill: December 25
Jeff: October 15
Millie: April 1
Max: September 9

Part 2 Answer Key *(cont.)*

Page 337
Nicole: flute for 40 minutes
Sean: drums for 30 minutes
Justin: clarinet for 35 minutes
Janis: piano for 45 minutes

Page 338
Matt: baseball
Brian: basketball
Jon: soccer
Neil: tennis
Jason: hockey

Page 339
Chelsea: B
Linda: C-
Marcia: A
Morgan: C
Casie: D

Page 340
A. J. Smith is 8.
Andy Jones is 9.
Andrew Rogers is 10.

Page 341
Bess May is 10.
Liz Smith is 8.
Beth Jones is 9.

Page 342
David jogs for 15 minutes.
Tom bikes for 30 minutes.
Rick golfs for 45 minutes.
Roger swims for 60 minutes.

Page 343
Katelyn likes the roller coaster and ate bratwurst.
Kenny likes the ferris wheel and ate a hot dog.
Emily likes the bumper cars and ate a hamburger.
Howie likes the carousel and ate a corn dog.

Page 344
Rita: May 12
Jenny: January 1
Millie: April 12
Andrew: February 3
Ralph: August 25
Scott: September 2
Andrea: July 13
Maeve: March 30

Page 345
Megan likes pizza.
Michael likes hot dogs.
Sergi likes hamburgers.
Jana likes chicken.

Page 346
Chad: Reds
Danny: Cardinals
Andrew: White Sox
Ryan: Dodgers
Will: A's

Page 347
1. Tom
2. David
3. Jordi
4. Greg
5. Jeff

6. Andrew
7. Luis
8. Phil
9. Carlos

Page 348
Becky: elephants and ice cream
Alexis: monkeys and snowcone
Lindsay: lions and popcorn
Brooke: horses and taffy

Page 349
Ms. Snow: Illinois, math, and Chinese
Mr. Hunter: Nevada, science, and Mexican
Mr. Wong: Wisconsin, English, and Italian
Mrs. Jackson: California, geography, American

Page 350
A.J. : peanut butter and jelly, orange
Nick: ham salad, banana
Jim: bologna and cheese, grapes
Tom: ham and cheese, apple

Page 351
1. Dad
2. Rachel
3. Christine
4. Andrea
5. Mom
6. Andrew
7. Greg
8. Rob

Page 352
1. Russ
2. Andrew
3. Jeff
4. Zac
5. Ryan
6. Danny
7. Alan
8. Mark

Page 353
1. Jack Smith, 130 points
2. Ron Ford, 100 points
3. Charles May, 120 points
4. Dave Thompson, 90 points

Page 354
Tammy Simpson, guitar
Gina Donaldson, trombone
Shannon Green, drums
Donna Thompson, sax

Page 355
Bev: frame, $40
Debbie: chair, $60
Janis: vase, $30
Mary Jo: lamp, $20

Page 356
Some answers may vary.
1. Los Angeles
2. afternoon
3. octagon
4. saw
5. Texas
6. bed
7. red

Part 2 Answer Key *(cont.)*

Page 356 *(cont.)*
8. cherries
9. Easter
10. mother
11. pancakes
12. see
13. chicken
14. Egypt
15. temperature
16. 100
17. floor
18. pilot
19. hungry
20. hive

Page 357
1. Bird
2. racket
3. Elizabeth
4. poem
5. tall (or long)
6. Abraham
7. Nut
8. soft
9. sand
10. window
11. read
12. teeth
13. Snow
14. cut
15. shoe
16. screw
17. ring
18. hands
19. Oink
20. minute

Page 358
1. Niece
2. hungry
3. library
4. hearing
5. December
6. large
7. Belt
8. vine
9. green
10. head
11. calf
12. dawn
13. Book
14. captain
15. ceiling
16. room (or house)
17. girl
18. curtain
19. Bird
20. water (or lake, ocean, or river)

Page 359
1. T
2. T
3. F
4. F
5. T
6. T

7. T
8. F
9. T
10. F
11. F
12. T
13. T
14. T
15. F
16. F
17. F
18. T

Page 360
1. T
2. F
3. T
4. F
5. F
6. T
7. F
8. T
9. F
10. T
11. T
12. T
13. F
14. T
15. T
16. T
17. F
18. F

Page 361
1. T
2. F
3. T
4. F
5. F
6. T
7. F
8. F
9. T
10. F
11. T
12. T
13. T
14. F
15. T

Page 362
1. the rear plate
2. 39
3. red
4. Thomas Jefferson
5. balls
6. right
7. 6
8. 90 degrees
9. five or nine
10. eight
11. denominator
12. autumn or fall
13. left
14. maximum

Part 2 Answer Key *(cont.)*

Page 363
1. six
2. Lincoln
3. buffalo
4. red and yellow
5. peacock
6. Captain
7. autumn
8. sheep
9. Dopey
10. yellow
11. glasses
12. your uncle
13. origami
14. joey
15. white

Page 364
1. escalator
2. once every four years
3. "Once upon a time"
4. quintuplets
5. tripod
6. stamps
7. break it open to get the treats
8. black
9. pride
10. port
11. stovepipe
12. a genie
13. moat
14. the eye
15. rabbit

Page 365
1. black, red, yellow, blue, and green
2. a mummy
3. Doc
4. southpaws
5. a mural
6. diamond
7. glider
8. gold
9. coins
10. Ramadan
11. ewe
12. Good Friday
13. the left shoulder
14. seven
15. John Arbuckle

Page 366
1. 12
2. 66
3. 24 or 25
4. 102
5. 132
6. 13
7. 5
8. 4
9. 206
10. 32
11. 88
12. 144
13. 13
14. 100
15. 1

Page 367
1. 1
2. 2
3. 5
4. 100
5. 90
6. 100
7. 4
8. 0
9. 110
10. 360
11. 6
12. 10
13. 14
14. 52
15. 64
16. 1000
17. 366
18. 500
19. 168
20. 11

Page 368
1. left
2. "and one for all"
3. Leonardo da Vinci
4. graphite
5. lion
6. bathyscaphe
7.
8. metronome
9. a good thing
10. Jesus
11. navel oranges
12. "a partridge in a pear tree"
13. pitchfork
14. Friday
15. "The land of the free and the home of the brave."

Page 369
1. Mt. Everest
2. redwood tree
3. Sears Tower
4. blue whale
5. ostrich
6. Asia
7. Greenland
8. anaconda
9. African bush elephant
10. killer whale
11. cheetah
12. peregrine falcon

Page 370
1. Lake Superior
2. Sauropod dinosaur
3. Russia
4. Pacific
5. redwood tree
6. South China Sea
7. blue whale
8. Sahara
9. Andes
10. giant clam
11. sailfish
12. Nile
13. king cobra

Part 2 Answer Key *(cont.)*

Page 370 *(cont.)*
14. pygmy shrew
15. gecko
16. bee hummingbird
17. Australia

Page 371
1. 8 sides
2. Florida
3. Oklahoma
4. 3rd president
5. Picasso
6. Quebec
7. 13
8. 10 sides
9. 12 months
10. tambourine
11. cumulus
12. Sacramento
13. 24 hours
14. 100 years
15. 4
16. May

Page 372
1. 90
2. 12
3. 144
4. Chile
5. da Vinci
6. 20
7. D
8. over 600
9. Shoo!
10. calculus
11. September
12. self-conscious
13. clarinet
14. Trudeau
15. 272
16. Pablo Casals
17. Oklahoma
18. yellow
19. 14
20. 360

Page 373
1. Florida
2. 16th
3. 50
4. 132
5. Springfield
6. Lincoln
7. Mississippi
8. 102
9. Michigan
10. 10
11. 33
12. Roosevelt
13. Pennsylvania
14. Lincoln
15. Ford

Page 374
1. Lincoln and Washington
2. July 4
3. November
4. November 11
5. Labor Day
6. to honor Americans who gave their lives for their country (some people also use the day to honor all loved ones who have died.)
7. Columbus Day
8. Dr. Martin Luther King, Jr.
9. January 15 (or the third Monday of January)
10. St. Patrick's Day
11. Grandparent's Day
12. Citizenship Day

Page 375
1. North America
2. east
3. red
4. Mississippi River
5. north
6. Alexander Graham Bell
7. atlas
8. Mt. Everest
9. island
10. Nina, Pinta, and Santa Maria
11. Mt. Rushmore
12. Huron, Ontario, Michigan, Erie, and Superior
13. Peru
14. Pacific
15. Honolulu

Page 376
1. Juneau
2. peninsula
3. six
4. John Wilkes Booth
5. Amerigo Vespucci
6. Lake Michigan
7. copper
8. Benjamin Franklin
9. west
10. France
11. Philadelphia
12. Hawaii and Alaska
13. Thomas Jefferson
14. Statue of Liberty
15. Betsy Ross

Page 377
1. monarchy
2. United States and Britain
3. Sahara
4. South America
5. Denmark
6. Christopher Jones
7. Cuba
8. Hernando Cortez
9. Himalayas
10. Russia
11. topographic
12. Australia
13. 1914-1918
14. twelve
15. China

Page 378
1. "out of many, one"
2. six years
3. Abraham Lincoln
4. San Antonio, Texas
5. 1861–1865

Part 2 Answer Key *(cont.)*

Page 378 *(cont.)*
6. Francis Bellamy
7. executive branch
8. Ronald Reagan
9. courage
10. John F. Kennedy
11. Eli Whitney
12. Hawaii
13. her right
14. Sir Francis Drake
15. "Hail to the Chief"

Page 379
1. Teddy
2. Washington
3. Delano
4. Madison
5. February
6. Adams
7. Honolulu
8. Carter
9. Lincoln
10. Nixon
11. Virginia
12. Mount Vernon
13. Alaska
14. Roosevelt (Theodore)
15. Congress

Page 380
1. John
2. Dwight
3. Ronald
4. Thomas
5. Richard
6. Abraham
7. Jimmy
8. Herbert
9. Theodore or Franklin
10. George
11. Calvin
12. Grover
13. Ulysses
14. Zachary
15. William or Benjamin
16. Harry
17. James
18. James
19. James
20. Lyndon or Andrew

Page 381
1. I
2. C
3. B
4. L
5. K
6. E
7. H
8. M
9. G
10. O
11. A
12. F
13. D
14. N
15. J

Page 382
1. Abraham Lincoln
2. James Madison
3. John Adams
4. Thomas Jefferson
5. Grover Cleveland
6. Zachary Taylor
7. Abraham Lincoln
8. John Kennedy and William Taft
9. Franklin D. Roosevelt
10. James Madison
11. Benjamin Harrison
12. James Buchanan
13. James Buchanan
14. Richard Nixon
15. John Garfield, Herbert Hoover, Harry Truman, Gerald Ford, Ronald Reagan, George Bush, and Bill Clinton

Page 383
1. 120
2. 10
3. triangle
4. tells time
5. 4, 000
6. colon
7. 12
8. 6
9. sum
10. 100
11. 6
12. octagon
13. 6
14. 10
15. 24

Page 384
1. graph
2. 90 degrees
3. time zone
4. 100
5. octagon
6. 10
7. 40
8. 21
9. no
10. 10
11. 6
12. length x width
13. 606
14. 70
15. 360 degrees

Page 385
1. no
2. 300
3. It means having the same size and shape.
4. They weigh the same.
5. CLXXVI
6. protractor
7. 5
8. 144
9. 10
10. 3/4
11. 9
12. obtuse
13. yes
14. a straight line
15. ordinal

Part 2 Answer Key *(cont.)*

Page 386
1. 1,000
2. M
3. tangram
4. 5,280
5. minimum
6. 12.5 or 12 1/2
7. 1/2
8. 24
9. radius
10. 7
11. 9
12. multiply the number by itself
13. 7 tenths
14. acute
15. prime number

Page 387
1. subject and predicate
2. apostrophe
3. nouns
4. fiction
5. Templeton
6. comma
7. opinion
8. comma
9. won't
10. glossary
11. sheep
12. opposite
13. maybe
14. fable
15. haiku

Page 388
1. autobiography
2. *Little Women*
3. Aesop
4. Beatrix Potter
5. author
6. adverb
7. Samuel Clemens
8. period
9. palindromes
10. Fudge
11. proper nouns
12. quotations marks
13. fairy tales
14. colon
15. four

Page 389
1. Harriet Beecher Stowe
2. thesaurus
3. conjunctions
4. imperative
5. guide words
6. author, subject, and title
7. Huck Finn
8. a vampire
9. heading, inside address, greeting, body, closing, and signature
10. alliteration
11. homophones
12. in a subway station
13. to sign your name
14. humble
15. nonfiction

Page 390
1. bibliography
2. epic
3. Black
4. Captain Ahab
5. Grimm
6. pen name
7. wolf
8. Lilliput
9. forty
10. sixth
11. hope
12. a disembodied brain
13. exclamatory
14. onomatopoeia
15. nonfiction

Page 391
1. thermometer
2. invertebrates
3. gills
4. oysters
5. telescope
6. Saturn
7. skunk
8. eight
9. hummingbirds
10. fog
11. tadpole
12. bats
13. school
14. toadstool
15. poles

Page 392
1. microscope
2. Jupiter
3. muscles
4. diamond
5. barometer
6. Earth
7. 98.6 degrees
8. orbit
9. Neptune until 1999, then Pluto
10. ribs
11. galaxy
12. iris
13. fossils
14. deciduous
15. heartbeat

Page 393
1. nervous system
2. Halley's Comet
3. solid, liquid, and gas
4. barometer
5. smog
6. elbow
7. chlorophyll
8. kinetic energy
9. earthquake
10. carnivore
11. oxygen
12. hot
13. esophagus
14. meteors
15. crater

Part 2 Answer Key (cont.)

Page 394
1. circulatory system
2. Venus
3. cold-blooded
4. solar and radiant
5. collarbone
6. 0 degrees Celsius
7. Mike Collins
8. tropical
9. mercury
10. Sirius
11. two
12. kangaroo
13. left ventricle
14. crater
15. herbivore

Page 395
1. F
2. G
3. B
4. E
5. A
6. C
7. D
8. I
9. J
10. H

Page 396
1. astronaut
2. earth
3. clouds
4. hibernate
5. insect
6. moon
7. hurricane
8. rain
9. stomach
10. microscope
11. flowers
12. snow
13. thermometer
14. mammals
15. gravity

Page 397
Colors will vary. Be sure the directions have been followed.

Page 398
Circled items should include the helicopter, surfer, paper boy, truck, and clown.

Page 399
A. 3
B. 4
C. 1
D. 2

Page 400
1. bicycle
2. bird on a branch
3. slide
4. umbrella
5. swing set
6. Statue of Liberty

Page 401
This is a depiction of man's first walk on the moon in 1969.

Page 402
This is the burial mask of King Tutankhamen.

Page 403
This is Benjamin Franklin.

Page 404
Answers will vary.

Page 405
1. Open up!
2. You're under arrest.
3. double cross
4. I understand.
5. a hole in one
6. Holy cow!
7. all mixed up
8. tricycle
9. good afternoon
10. Big Mac
11. highchair
12. touchdown

Page 406
1. Jack-in-the-box
2. Tiny Tim
3. a pair of dice
4. long underwear
5. reading between the lines
6. Get up!
7. just in time
8. G.I. overseas
9. going on a diet
10. sandbox
11. downtown
12. man in the moon

Page 407
1. skating on thin ice
2. right in the middle of everything
3. double vision
4. check up
5. crossroads
6. mind over matter
7. I am beside myself.
8. bottoms up
9. deep beneath the sea
10. hand in hand
11. uptown
12. H2O

Page 408
1. driving up a wall
2. half an hour
3. just between you and me
4. smallpox
5. man on the moon
6. worn out
7. long overdue
8. loosen up
9. turkey in the straw
10. going around in circles
11. quit following me
12. Minnesota

Page 409
1. face to face
2. man overboard
3. split level

Part 2 Answer Key *(cont.)*

Page 409 *(cont.)*
4. barrel full of monkeys
5. deer crossing
6. upstairs
7. business before pleasure
8. order in the court
9. I'm under the weather
10. banana split
11. three degrees below zero
12. full-length mirror

Page 410
1. scatterbrained
2. six feet below the ground
3. a square meal
4. neon light
5. little league
6. big man on campus
7. pain in the neck
8. sleeping on the job
9. high-rise
10. once over lightly
11. keep it under your hat
12. high school

Page 411
1. I'm on the top of the world.
2. backwards glance
3. forum
4. She's on cloud nine.
5. Raindrops keep falling on my head.
6. down and out
7. pie in the face
8. circles under the eyes
9. long time, no see
10. age before beauty
11. double date
12. split decision

Page 412
1. What goes up, must come down.
2. life after death
3. talking in his sleep
4. one in a million
5. eggs over easy
6. three-ring circus
7. Go for it!
8. no two ways about it
9. good over evil
10. one on one
11. slow down
12. stand in the corner

Page 416
1. "Moon River"
2. "Yellow Submarine"
3. Ringo Starr
4. Jefferson Airplane
5. "Cathy's Clown"
6. Rolling Stones
7. Woodstock
8. Three Dog Night
9. "California Dreamin'"
10. "I Left My Heart in San Francisco"

Page 417
1. Chuck Berry
2. "Rock Around the Clock"
3. "Teen Angel"
4. "Sixteen Tons"
5. "Unchained Melody"
6. Fats Domino
7. "Jailhouse Rock"
8. "Tears on Your Pillow" (or is that "my" pillow?)
9. "Heartbreak Hotel"
10. "Sixteen Candles"

Page 418
1. ill Bill
2. bad lad
3. glum chum
4. shy fly
5. funny bunny
6. plump ump
7. fat cat
8. sad dad
9. wet pet
10. pink drink
11. big pig
12. lazy daisy
13. wee flea
14. sick chick
15. fat rat

Page 419
1. bony pony (or spare mare)
2. hid kid
3. slick chick
4. legal beagle
5. roast toast
6. grape ape
7. sad dad
8. boulder holder
9. Swiss miss
10. bug hug
11. rude dude
12. fender bender
13. pooch smooch
14. fright night
15. darling starling
16. shy guy
17. mouse house
18. big pig
19. glad lad
20. lazy daisy

Page 420
1. late date
2. red head
3. crass bass
4. crude dude
5. bug mug
6. long song
7. dog jog
8. double trouble
9. big dig
10. wish fish
11. fake flake
12. bright light
13. sweet treat (or eat)
14. rocks box
15. book crook
16. flat hat
17. sun done
18. no dough
19. cross boss
20. funny money

Part 2 Answer Key *(cont.)*

Page 421
1. britches itches
2. same game
3. sassy lassie
4. prone clone
5. cozy posy
6. pale male
7. hot yacht
8. pink mink
9. slender mender
10. fine dine
11. flat mat
12. clean queen
13. merry dairy
14. hen pen
15. sad lad
16. light bite
17. loud crowd
18. gory story
19. sweet tweet
20. witty kitty

Page 422

1. H		11. H
2. A		12. S
3. S		13. A
4. A		14. S
5. S		15. H
6. A		16. A
7. H		17. S
8. S		18. A
9. S		19. S
10. S		20. H

Page 423
1. noon
2. madam
3. level
4. Bob
5. ma'am
6. peep
7. eye
8. pop or dad
9. dud
10. toot
11. bib
12. gig
13. mom or mum
14. bob
15. Pip
16. pop
17. kook
18. pup
19. deed
20. bub

Page 424
1. photography
2. *The Nutcracker*
3. Beethoven
4. impressionism
5. Mark Twain
6. Mildred D. Taylor
7. *Mona Lisa*
8. The Beatles
9. Charles Dickens
10. *Aida*
11. *American Gothic*

12. Duke Ellington
13. Jane Austen
14. the Sistine Chapel
15. Edgar Allan Poe

Page 425
Questions will vary.

Page 126
Questions will vary.

Page 427
Questions will vary.

Page 428
Questions will vary.

Page 429
Men and Women at Work and Play
1. You can't dig half a hole!
2. The two men were not playing against each other.
3. The bear is white because it is at the North Pole.
4. nine
5. Zero. Moses never took any animals into an ark, Noah did.
6. meat
7. The boss hired her because she was smart enough to see that the second rate of pay was much better. At the end of the tenth day, with the first rate of pay, she would have earned $100. With the second rate of pay, she would have earned 2x2x2x2x2x2x2x2x2 cents which is 512 cents on the tenth day. Her total earnings would be $10.23 for ten days of work. On the 27th day she would have earned $270 with the first rate, and with the second rate she would be a millionaire! She would have earned a total of two times itself twenty-seven times, less one cent, or $1,342,177.27!
8. People who lived during the years we now call B.C. did not call them that themselves.
9. The men paid twenty-seven dollars. Where did it go? The manager has twenty-five dollars and the bellhop has two.
10. In exactly one week it will also be midnight, and the sun will not be shining.

The Passing of Time
1. Yes! Did you think they skipped from July 3 to July 5?
2. He was born on February 29, 1792, a leap year. He only had a birthday every fourth year.
3. One hour; the first is taken immediately, the second in thirty minutes, and the third one thirty minutes later — one hour.
4. All of them
5. A person has only one birthday; the rest are anniversaries of the birth.

Page 430
Mathematical Mayhem
1. a fifty-cent piece and a nickel (One is not a nickel, but the other one is!)
2. Two—the apples you took away
3. $99 + 9/9 = 100$
4. 12
5. 12 (30 divided by 15 = 2 + 10 = 12)
6. The weight would be the same since the stone and mortar were already on the earth before the wall was built.

Part 2 Answer Key *(cont.)*

Page 430 *(cont.)*

7. Jackie wrote 120 threes. She wrote 100 threes in the hundreds places, 10 threes in the tens places, and 10 threes in the ones places.

If You're Not Groaning Already, These Will Do the Trick

1. He cannot be buried because he is living.
2. He can only run in halfway, because after that, he is coming out of the woods.
3. The match
4. Push the cork in
5. Survivors don't need to be buried!
6. The beggar is a female.
7. Just do it in the daytime!

Page 421

1. sight, hearing, touch, taste, and smell
2. Papa Bear, Mama Bear, and Baby Bear
3. red, orange, yellow, green, blue, indigo, and violet
4. reading, 'riting, and 'rithmetic
5. Dasher, Dancer, Prancer, Vixen, Comet, Cupid, Donner, Blitzen, and Rudolph
6. Heron, Ontario, Michigan, Erie, and Superior
7. April, June, September, and November
8. yellow, red, and blue
9. white and red
10. Dopey, Grumpy, Happy, Sleepy, Sneezy, Bashful, and Doc

Page 432

1. Mercury and Venus
2. New York City, Philadelphia, and Washington, D.C.
3. Casper, Melchior, and Balthasar
4. George Washington, Thomas Jefferson, Abraham Lincoln, and Theodore Roosevelt
5. Mercury, Venus, Earth, Mars, Jupiter, Saturn, Uranus, Neptune, and Pluto
6. who, what, where, when, why, and how
7. Pyramids of Egypt, Hanging Gardens of Babylon, Statue of Zeus, Temple of Diana at Ephesus, Mausoleum at Halicarnassus, Colossus at Rhodes, and the Lighthouse at Pharos
8. Asia, Africa, North America, South America, Europe, Australia, and Antarctica
9. Alberta, British Columbia, Manitoba, New Brunswick, Newfoundland, Nova Scotia, Ontario, Prince Edward Island, Quebec, Saskatchewan, Northwest Territories, and the Yukon Territory
10. Virginia, Massachusetts, New Hampshire, New York, Connecticut, Maryland, Rhode Island, Delaware, Pennsylvania, North Carolina, New Jersey, South Carolina, and Georgia

Page 433

Answers will vary.

Page 434

1. 35,001; loose
2. 38,076; globe
3. 5338; bees
4. 710; oil
5. 3504; hose
6. 771; ill
7. 0.04008; boohoo
8. 7718; Bill
9. 35,108; Boise
10. 618; big

Page 435

1. 771; ill
2. 7735; sell
3. 35001; loose
4. 710; oil
5. 0.7734; hello
6. 0.02; zoo
7. 376616; giggle
8. 3045; shoe
9. 808; Bob
10. 0.40404; hohoho
11. 3704; hole
12. 7105; soil
13. 638; beg
14. 505; SOS
15. .09; go

Page 436

1. add
2. sum
3. zero
4. half
5. plus
6. minus
7. addition
8. negative
9. digit
10. mathematics
11. subtract
12. times
13. divide
14. fraction
15. number

Page 437

1. 6+4-1-2+6+2=15
2. 9+1-3+1-4+1=5
3. 9-3+4-1+2+3=14
4. 5-1+1+3+4+6=18
5. 9-8+6+3-5+3=8
6. 2-1+8+9-3+5=20
7. 5+3+2-4+1+5=12
8. 4+9+3-7+3-1=11
9. 7-6+2+8-7-1=3
10. 9+9-9+2-2-8=1

Page 438

1. 9-8+6+3-5+1=6
2. 5-3+4+4-2+9=17
3. 5+3+2-4+1-5=2
4. 3+2-1+4+1-3=6
5. 5-1-1+3+4+8=18
6. 4+9-3+7+3-1=19
7. 2-1+8+9-3+5=20
8. 8+7+1-4-4+6=14
9. 7-6+2+9-9-3=0
10. 3+5-3+9+6-5=15

Page 439

8 ounces
2.54 centimeters
5 cents
60 seconds
16 ounces
1 cent
4 weeks
12 inches
2 cups

Part 2 Answer Key *(cont.)*

Page 439 *(cont.)*

25 cents
3.3 feet
60 minutes
3 feet
36 inches
100 cents
24 hours
2 pints
12 months
2,000 pounds
4 quarts

Page 440

1. aviator
2. prophet
3. authors
4. senator
5. peanuts
6. flights
7. candies
8. pianist
9. Dodgers
10. New Deal
11. Braille
12. soldier
13. painter
14. skating
15. general

Page 441

1. vaccine
2. villain
3. dancing
4. chemist
5. college
6. gymnast
7. gorilla
8. Windows
9. teacher
10. physics
11. tourist
12. ceiling
13. leaders
14. stories
15. almanac

Page 442

Answers will vary.

Page 443

1. 1 silver dollar
2. 3q, 2d, 1n
3. 2q, 5d
4. 10d
5. 5d, 10n
6. 2q, 4d, 10p
7. 7d, 5n, 5p
8. 9d, 10p
9. 1q, 3d, 6n, 15p
10. 3q, 25p

Page 444

Answers will vary.

Page 445

1. 11
2. 5
3. 64
4. 5
5. 1
6. 100
7. 5
8. 6
9. 10
10. 20
11. 9
12. 52
13. 162
14. 1000
15. 5280
16. 1000
17. 8
18. 5
19. 8
20. 3

Page 446

Woodrow Wilson

Page 447

Students may find a variety of paths, but the only boxes included in the maze should be the following:
First column: boxes 2 and 3
Second column: boxes 4, 5, and 7
Third column: boxes 3, 4, 6, and 7
Fourth column: boxes 2, 5, and 7

Page 449

For metric answers, convert the following U.S. customary responses accordingly.

A1. 7,000,000,000
A2. the population of the United States
A3. an almanac
A4. Divide the number of cookies by the population figures.
B1. 90 million over 150 million; three-fifths
B2. 50 million; find out what fraction 30 million is of 90 million — one-third — and find one-third of 150 million to get 50 million
C1. Divide 150 million pounds by 10 to get 15 million pounds.
C2. One solution: You already know that 150 million cookies equals 10 times around the globe. Fifteen times is half again as much as ten, so divide 150 million by 2. Add that figure to 150 million. The equation will read 150 million + 75 million = 225 million.
D1. Multiply 33,000 by 7, which is the number of days in a week, to get 231,000.
D2. Divide 33,000 by 24 to get 1,375.

Page 450

1. motion
2. kinetic
3. Wind
4. energy
5. Heat
6. Sound
7. Electricity
8. changed

Part 2 Answer Key *(cont.)*

Page 451
1. Pigs
2. Bears
3. Billy
4. Snow; Seven
5. Little
6. Beast
7. Lamp
8. Jack
9. Goose; Egg
10. Town
11. Sleeping
12. Little
13. Tin
14. Rabbit

Page 452
1. bed
2. lamp
3. oven
4. television
5. table
6. sink
7. glass
8. chair
9. towel
10. plate
11. tub
12. fork
13. window
14. couch
15. patio
16. bookcase
17. dresser
18. frying pan
19. spoon
20. painting

Page 453
1. catcher
2. catsup
3. duplicate
4. medication
5. scat
6. catacombs
7. vacation
8. Catholicism
9. vocation
10. copycat
11. decathlon
12. dedicated
13. cattle
14. educate
15. catastrophe

Page 454
1. Connecticut
2. Connie
3. conclusion
4. condiments
5. conceal
6. continue
7. congratulate
8. confused
9. concoct or construct
10. concert
11. consonants
12. continents
13. reconcile
14. concrete
15. confetti

Page 455
1. cartoons
2. caramel
3. Cardinals
4. carton
5. carnival
6. carnation
7. carpet
8. carnivores
9. carat
10. carousel
11. carburetor
12. discard
13. cardigan
14. caricature
15. incarcerate

Page 456
1. nobody
2. Knoxville
3. knock
4. nomad
5. knowledge
6. novel
7. noise
8. Noah
9. equinox
10. snout
11. gnome
12. noose
13. nonsense
14. nose
15. noodles

Page 457
1. barbecue
2. barrack
3. barbells
4. barbarian
5. barn
6. barberry
7. (Clara) Barton
8. bargain
9. baritone
10. baroness
11. Barbie
12. barge
13. barracuda
14. bareback
15. Barcelona

Page 458
1. bicentennial
2. price
3. slice
4. mice
5. iceberg
6. licorice
7. spice
8. Iceland
9. rice
10. triceratops
11. vice-president or vice-chancellor
12. *Alice in Wonderland*
13. advice
14. office
15. juice
16. biceps
17. device
18. entice
19. police
20. dice
21. choice

Part 2 Answer Key *(cont.)*

Page 458 *(cont.)*
22. notice
23. thrice
24. lice
25. *The Price Is Right*

Page 459
1. *Goldfinger*
2. goldfish
3. goldbrick
4. Gold Coast
5. Goldilocks
6. gold digger
7. gold dust
8. golden
9. goldeneye
10. Golden Rule
11. gold mine
12. Gold Rush
13. golden anniversary
14. gold reserve
15. goldenrod
16. goldsmith
17. goldfinch

Page 460
1. green thumb
2. Tom Thumb
3. thumbs-up
4. Thumbelina
5. thumbprint
6. thumb a ride
7. thumbs down
8. thumb through
9. thumbtack
10. rule of thumb
11. all thumbs
12. under someone's thumb
13. thumb one's nose

Page 461
1. goat, goose, or gopher
2. golf
3. gondola
4. gold
5. gone
6. Golden Rule
7. golden retriever
8. goal
9. goober
10. go-between
11. gobble
12. goblin
13. gorgeous
14. gorilla
15. goulash
16. to get one's goat
17. goblet
18. goggles
19. *Gone With the Wind*
20. Goliath
21. gown
22. mango
23. tango
24. gourd
25. goldfinch

Page 462
1. aspirin
2. guarantee
3. medicine
4. settlement
5. important
6. condition
7. overtone
8. earliest
9. limousine
10. different
11. bravery
12. radium
13. prisoner
14. informal
15 vitamins

Page 463
1. cow or sow
2. oyster
3. ape
4. hen
5. lion
6. deer
7. cat
8. seal
9. bear
10. goat

Page 464
1. cat
2. frog
3. goat
4. kid
5. dog
6. weasel
7. camel
8. ferret
9. deer
10. gnu and owl
11. hen
12. tiger
13. fish
14. seal
15. ape

Page 465
1. cornucopia
2. cornerstone
3. corner
4. corned beef
5. corncob
6. corncrib
7. cornerback
8. corn oil
9. cornet
10. corny
11. cornea
12. cut corners
13. cornstarch
14. cornice
15. corn flakes

         #3670 Brain Games

Part 2 Answer Key *(cont.)*

Page 466
1. fare
2. farm team
3. farm hand
4. farrow
5. farther
6. farmer
7. faraway
8. farewell
9. farthing
10. far-fetched
11. Far East
12. so far so good
13. farce
14. to go too far
15. far-reaching

Page 467
1. Peter
2. petrified
3. petal
4. carpet
5. repetitious
6. puppet
7. petite
8. petunia
9. petticoat
10. petroleum
11. petty officer
12. petty cash
13. petition
14. petri dish
15. petit four

Page 468
1. shore
2. forefather
3. galore
4. Oregon
5. swore
6. forefinger
7. chore
8. snore
9. oregano
10. adore
11. forecast
12. forest
13. more
14. carnivores
15. ignore

Page 469
1. thermos
2. thereabouts
3. mathematics
4. thermometer
5. theme song
6. gather
7. theft
8. thesaurus
9. thesis
10. bathe
11. theory
12. then
13. panther
14. weather
15. theater

Page 470
1. Praying mantis
2. mango
3. mantel
4. manger
5. Manitoba
6. manufacture
7. many
8. mandarin
9. mandolin
10. manicure
11. manhole
12. manager
13. mansion
14. manhandle
15. mannequin

Page 471
1. snow
2. clear
3. mild or dew
4. thunder
5. heat
6. sun
7. rain
8. tornado
9. cloud
10. season
11. warm
12. cold
13. hail
14. wind
15. hot

Page 472
1. out
2. step
3. head
4. side
5. pot
6. fire
7. ball
8. down
9. store
10. friend
11. light
12. side
13. out
14. back
15. how

Page 473
schoolroom
anyone
backbone
blackboard
newspaper
homemade
bedtime
everyday
grandfather
elsewhere
cowboy
snowball
whoever
seashore
headline
railroad

Part 2 Answer Key *(cont.)*

Page 473 *(cont.)*
afternoon
outdoors
southeast
understand

Page 474
anywhere
baseball
campground
downtown
eyelid
flagpole
grandfather
handshake
inside
lighthouse
junkyard
mailbox
northeast
overcome
paintbrush
quarterback
railroad
seaport
textbook
underline

Page 475
1. telephone
2. champion
3. gasoline
4. veterinarian or veteran
5. popular
6. bicycle
7. airplane
8. tuxedo
9. mathematics
10. referee
11. automobile
12. refrigerator
13. submarine
14. promenade
15. gymnasium
16. taxicab
17. hamburger
18. spectacles
19. limousine
20. examination

Page 476
1. tale
2. hare
3. fare
4. scent
5. buy
6. lone
7. too
8. aide
9. beach
10. pair
11. great
12. alter
13. air
14. mourning
15. isle

Page 477
1. desert
2. thorough
3. their
4. all ready
5. proceed
6. stationery
7. latter
8. principle
9. quiet
10. it's
11. lie
12. effect
13. preposition
14. anyway
15. sit

Page 478
1. except
2. capitol
3. counsel
4. imply
5. latter
6. phobia
7. former
8. stationary
9. birth
10. weather
11. annual
12. disposition
13. moral
14. your

Page 479
1. clock
2. cup
3. cupboard
4. dish
5. frying pan
6. candlestick
7. tub
8. Mirror
9. bowl
10. range
11. plate (or light)
12. iron
13. closet

Page 480
1. damp + pen = dampen
2. sea + son = season
3. cot + ton = cotton
4. pea + nut = peanut
5. sun + dry = sundry
6. son + net = sonnet
7. off + ice = office
8. rat + tan = rattan
9. men + ace = menace
10. Jack + son = Jackson

Page 481
1. par + take = partake
2. bud + get = budget
3. ash + ore = ashore
4. rot + ate = rotate
5. leg + end = legend
6. car + pet = carpet
7. don + key = donkey
8. win + try = wintry

Part 2 Answer Key (cont.)

Page 482
1. Golden Gate
2. brownie
3. violet, rose, iris, or bluebells
4. bluebird
5. greenhorn
6. orange
7. pinkeye or black death (or plague)
8. yellow jacket
9. greyhound
10. blackboard
11. whitewall
12. red meat
13. Purple Heart
14. Blackbeard

Page 483

We must hurry to get to school on time.

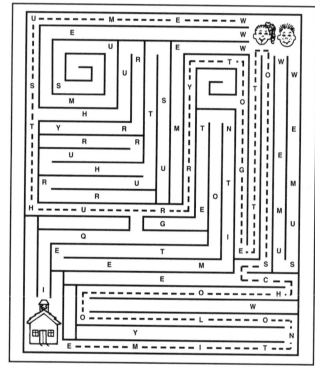

Page 484
1. tears
2. be merry
3. spoon
4. night
5. pop
6. away
7. the candlestick maker
8. a jump
9. sinker
10. Nod
11. tomato
12. the American way
13. children
14. wise
15. Baby Bear
16. maybe
17. blew the house down
18. thing

Page 485
1. north
2. Street or Saint
3. railroad
4. Bachelor of Arts
5. Master of Ceremonies
6. cash on delivery
7. Wednesday
8. ante meridiem (before noon)
9. chapter
10. dozen
11. quart
12. package
13. Pacific Standard Time
14. Avenue
15. September
16. year
17. building
18. number
19. temperature
20. post office

Page 486
1. president
2. as soon as possible
3. adjective
4. pounds
5. maximum
6. et cetera
7. December
8. Master of Arts
9. I owe you.
10. before Christ
11. post meridiem (after noon); post mortem
12. Respondez s' il vous plait. (Please respond.)
13. self-addressed, stamped envelope
14. South America
15. building
16. railroad
17. preposition; preparatory
18. headquarters
19. District Attorney
20. Daylight Saving Time

Page 487

Answers will vary. Here is one example for each.
1. canoe
2. pans or naps
3. brain
4. low
5. lemon
6. stop or post
7. leaf
8. grin
9. tar or rat
10. mug
11. earth
12. tab
13. wasp or swap
14. pea
15. note
16. pat or apt
17. pots or tops
18. ton
19. rope
20. ewe

Part 2 Answer Key *(cont.)*

Page 488
1. makes a man healthy, wealthy, and wise.
2. before they hatch.
3. flock together.
4. is a penny earned.
5. don't make a right.
6. the mice will play.
7. you leap.
8. in the mouth.
9. what you can do today.
10. makes Jack a dull boy.

Page 489
1. what you can do today.
2. is a friend indeed.
3. spilled milk.
4. saves nine.
5. are better than one.
6. grow fonder.
7. is not gold.
8. on the other side.
9. catches the worm.
10. waste.

Page 490
Don't put off until tomorrow what you can do today.

Page 491
1. eggs
2. hide
3. these
4. lone
5. sorry
6. koala
7. rather
8. new
9. toss
The grass is always greener on the other side.

Page 492
Answers will vary.

Page 493
Answers will vary.

Page 494
1. EZ
2. IC
3. CU
4. P
5. C
6. K or D
7. O
8. I
9. U
10. TP
11. IV
12. Y
13. T
14. B
15. DJ

Page 495
1. Q
2. XTC
3. NME
4. NV
5. B, D, K or L
6. O
7. SA
8. FX
9. J
10. CU
11. AT
12. T
13. G
14. XL
15. DK

Page 496
1. cold
2. colt
3. bolt
4. bold
5. bald
6. ball
7. bell
8. belt
9. melt
10. molt
11. mold
12. mole
13. hole
14. hold
15. gold
16. fold
17. food
18. fool
19. tool
20. pool

Page 497
1. sharp
2. shark
3. share
4. care
5. chart
6. charm
7. hard
8. hare
9. fare
10. farm
11. alarm
12. lark
13. bark
14. dark
15. dare
16. date
17. late
18. lane
19. cane
20. cone

Page 498
1. aardvark; poodle; raccoon; etc.
2. summer or fall
3. football or baseball
4. intelligence
5. doodle
6. buccaneer
7. butterfly
8. giraffe
9. beggar
10. moon
11. pepper

Part 2 Answer Key *(cont.)*

Page 498 *(cont.)*
12. gaggle
13. wiggle
14. borrow
15. sorrow
16. sonnet
17. ballot
18. classic

Page 499
1. chew
2. ewe
3. weed
4. edible
5. letter
6. erase
7. season
8. once
9. celebrate
10. telegram
11. amour
12. Uranus
13. usual
14. allow
15. owl

Page 500
1. Adams
2. Ford
3. Madison
4. Garfield
5. Jefferson
6. Eisenhower
7. Armstrong
8. Vespucci
9. Edison
10. Earhart

Page 501
Answers will vary.

Page 502
Answers will vary.

Page 503
Use the key on the page to check the work.

Page 504
1. windows
2. haste
3. expenses
4. visitors
5. example
6. melons
7. enemy; friend
8. secret
9. vinegar

Page 505
1. bullet
2. italics
3. stock
4. widow
5. copy
6. dingbats
7. thumbnails
8. dummy
9. folio
10. characters

Page 506
1. cardinal directions
2. female relatives
3. odd numbers
4. words for pretty
5. continents
6. months (or months with 30 days)
7. states in the U.S.
8. astronauts
9. boy's names starting with P
10. planets
11. flowers
12. things that have three of something
13. some of the Seven Dwarfs
14. primary colors
15. reference books

Page 507
1. trees
2. sports
3. cities (cities in Europe)
4. members of the cat family
5. desserts
6. tools
7. feelings
8. make-believe characters
9. products from a cow
10. words that mean "one"
11. round objects
12. transportation
13. vegetables
14. candy bars
15. girls' names beginning with C

Page 508
Answers will vary.

Page 509
Answers will vary.

Page 510
Answers will vary.

Page 511
Answers will vary.

Page 512
Answers will vary.

Page 513
Answers will vary.

Page 514
Answers will vary.

Page 515
Answers will vary.

Page 516
Answers will vary.

Page 517
Answers will vary.

Part 2 Answer Key (cont.)

Page 518
1. litterbug
2. hello
3. happy
4. gobble
5. difficult
6. puddle
7. terrible
8. mallard
9. good-bye
10. baboon
11. pillow
12. chatter
13. offense
14. moose
15. address

Page 519
1. opportunity
2. look
3. blizzard
4. intelligence
5. innocent
6. wiggle
7. vacuum
8. pessimist
9. borrow
10. football
11. syllable
12. bazaar
13. exaggerate
14. pennant
15. afternoon

Page 520
1. hopscotch
2. Asia, Africa, Antarctica, Australia, or Europe
3. solos
4. eagle
5. gong
6. reindeer
7. eye
8. Bob
9. hush
10. aqua
11. peep
12. noon
13. oleo
14. diamond
15. yesterday

Page 521
1. amnesia
2. hearth
3. eagle
4. kayak
5. Alberta
6. maximum
7. tourist
8. greeting
9. recover
10. nitrogen
11. wallow
12. doubled
13. erase
14. neon

Page 522
1. Antarctica
2. dividend
3. abracadabra
4. exercise
5. episode
6. critic
7. blurb
8. arena
9. surplus
10. classic
11. moonbeam
12. lentil
13. tolerant
14. penmanship
15. stress
16. register
17. millennium

Page 523
Answers will vary.

Page 524
Answers will vary.

Page 525
Answers will vary.

Page 526
Answers will vary.

Page 527
Answers will vary.

Page 528
Answers will vary.

Page 529
Answers will vary.

Page 530
Answers will vary.

Page 531
Answers will vary.

Page 532
1. jazz
2. quiet
3. yucca
4. extra
5. violin
6. bashful
7. grown
8. defeat
9. koala
10. molar
11. porcupine

Page 533
1. model
2. backward
3. uncle
4. squint
5. return
6. gopher
7. jackal
8. x-ray
9. voice
10. relief
11. zoom

Part 2 Answer Key *(cont.)*

Page 534
Answers will vary.

Page 535
Answers will vary.

Page 536
1. country
2. city
3. city
4. continent
5. city
6. continent
7. state/province
8. country
9. city
10. state/province
11. continent
12. city
13. country
14. state/province
15. continent
16. country
17. continent
18. city
19. state/province
20. country

Page 537
1. tease
2. stand
3. aunt
4. need
5. attend
6. ten
7. test
8. sun
9. ate
10. taste
11. sand
12. sea
13. unite
14. tent
15. den
16. tuna
17. sunset
18. seat
19. tune
20. end

Page 538
1. Chicago, United States
2. Paris, France
3. Tokyo, Japan
4. Buenos Aires, Argentina
5. Lima, Peru
6. Johannesburg, South Africa
7. Marrakech, Morocco
8. Rome, Italy
9. Quebec, Canada
10. Lagos, Nigeria
11. Hanoi, Vietnam
12. Sydney, Australia
13. Christchurch, New Zealand
14. Moscow, Russia
15. Peking, China
16. London, England
17. Stockholm, Sweden
18. Berlin, Germany
19. New Delhi, India
20. Guadalajara, Mexico

Page 539
North America: Bahamas, Canada, Costa Rica, Cuba, Guatemala, Jamaica, Mexico, Nicaragua, Panama, and United States
South America: Argentina, Bolivia, Brazil, Chile, Colombia, Ecuador, Paraguay, Peru, Uruguay, and Venezuela
Europe: Austria, Belgium, Denmark, France, Germany, Greece, Italy, Norway, Portugal, and Sweden
Asia: China, India, Israel, Japan, Lebanon, Nepal, Pakistan, Philippines, Thailand, and Turkey
Africa: Congo, Egypt, Ghana, Ivory Coast, Liberia, Morocco, Nigeria, Somalia, Swaziland, and Zambia

Page 540
1. Sweden
2. Argentina
3. Canada
4. South Africa
5. Austria
6. Spain
7. Brazil
8. Ireland
9. China
10. United Kingdom
11. India
12. Russia
13. Mexico
14. Japan
15. Germany
16. Italy
17. Morocco
18. Australia
19. France
20. Egypt

Page 541
1. France
2. Germany
3. Mexico
4. France
5. Italy
6. Netherlands
7. Spain and California
8. Germany
9. Pennsylvania
10. England
11. South America
12. England
13. France
14. Border of Europe and Asia
15. England

Page 542
Answers may vary.

Page 543
Answers may vary.

Page 544
Answers may vary.

Page 545
1. Arizona
2. Wyoming
3. Texas

Part 2 Answer Key (cont.)

Page 545 (cont.)
4. Colorado
5. Kentucky
6. Oregon
7. Florida
8. Alaska
9. California
10. Arkansas
11. Hawaii
12. Washington
13. South Dakota
14. Virginia
15. New Mexico

Page 546
1. Manitoba, Canada
2. Nevada, USA
3. New York, USA
4. Louisiana, USA
5. Montana, USA
6. North Carolina, USA
7. Alberta, Canada
8. Alaska, USA
9. Texas, USA
10. Sonora, Mexico
11. Oregon. USA
12. Ontario, Canada
13. New Mexico, USA
14. Durango, Mexico
15. Maine, USA
16. Nuevo Leon, Mexico
17. British Columbia, Canada
18. California, USA
19. New Hampshire, USA
20. Tamaulipas, Mexico

Page 547
1. South Australia
2. Papua New Guinea
3. Queensland
4. Australia
5. New Zealand
6. Western Australia
7. Indonesia
8. Tasmania
9. Northern Territory
10. Malaysia
11. New South Wales
12. Victoria

Page 548
1. Egypt
2. Zaire
3. Mali
4. South Africa
5. Ivory Coast
6. Chad
7. Angola
8. Ethiopia
9. Libya
10. Zambia
11. Sierra Leone
12. Morocco
13. Madagascar
14. Uganda
15. Togo

Page 549
1. Ecuador
2. Brazil
3. Guyana
4. Argentina
5. French Guiana
6. Chile
7. Colombia
8. Paraguay
9. Peru
10. Uruguay
11. Suriname
12. Venezuela
13. Trinidad and Tobago
14. Bolivia
15. Falkland Islands

Page 550
1. Thailand
2. Mongolia
3. Saudi Arabia
4. Pakistan
5. Bangladesh
6. China
7. South Korea
8. Iran
9. Israel
10. Vietnam
11. India
12. Japan
13. Jordan
14. Turkey
15. Syria

Page 551
1. Paris, France
2. London, England
3. Madrid, Spain or Lisbon, Portugal
4. Athens, Greece
5. Moscow, Russia
6. Amsterdam, Netherlands
7. Rome, Italy
8. Bern, Switzerland or Vienna, Austria
9. Cork, Ireland
10. Vienna, Austria
11. Oslo, Norway
12. Edinburgh, Scotland
13. Berlin, Germany
14. Oslo, Norway or Helsinki, Finland
15. Brussels, Belgium

Page 552
1. Africa
2. weather
3. river
4. temperature
5. Antarctica
6. hemisphere
7. meadow
8. vegetation
9. Germany
10. monsoon

Part 2 Answer Key *(cont.)*

Page 553
1. volcano
2. South Pole
3. earthquake
4. France
5. lake
6. Hawaii
7. Australia
8. map
9. mountains
10. jungle

Page 554
1. The Statue of Freedom
2. The Statue of Liberty
3. The Jefferson Memorial
4. Jefferson, Lincoln, and Washington
5. St. Louis, Missouri
6. Arlington National Cemetery, Arlington, Virginia
7. the military might of the United States
8. The Washington Monument
9. north of Arlington National Cemetery in Washington, D.C.
10. servicemen raising the American flag on Iwo Jima during WWII
11. Vietnam Veterans Memorial (The Wall)
12. Philadelphia

Page 555
1. Turkey; not in Africa
2. India; not an island
3. Alaska; not a country
4. Mediterranean; not an ocean
5. Chad; not on the Mediterranean
6. Canary; not in the Pacific
7. Antarctica; no inhabitants
8. New Zealand; not in Australia
9. South Africa; not on the equator
10. Angola; not bordered by the Indian Ocean

Page 556
1. 11,777,000
2. 11,518,000
3. 11,663,000
4. 20,207,000
5. 14,622,000
6. 13,826,000
7. 18,052,000
8. 16,268,000
9. 26,952,000

Page 557
1. peso
2. dollar
3. rand
4. pound
5. franc
6. mark
7. drachma
8. rupee
9. yen
10. lira
11. peseta
12. shekel
13. schilling
14. won
15. balboa
16. bolivar
17. guilder
18. ruble
19. markka
20. krona

Page 558
1. Alabama
2. South Dakota
3. Lake Michigan
4. Connecticut
5. Red River
6. Nevada
7. Rio Grande River
8. Indiana
9. New Mexico
10. Mississippi River
11. U.S.A.
12. New Hampshire
13. Iowa
14. California
15. Oregon

Page 559
1. Poland
2. Pyrenees Mountains
3. Liechtenstein
4. English Channel
5. Mediterranean Sea
6. Norwegian Sea
7. Strait of Bonifacio
8. Adriatic Sea
9. Ural Mountains
10. Baltic Sea
11. Sea of Crete
12. North Sea
13. Latvia
14. Danube River
15. Belgium

Page 560
1. Atlantic Ocean
2. Equator
3. Tasman Sea
4. New Mexico
5. Indian Ocean
6. Central America
7. Prime Meridian
8. Indian Ocean
9. Mediterranean Sea
10. Pacific Ocean
11. Atlantic Ocean
12. Equator
13. Red Sea/Indian Ocean
14. Drake Passage
15. Pacific Ocean